LIFE ABOARD
A WARTIME
LIBERTY SHIP

LIFE ABOARD A WARTIME LIBERTY SHIP

IAN M. MALCOLM

AMBERLEY

First published 2010

Amberley Publishing
Cirencester Road, Chalford,
Stroud, Gloucestershire, GL6 8PE

www.amberleybooks.com

British Library Cataloguing in Publication Data.
A catalogue record for this book is available from the British Library.

ISBN 978-1-4456-0020-8

Typeset in 10pt on 12pt Sabon.
Typesetting and Origination by Amberley Publishing.
Printed in the UK.

CONTENTS

CHAPTER 1

THE TURNING POINT

With the Second World War imminent, my ten-year-old brother, Eric, and I were evacuated to St Cyrus in Kincardine. This was towards the end of the summer of 1939, but, as the weeks passed without Dundee receiving any attention from the Germans, our parents brought us home and a week or two later, at the age of fourteen, I began my working life as an apprentice clerk in the jute office of A. & S. Henry & Co. Ltd in Victoria Road.

By the end of 1942, when my call-up at eighteen was approaching, I began to wonder which Service I would prefer to join. Flying was out of the question because I wore glasses, but as I played the bagpipes in the 3rd Boys' Brigade Pipe Band, I thought of becoming a piper in a Highland regiment. Then, quite by chance, another possibility presented itself.

I was in Johnston's snooker hall at the foot of Blackness Avenue when some young chaps came in carrying earphones. My curiosity was aroused and on learning that they were evening class students at the nearby Wireless College in Windsor Street, training to become radio officers in the Merchant Navy, my imagination was fired. I found out what the job entailed, presented the case to my parents and, because my call-up was not far off, they agreed that I should attend the College as a full-time day student.

During the war, when a continuous human wireless watch was kept on all merchant ships, possession of a Special Postmaster General's (PMG) Certificate in Radiotelegraphy was sufficient to allow the holder to become a radio officer in the Merchant Navy, but not the R/O in charge. And a 2nd Class Certificate could be sat after only six months' sea experience. I attended the College from mid-January to mid-June 1943 and, as my eighteenth birthday fell on 27 April, a local tribunal granted a postponement of call-up to allow me to sit the June exam.

We had to be able to send and receive Morse at twenty words a minute, demonstrate our ability to operate marine radio equipment, and answer questions on wireless theory and the regulations applying to radio communications to the satisfaction of a GPO examiner. There was no written examination. The Merchant Navy needed radio officers in a hurry and this was how it was done. The 'wastage' at sea was considerable, but there was never a shortage of young recruits.

The majority of radio officers were employed by the Marconi Company, Siemens and International Marine Radio, which were wireless companies supplying both personnel and equipment to the shipping lines. Long before I became interested in the sea, however, I had heard my father, an engineering fitter in the Caledon Shipyard, extolling the virtues of the ships they built for Alfred Holt & Company of Liverpool, who owned the Blue Funnel Line and the Glen Line. And as Holts employed their men direct, I applied to them as soon as I qualified.

As the situation at sea was not as desperate as it had been during the earlier years of the war, I expected to have a holiday between passing the exam and going to sea. But this proved woefully inaccurate. I collected my Certificate at the Wireless College on the afternoon of 30 June 1943 and was still in bed the following morning when a telegram arrived calling me for interview at Holt's office at 9 a.m. next morning. It is one thing preparing to enter a heroic service and basking in its limelight, but quite another thing going. But, like thousands of others, I was caught in the tide of events and within two hours of receiving that telegram I boarded a crowded train for Liverpool.

Wartime trains were always crowded. I changed trains at Perth and Preston and arrived in Liverpool's Lime Street Station at about 5 p.m. A friend of my parents had given me an address in Aintree and I set about finding my way there through an unknown city at a time when people were returning home from work. Carrying my small suitcase, I walked past buildings gutted by enemy bombs to the Pier Head where I boarded a tram for Aintree. I did not know the people who lived at the address I had been given and, equally, they did not know me or even that I was coming. We did not enjoy the luxury of a telephone in those days and my summons to Liverpool had been too precipitous to allow the sending of a letter.

When I gave the address to the tram conductor, he said I had to get off at the Black Bull and that he would tell me when to get off. The tram ride seemed a long one and, becoming anxious, I reminded him of my destination. A small bespectacled lady, standing beside me on the platform, overheard my remarks and said that she lived nearby and would show me where to go. I therefore disembarked in her company and told her what I was doing in Liverpool and how I had been given the address of Mrs J. Murphy, 11 Fir Grove, Aintree. She responded by saying that she lived with her mother and that, if I found that I could not be put up for the

Photo for Special Certificate, June 1943.

night there, I had only to come to her home. This was indeed kindness to a stranger, but I have since then had additional reason to associate generosity with the people of Merseyside.

After walking alongside Aintree Race Course (occupied by the US Army) for some way with my companion, I left her and arrived at Mrs Murphy's door. The house turned out to be a fairly new villa occupied by a young pregnant woman with a son who must have been about three years old. Her husband was in the Army and I learned that he had been billeted on my parents' friend in Dundee. She had no hesitation in welcoming me into her home. I was young and immature and the little boy embarrassed me by following me about the house. To him, I was no doubt a replica of his dad.

I remember my first morning at the Holt's office in Ullet Road very clearly. I had been called there with such urgency that I expected it to continue. In this I was much mistaken. 54 Ullet Road had been Richard Holt's mansion house and, together with Lawrence Holt's mansion next door (No. 52), became Company Headquarters when India Buildings was reduced to a shell by fire, following the air raid on the night of 3 May 1941. I was ushered into the Steamship Department on the ground floor where typists banged at their machines and important-looking clerks busied themselves with their papers. A Mr Calverley dealt with radio officers. He was similar to my father in appearance, but seemed somewhat nervous and spoke of 'wireless operators' rather than 'radio officers', which appeared to be company policy. There was no welcoming smile as he told me to take a seat, thus suggesting that I should wait while he completed an item of business. Behind where I sat were large windows overlooking a lawn while before me was the entire Steamship Department. Everyone was busy, except me. After my dash from Dundee, I had nothing to do but survey the activity or read the pile of PLA (Port of London Authority) magazines on the table by my side. When I heard Calverley mention the loss of Radio Officer Robert Laird on the *Centaur* to a colleague, I blurted out that Bob and I had been pipers together in the Boys' Brigade. The interruption was met with a stony stare and he made no comment.

The minutes that I had expected to wait developed into hours and I was then told that I could go for lunch either to the canteen within the building or elsewhere. I jokingly remarked that, being a Scotsman, I would go to the cheaper canteen within the building, but this remark again met with the stony stare. I had a distinct feeling of being an outsider and did not feel at all welcome.

After a solitary lunch in a noisy canteen in the basement, I returned to the Steamship Department and then had a busy afternoon where I was medically examined by Dr Wilson and interviewed by Mr Stocks, the Company's Radio Superintendent. I travelled by tram and train to

Mr Stock's office in Birkenhead and remember that he asked me why a transmitter motor required a starting resistance. I confidently gave my parrot answer, 'in order to allow the back EMF (Electro-Motive Force) time to build up', but when he followed this up by asking what was meant by the back EMF, I didn't know and my superficial knowledge was exposed. But he must have come across many novices like me. I was accepted into the Company and on returning to India Buildings, Calverley told me to come back the following morning. Where I was to spend the night seemed of no concern to him, but Mrs Murphy had told me to come back if necessary and so I spent another night at Aintree.

When I saw Calverley again on the Saturday morning, I discovered that he thought that I was ready for sea and, when I told him that I was not, he appeared irritated and said to get back to Dundee, get myself kitted out and to report at the dock gate at Greenock on the morning of 7 July with my luggage labelled with the letter M. I returned to Dundee overnight and travelled the last part of the journey with a young Dundee radio officer returning home from an Atlantic crossing. It was Sunday morning when the train arrived in the West Station and I had only Monday and part of Tuesday to get ready.

My mother accompanied me to the Mercantile Marine Office in Dock Street where I joined the Merchant Navy and was given my Seaman's Identity Card and my Continuous Certificate of Discharge, the latter between thin, light blue, wartime cardboard covers and bearing the embossed stamp of the Ministry of War Transport. I was also given the silver MN lapel badge (the only 'uniform' of MN ratings), MN clothing coupons and a National Service (Armed Forces) Act, 1939 Certificate of Registration. My mother also came with me to buy my uniform at the large main shop of Dundee Eastern Co-operative Society in the Seagate, and the bare minimum of clothes – which did not include white tropical uniform as we thought only of the North Atlantic. (The Co-op was unable to supply me with a greatcoat at such short notice, but one was ordered and I was to collect it after my first voyage. But the voyage lasted so long, and I came to realise that I had no real need of a greatcoat, that the order was cancelled.)

I was ready by the evening of Tuesday 6 July and, wearing my new uniform with its one wavy gold band, said goodbye to my grandparents in their house on the tenement landing below, and lastly to my mother and Eric.

My father went with me on the evening train to Glasgow where we found it almost impossible to find overnight accommodation and ended up on chairs and a settee in the sitting room of a guesthouse. While looking for a place to stay, we found ourselves in the foyer of a hotel with a group of men in

Clothing coupon book.

civilian clothes, whom we took to be Merchant Navy officers. I was to learn that, even during the war, few senior MN officers ever wore uniform ashore as this had not been their custom in peacetime. That same evening, when we visited a public toilet, a drunk man staggered on to a weighing machine and asked me to read his weight. I had little experience of drunk men and the incident emphasised the fact that I was entering a very different world.

On the morning of Wednesday 7 July we took the train to Greenock and, when we arrived at the dock gate, the place seemed deserted. There was little sign of traffic and, apart from the policeman on duty at the gate, there was nobody about. On showing my pass to the policeman, I was directed to a large shed at some distance from the dock gate. As my father was not allowed into the dock area, I said to him that I would probably be able to come out again once I had reported myself present and set off down that lonely dock road carrying my one suitcase and feeling awkward in my brand new uniform, covered by the standard dark-blue merchant navy raincoat. I didn't look back. I had a pretty shrewd idea that I would not be allowed to return to the dock gate, but felt that this was an easier way to say farewell. My assumption proved correct. My father waited at the gate for two hours before beginning his journey back home, and I didn't see him or Dundee again until Thursday 19 October 1944.

CHAPTER 2
MY LIFE AT SEA BEGINS

On arriving at the large shed or warehouse to which I had been directed, I was surprised to find it full of Merchant Navy personnel. I had been told that I was to be 3rd Radio Officer of *Liberty Ship D* and I quickly found myself in line with the other men of this somewhat mythical vessel who had travelled overnight from Liverpool by train. Holts had told me nothing about where I was going, but a radio officer whom I had met in Liverpool had informed me that crews were being sent to the States to pick up new ships and so I had a fair idea of what was happening. Along with hundreds of others, we waited to undergo the formality of passing through Customs and then to board a tender to convey us to a grey-painted ship which lay at anchor in the Clyde.

After Customs officers had scribbled chalk marks on our cases, names were called and men assembled on the jetty to board a tender. My companions departed, but my name was not called. The number of men around me dwindled. Everybody was leaving except me and I began to feel anxious. Then somehow or other I came in contact with Captain Turner who was Holt's representative and their Marine Superintendent in Glasgow. He was in no way sympathetic to my youth, my inexperience or my feelings of inadequacy and rounded on me for not contacting him sooner. Because of my hurried entry into the Company, the Articles of *Liberty Ship D* did not carry my name and this is why it had not been called. I learned later that this was the notorious 'One Egg' Turner who, during the Depression prior to the war, had commanded a ship on the Pacific run. It had been the custom to serve two eggs for breakfast, but Captain Turner, in order to reduce costs, had ordered that only one egg be served, thus earning himself the sobriquet. On his intervention, an RNVR Sea Transport Officer scribbled my boarding pass on the back of a pink cardboard slip concerning boat-stations and I was allowed to board the tender which proceeded out into the Clyde. As we neared the vessel at anchor, I asked one of the few civilian passengers (excluding the merchant seamen) if he knew what ship it was. When he replied that he thought it was the *Queen Elizabeth*, I said that she didn't seem all that big to me. He laughed at this and said that I'd find her large enough once I got on board. The vessel did indeed prove to be the *Queen Elizabeth* and, as the day of the super-tanker had not yet dawned, her gross tonnage of 83,673 tons made her the largest merchant ship in the world at that time.

My boarding pass assigned me to Cabin 127 on 'M' Deck – a first-class cabin originally designed for two people travelling in luxury, but now containing something like fifteen plain wooden bunks in tiers of three. Although there were thousands on board, the ship was not filled to her capacity of twenty thousand servicemen on this outward voyage and consequently two or three bunks in the cabin were unoccupied. I took a bottom bunk with nobody above me and when I rose the following morning the ship was well out at sea.

I was given a blue card directing me to have my meals at Table No. 6 in the Officers' Dining Room on 'R' Deck Aft during the Second Sitting. This last aspect proved to be fortuitous as all the other officers in the cabin held First Sitting cards. The cabin contained a small washbasin and, while they scrambled for this, I slumbered on until they had all departed for the dining room. I then rose and washed in comfort in a deserted cabin. The Officers' Dining Room/First Class Saloon was extremely large and could be compared with the dining room of the most prestigious hotel. At some distance from where I sat was a grand piano, in a somewhat elevated position and at which a junior engineer officer of Clan Line, who came from Broughty Ferry, sometimes entertained us. The meals were excellent and not at all what we were accustomed to in wartime Britain. This was because the ship replenished her stores in either Canada or the United States and the white linen tablecloths were changed after every sitting. I did justice to those lovely meals, but I was not yet a seasoned sailor and there was one occasion when I had hastily to excuse myself and head for my bunk after having only the soup!

Throughout the passage, however, the sea was never rough and the *Lizzie* ploughed towards North America at a speed of about 30 knots. Because of her fast speed, she was unescorted, i.e. travelling alone and unaccompanied by ships of the Royal Navy. Standing on her boat deck in brilliant sunshine along with other passengers, I watched her foaming wake. DEMS (Defensive Equipment Merchant Ships) gunners of the Royal Navy and a Maritime Regiment of the Royal Artillery manned her many guns and experienced Merchant Navy officers guessed at the speed she was doing. I spent many hours walking the decks and getting the feel of

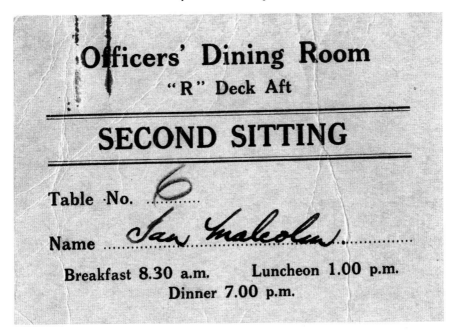

Officers' Dining Room

"R" Deck Aft

SECOND SITTING

Table No. 6

Name *Ian Malcolm*

Breakfast 8.30 a.m.   Luncheon 1.00 p.m.
Dinner 7.00 p.m.

Dining ticket.

the sea. Sailors are so accustomed to being out of sight of land that it is commonplace to them, but it was a new experience for me to gaze at the immensity of the ocean.

We had nothing to do but eat and sleep. Strangely enough, although many people enjoy cruises, merchant seamen prefer to be working and part of the crew. This crossing of the Atlantic lasted only about four days, but almost everyone complained of boredom. Long hours were spent in the saloon drinking Pepsi Cola (no intoxicating liquor was available) and playing cards. I got to know two senior engineer officers who spent their time playing interminable games of cribbage in the saloon. On learning that I spent much of my time writing letters, one of them asked me to write to his wife on his behalf. This I did and took the letter to the saloon for him to sign. He barely took his eyes off his cards as he said, 'You sign it for me.' I thought that this was a bit much and persuaded him to break off his game just long enough to put his signature to the letter. Strangely enough, word got around that I had written a letter for this man and I was then approached by the junior engineer, who played the piano, to write a letter for him! This I declined to do although I might have earned some money as a scribe if I had been so inclined.

As my acquaintance on the tender had prophesied, I did find the *Queen Elizabeth* a big ship. She had ten decks and I once went to what I thought was my cabin only to find a different number on the door, thus signifying that I was on another deck laid out in exactly the same way. As on all merchant ships, we had boat-drill so that, at a given signal, we reported to the lifeboat we were to go to if we had to abandon ship. The boat-drill was over before I managed to find my boat station!

In addition to the Merchant Navy crews, travelling to collect new Liberty Ships in the States and Fort 'Boats' in Canada, the *Queen Elizabeth* carried RAF personnel going to Canada to train as aircrew. Canada, being remote from the war, had the unlimited space of the flat prairies where learner pilots and navigators could make mistakes without bumping into anything such as towns, hills or mountains. One of these trainee navigators later told me of an occasion when his plane landed to enquire of a farmer where they were! Among these men, I was delighted to meet Peter Bruce, who lived near me in Dundee.

One evening, when in the middle of the Atlantic, a special ceremony took place in the first-class saloon. Some United States servicemen were to receive medals and there was a queue of men wishing to witness the ceremony. It was a novelty and there was nowhere else to go. Nobody seemed to know how the medals had been earned and rumour had it that they were being given for crossing the Atlantic! This humorous suggestion was due to the fact that US servicemen seemed to be given medals for any reason at all. I did not, however, feel inclined to join the long queue and decided to take a bath instead.

Our cabin had its own bathroom. Every morning when I washed at the washbasin, I poured in the water from a metal container which had been carried by one of my 'first sitting' cabin mates from a kitchen along the passage and at some distance from the cabin. Knowing that the water had to carried in this way, I began to collect it but, after two or three journeys, something prompted me to try the taps over the bath and I found that both taps were working and water poured into the bath. This was a revelation to me. Why carry water when you merely had to turn on the taps? So I filled up the bath from the taps and clambered in only to find that I could get no lather from the soap because the water was salt!

Momentous news which reached the ship on 10 July 1943 was that of the Allied invasion of Sicily and my copy of the ship's single-sheet newspaper *Ocean News*, dated 14 July 1943, has the headline 'British Extend Lines On Sicily Coast'. It was on the evening of the same day that I retired early, only to be told by someone entering the cabin that we were entering port. I hastily donned my uniform over my pyjamas and went on deck. The lights of the port were clearly visible, but where were we? Even in the dark, experienced eyes recognised it as Halifax, Nova Scotia.

The following day was a busy one on board the ship, although I had nothing to do after packing the few things I had taken from my suitcase during the crossing. Canadian troops came on board and stood on guard at various points throughout the vessel while both RAF and Merchant Navy personnel disembarked. The ship began to take on a deserted look, but my party remained on board. I had lunch in an almost deserted saloon and sat alone at the table waiting for the steward to come and get my order for pudding. When at last he appeared from the recesses of the kitchen, he feigned surprise that I was still there. But I saw no reason to do without pudding just because we had arrived in Canada!

Eventually it was the turn of the crew of *Liberty Ship D* to disembark and we boarded a bus to convey us to accommodation in the town. On the way, cheers went up as we drove past a fruit shop displaying luxuries not seen in wartime Britain – such as oranges.

The *Queen Elizabeth* remained in Halifax for a few days. Astern of her lay the French liner *Pasteur* and ahead of her, her sister ship, the *Queen Mary* which was similarly employed. It was an impressive sight to see these great ships lying in line together and I was too overawed by security precautions to return to the *Queen Elizabeth* to try to retrieve the mouth organ I had left under my pillow. It was the finest mouth organ I had ever possessed, with double octaves on two sides. It hurt me to lose it, but I like to think that some Canadian soldier made use of it on the way to his war in Europe.

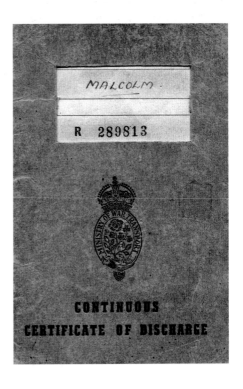

Discharge Book.

CHAPTER 3

HALIFAX, NOVA SCOTIA

Along with other junior officers of *Liberty Ship D*, I was installed in the small all-timber Gainsboro Hotel in Hollis Street where I shared a room with Neville Caro, the 2nd R/O. We did not eat in the hotel and were given $2 a day so that we could eat at any restaurant of our choosing. I usually ate at the Green Lantern situated on Barrington Street, Halifax's main thoroughfare. The food was good and reasonably priced and the uniformed waitresses were smart.

I remember two specific things about the Green Lantern. One is that food dishes were given numbers so that a customer could order merely by stating them. Number 1 might be soup, 3 fish and chips and 6 a sweet/pudding of some sort. To begin with, I did not understand the drill and so did my best to pronounce what was billed as Potage Parmentier. This completely nonplussed the waitress who eventually realised that I wanted soup. The rocky coast of Nova Scotia is noted for its shellfish and it was at this restaurant that I came to know and like clam chowder, a soup I have never seen in Britain. My second specific memory of the Green Lantern is that of a Scandinavian sailor who wished to 'date' what seemed to me to be an older waitress who was probably in her thirties. He was sitting at my table when he asked her to go out with him and when she answered that she was 'not sure', he asked her to 'fink about it'. Since that time, I have never heard anyone use the phrase 'to think about' something without recalling that incident in the Green Lantern. The waitress did her 'finking' during a quick trip to the kitchen and agreed to go out with the sailor.

Halifax was no great shakes of a town and most sailors had little good to say about it. Together with Saint John, New Brunswick, it is an eastern terminus of the vast Canadian railroad system which spans the country from Prince Rupert and Vancouver on the west coast. This makes Halifax extremely important, especially so in winter when the St Lawrence Seaway is frozen over and closed to shipping. In war, Halifax had even more significance as it was the most important western convoy port of the North Atlantic. Convoys sailed to and from Halifax and maintained the vital lifeline with Britain.

But, for six whole weeks as it turned out, I had nothing to do but enjoy Halifax and I found it a very agreeable place. The weather was glorious and I soon learned that the local people spent much of their leisure time at the extremely pleasant Northwest Arm, an inlet of the Atlantic. The Arm was particularly busy at weekends with families picnicking, sailing and bathing. I went there many times so that the journey became familiar.

The first stage of the journey was by tramcar. Unlike the trams in Britain at that time, these were single deckers. There was no conductor and the driver saw that the correct fare was dropped into a glass container when a passenger boarded. It was possible to buy a number of tickets held together by perforations and, if a change of trams were necessary in order to reach your destination, 'transfer' tickets allowed you to do this at a lower price than that charged for the individual journeys.

On arriving at the tram terminus near the Northwest Arm, I walked to the ferry which conveyed passengers across to the Dingle. This ferry was merely a coble with an engine operated by a surly man who never spoke, but who seemed to resent ferrying me across on weekdays when I could be the only passenger. No doubt this stemmed from the fact that the fare was only five cents! Obviously, he required a certain number of passengers to

With deck apprentices and radio officers, Northwest arm.

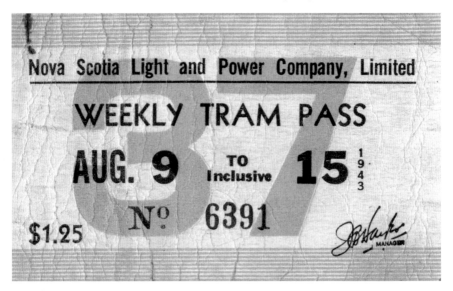

Tram Pass, Halifax.

make a profit, but how pleasant it was to chug back and forth across the Northwest Arm.

The Dingle had a few shops selling ice cream, soft drinks, etc., and at weekends was pleasantly noisy with families enjoying themselves. My first visit there was made in the company of nine young radio officers and deck apprentices who had also crossed on the *Lizzie*. Some of them knew the area and we climbed the path behind the Dingle until we came to Lake Target, a freshwater lake which sported a diving board and was excellent for swimming.

Lake Target became my regular venue. It was quiet and pleasant and, to me, somewhat typical of Canada as there were fir trees all around. It was similar also to Scotland as there were blaeberries and heather. On a later occasion, George McPherson, Ron Kenyon and I swam naked in the lake by moonlight and walked back on the road through the forest singing at the top of our voices. As the ferryboat would, most certainly, not be available, there must have been another route back to Halifax.

There was one occasion when Neville Caro and I went canoeing on the Arm. The hired canoe was heavy and difficult to manage so I suspected that Neville, sitting behind me, was not pulling his weight! We paddled down the Arm to the open sea and found that we could go no further as the incoming tide carried us ashore. We then tried to re-enter the Arm, but this proved to be impossible so we ended up by beaching the canoe and dragging it through a park in order to re-enter the Arm at some distance from the sea. It was a warm sunny afternoon and we felt very foolish dragging our heavy canoe past families picnicking in the park.

I became friendly with George McPherson, from Glasgow, who was also a 3rd R/O, but who had been at sea for some time. George, who also stayed at the Gainsboro, was one of the group during that first visit to the Northwest Arm and he had asked a girl if he might borrow her camera to take a snapshot of the group. I suppose it was a bit of a cheek, but when I met up with George in Baltimore about six weeks later he gave me a copy of the picture which I still have and value although George, of course, is not on it. He was a friendly extrovert who got to know people and it was through him that I met Ron Kenyon, whose parents owned an antique shop in the town. Ron, a quiet young man with bad eyesight, worked in the shipyard at Dartmouth. A keen photographer, it was he who produced the copies of the pictures taken of the group. The three of us sometimes met in his photographic studio at the rear of the shop where prints were drying after being developed and enlarged. I had meals in Ron's house and met his English parents, but when his mother recommended Canada as a land of opportunity, his father reminded her of the 1930s when university graduates had tried to scrape a living by selling 'round the doors'.

Halifax had no pubs, but a ration of intoxicating liquor could be obtained at a provincial liquor store of rather bare and forbidding appearance. I had no interest in 'drink', but others persuaded me to collect my ration for their use. I completed and presented the application form, but the clerk behind the counter took one look at me and pronounced that I was too young.

The Gainsboro Hotel was run by an elderly lady, who, I heard saying, had a desire to visit Europe and Scotland in particular. This brought home to me that Scotland is in Europe, although people in the UK have continually referred to Europe as if it were those countries on the mainland to the east of the British Isles. On one occasion, when I was tinkering with the piano in the lounge, I heard her having a long conversation with a Canadian soldier who had not enough money to pay his bill. The soldier said that he had wired home for money so that she enquired as to how much the telegram had cost. Apparently the cost would have gone a long way to paying the bill, so she railed at the soldier for his foolishness. Following the discussion, she entered the lounge and said to me, 'What do you think of that?' But when I pretended not to have heard, she said no more.

Her hotel was not palatial, but the atmosphere was homely. I sometimes enjoyed buying a magazine at a drug store and going to bed early to read it, although I sometimes had to interrupt my reading to deal with the odd bed bug.

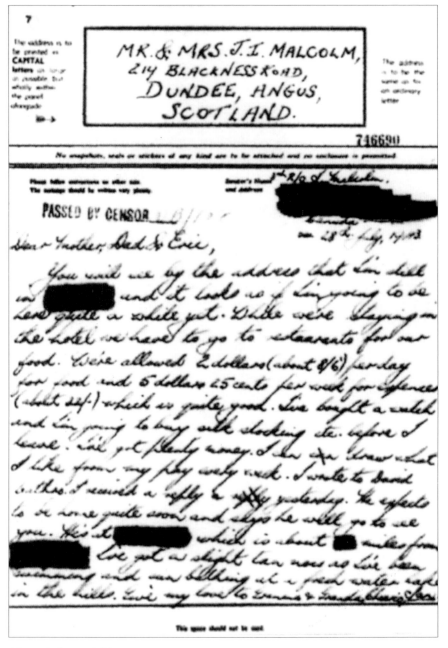

Airgraph from Halifax.

I wrote home on Airgraph forms, used only during the war. These forms, approximately 6½ x 8 inches, were photographed and then carried by 'plane as small negatives, in order to conserve both weight and space. The reproductions from the negatives which went through the letterboxes were roughly 4 x 5½ inches. Our letters were, of course, censored, and in the one I sent on 21 July, Censor 106 obliterated my hotel address and a reference to Halifax in the letter. A week later, Censor 108 did likewise except for the word Canada in the address, but, on 14 August, the same person left in the whole address and a reference to the Northwest Arm.

When having a meal in a restaurant one day, I found myself in the company of young men and women of the Royal Canadian Navy. We got talking and when a lady member of the Service asked how long I had been in the Merchant Navy and I said just over two weeks, they all laughed and thought I was having them on. Ships did not generally cross the Atlantic in only four days.

In addition to the $2 a day for food, we were paid $5.25 a week subsistence money and these payments were made every Monday at a Merchant Navy hostel near Bedford Basin, on the north side of Halifax. By living cheaply, I saved enough to buy myself a watch costing $20. I remember lounging in an armchair in the hostel, where ratings were accommodated, and listening for the first time in my life to commercial radio advertising.

Eventually, the day came to leave. We had to take only the bare essentials with us in a small suitcase or grip and the rest of our luggage was to go in the luggage car of the train on which we were to travel. Dressed in our best uniforms (I had only the one!) we loaded our luggage into a van when, to my embarrassment, my colleagues laughed at the leather money belt I had put on, which was exposed because I had my jacket off. The belt was my father's idea. His First World War experience had taught him that money had to be guarded, but my later and very different experience taught me why my colleagues had laughed. It was only in port that valuables could not be left unguarded. Throughout my time at sea I never gave a thought to anything being stolen and nothing ever was.

We now knew that we were to join *Liberty Ship D* in Baltimore, Maryland, but this first train was to convey us only as far as Montreal. I left Halifax with some regret. Although experiencing some loneliness, my stay there had been safe and pleasant and I was off again into the unknown. But it was this going into the unknown which I came to regard as the spice of life. Without it, life becomes a bore.

Although I had previously heard of only the Canadian Pacific Railway Co. (CPR), I found myself on a Canadian National Railway Co. (CNR) train. It was higher, wider and more comfortable than any train on which

I had travelled in Britain, but the latter attribute owed something to the fact that, for the first time in my life, I was travelling first class. We sat in wide lounge-type chairs which, at night, were transformed into beds while upper beds were pulled out from the wall.

When the train stopped at Moncton, New Brunswick, I leapt out with the intention of trying to phone David Cathro, a former colleague in the Dundee office, who was stationed there with the RAF. But the telephone system was strange to me and the RAF officer on the platform, whom I asked for help, was caught unawares. The train was about to leave, I reboarded regretting that I had not been able to make contact and the train continued its journey. The route took us along the southern shore of the St Lawrence and we passed close to the city of Quebec, where I recognised the Hotel Frontenac which I had seen in newsreels.

We arrived at Montreal at about 8 a.m. the following morning and a coach conveyed us to the Carlton Hotel which was to be our base for that day only as we were due to board another train in the evening. After being allocated rooms and breakfasting in the hotel, we were free to spend the day as we liked.

My day in Montreal was not spent to the best advantage. I wanted to see as much as I could, but was not experienced enough to know how to go about it. I spent the morning walking by myself through uninteresting streets, yet something occurred which impressed me. I had lost a button off my uniform jacket and entered a draper's shop to buy a replacement. As I stood waiting to be served, the young lady shop assistant spoke French to the gentleman before me. But, when it came to my turn, she addressed me in English. I have always been impressed by people who can speak fluently in a language other than their own as few can do this in Britain. Yet here was a shop assistant who was bilingual and no doubt had to be in order to hold her very ordinary job.

In the afternoon, I visited the centre of the city with Charlie Duncan, our 3rd Engineer Officer. I was eighteen and Charlie was in his early thirties, but we were to become buddies during the voyage. Charlie wanted to buy something for his young wife, but although he thought the world of her, he could never resist flirting and was extremely proud of his looks. When we entered a large department store on St Catherine Street, a good-looking young assistant rushed past the efficient looking older lady heading towards us. I then stood idly by while they flirted in a long conversation which did something for Charlie's ego, but nothing for mine!

Before we left the Carlton Hotel, I asked our room waiter for needle and thread to sew on my jacket button, whereupon he insisted on taking away the jacket for one of the staff to do the job. While I appreciated this, I realised that the service required a tip and, because of this, would rather have sewn on the button myself. I know that I under-tipped, but the small man who wished to be of service remained extremely courteous. I have always hated tipping which, I believe, demeans both parties and encourages the payment of low wages.

We left Montreal that evening on a United States train bound for Baltimore via New York and Philadelphia. This was the 'Chattanooga Choo Choo' of the tune played by the Glen Miller Orchestra, but we were not going as far as Chattanooga in Tennessee. As with our CNR train to Montreal, this train also had air-conditioning, but it was 'out of order'. Travelling south in midsummer, this was somewhat unfortunate. Once again a Negro attendant transformed our carriage into a sleeping car and I occupied a wide and comfortable bottom bunk. But it was stifling without the air-conditioning and, during the night, I released the spring-loaded roller blind which the attendant had pulled down. This allowed air to enter the window and I was able to get some sleep. When I awoke in the morning, I learned the reason for the blind being pulled down. My clothes, lying at the foot of the bed, were covered with soot which had blown in from the engine. Our white uniform shirts had detached, starched collars which we fixed on with studs and, as my other shirts were in my suitcase in the luggage van, I turned the collar inside-out to hide the dirt before presenting myself for breakfast.

Breakfast, and every meal on the train, was extremely enjoyable. I sat beside an elderly lady and a US serviceman wearing a uniform of a lighter blue than anything I had seen before. The lady was bound for Philadelphia and invited us both to dine at her home. I could not accept her invitation, but it was appreciated.

When the train stopped in New York's Grand Central Station, we were able to get out to stretch our legs. Some of the crew bought magazines from a bookstall on wheels and hurriedly reboarded the train in some excitement. They had paid for magazines with Canadian coins and were anxious that the train should leave before their deceit was discovered.

CHAPTER 4

BALTIMORE, MARYLAND

Baltimore is a large city and seaport, and when we arrived it was extremely hot with temperatures well into the eighties Fahrenheit. The officers and crew of *Liberty Ship D* were conveyed by coach from the railway station to two hotels. The senior officers went to the Southern Hotel while I, together with other juniors and ratings, went to the Biltmore, at the corner of Fayette Street and Paca Street. There were five of us in a very large room. We had only our heavy blue uniforms to wear. I still had to suffer my dirty shirt and we had no US money. Our luggage had not yet arrived and I felt that not having lighter clothes to wear in such heat was bad enough, but the lack of money suggested neglect on the part of our Captain. I therefore walked to the Southern Hotel, at the corner of Light Street and Redwood Street, and sought him out in his room a number of flights above ground level. I knocked at the door somewhat nervously and he appeared taken aback by the temerity of a junior officer who said he required some money. But he lent me $5 and so I had money before anyone else did. My associates were equally surprised by my behaviour.

We were in Baltimore for almost three weeks and, until our ship was ready to receive us, we stayed for over a week at the hotels. As in Halifax, we did not eat in the hotels, but were now given $4.50 ($1 = 5s 25d) a day and I sometimes patronised Child's Restaurant, at the corner of Charles Street and Fayette Street.

During my stay at the Biltmore, I became friendly with a young Baltimore fellow of my own age who addressed me when I was looking in a shop window. He made out that he mistook me for a friend of his, but I knew he did not and merely wished to become acquainted. He said that he was English and that his name was Robert Mitchell. His grandparents were English and called Mitchell, but he was American and his name was Philip Robert South. Yet he was a pleasant enough fellow who brightened up my

Identification card.

time in Baltimore and I later learned the reason behind the untruths. His father had married again and he didn't approve.

Like so many Americans, Robert was very generous. He worked in the gents outfitter's shop of the Schwartz Manufacturing Co. and the first time he called at the Biltmore he gave not only me, but each of my four room-mates, a tie. This was, of course, courting popularity, but, instead of appreciating the gift, they thought it unnatural that a complete stranger should be so generous and laughed about it behind his back. His ambition was to head for Hollywood and be a movie star. One evening, he donned my uniform and we went to Baltimore Street together. He had his photograph taken in an automatic kiosk and, pipe in hand, spun a yarn to a young lady attendant while I stood by in 'civvies' (civilian clothes) witnessing how a uniform could impress.

The Biltmore was a smaller, older and inferior hotel compared to the Southern, but the staff were kind and it possessed one special feature which the Southern did not. It had a swimming pool in the basement and during those hot summer days I revelled in its use. Strangely enough, nobody else seemed to use it and it certainly had a disused look as a great deal of furniture was stored beside it and the light 'switch' was two bare wires which had to be crossed! The desk clerk allowed Robert to use the pool with me and, after I had left the hotel and was living on board the ship, he allowed us both to use the pool – even supplying towels.

I spent most of my time wandering about the centre of the city, looking at the shops which were so full of goods not available in wartime Britain.

I was always looking for small gifts to take home to my parents and Eric. Baltimore Street was the main venue and I drank innumerable glasses of lemonade from open-air stalls. The vendors had large round glass tanks in which halved lemons or oranges floated and a glass cost only a nickel or 5¢. I was not accustomed to such heat and, for once in my life, did not eat much. A letter home informed my parents that I had eaten my first banana. I had not seen bananas in Halifax and ships could not be spared to bring such a luxury to Britain. For the first time I enjoyed freshly made popcorn, which Robert and I purchased before entering a cinema. One shop selling watches had an attractive advert for the Rolex Oyster watch which caused a group of people to gather at the window. The watch was advertised as shockproof, anti-magnetic and waterproof and went through an electrically operated automatic sequence which showed it continuing to work as it was dropped past a magnet into a jar of water.

Burlesque theatre ticket, Baltimore.

At night, Baltimore Street had a different life as it contained a number of burlesque theatres. I attended a show in the largest of these with the 4th Engineer and we thoroughly enjoyed the evening. The whole performance was good. It was good 'variety' and there was a 'striptease' act included. On another evening I went on my own to the smaller and rather seedy theatre across the street. Here there was a vulgar and suggestive stage show followed by a film and, unknown to me, some of my shipmates were also in the audience so that they afterwards ribbed me for sitting near the front during the striptease!

On two occasions I visited Greenmount Cemetery at some distance from the centre of the city. The first visit was not intentional as I boarded a tramcar merely to see if it would convey me to some green countryside. When I saw the large area of green grass and devoid of buildings, I disembarked from the tram and enjoyed sitting on a bench in the quietness of the cemetery. It was not until many years later that I learned that Johns Hopkins, the founder of Baltimore's University and world-famous teaching hospital which bear his name, is buried there, as is a Miss Patterson of Baltimore who, on marrying Jerome Bonaparte, brother of Napoleon, became Mme. Patterson Bonaparte.

Robert took me to the Walters Art Gallery, which contains one of the finest private art collections in the United States. I still have the handbook of the collection and a leaflet dated 1942 which contains brief notes about the collection. On the front of the leaflet is printed: 'Approximately thirty-five hundred objects have been evacuated to safer places for the duration of the war.' How the custodians could have considered Baltimore to be in any danger is beyond me.

Baltimore is south of the Mason–Dixon Line and has a considerable Negro population, although I did not come into contact with many as they lived in the poorer areas which I did not frequent. On one occasion, however, I strayed into a Negro district when a young man asked me for money and I found myself surrounded by a group of his friends. I felt a bit frightened and gave the man something like 10¢. They then made way for me to pass and I heard one of them ask, 'How much did he give you?'

On another occasion I saw two Negro boys of about twelve years of age fighting and rolling together on the ground when one called the other a black bastard. It is the adjective used by one black boy to another which has made me remember the incident.

Because others of my colleagues were staying at the palatial Southern Hotel, I was there quite often. The hotel lift was operated by a pleasant Negro lady who may have been about forty. On descending with her one day, she said to me, 'I'll miss you boys when you go.' I replied that there would no doubt be another lot following us. 'They won't be as nice as you boys,' she replied. I appreciated her remark. It indicated that the British merchant seamen had been kindly and friendly towards her and she, as a second class US citizen, was grateful. I would like to have visited her home and seen the circumstances in which she lived.

But the other side of the coin was an incident which took place after we had taken residence on board ship. We had Negro stevedores and the routine of loading was shattered one day by the Negro foreman storming up to the Mate's cabin in a fury. 'Nobody calls us niggers,' I heard him shout. 'We're coloured men, not niggers.'

I believe it was Robert who suggested that we spend a weekend out of town. This was to be at some coastal resort some thirty miles from Baltimore, but ended up being Washington, DC. We were to leave early Saturday afternoon and I can remember my frustration when he didn't appear at the hotel until early evening. This was typical of Robert. No doubt he had to work until 5 p.m.

The journey by train took about an hour. We found downtown Washington extremely busy and full of servicemen and I was amused to see a long queue of them waiting to be tattooed. Our problem was finding a room for the night and we visited so many 'full up' hotels that we considered a doss house consisting of long rows of trestle beds where the price of 50¢ suited us, but where, we suspected, the company might not. Eventually, we found a hotel where a room was available at an exorbitant price and where there was a single bed in addition to the double bed we were to occupy. Like so many more, the hotel manager had no respect whatever for those involved in the war. When we hesitated because of the price, he clearly displayed his impatience by his 'Well, do ya want it or don't ya?' But we had little choice and took it with cash 'up front'. If someone came to occupy the single bed, we would each get $1 back. We took the double bed and about 1 a.m. in the morning someone came stealthily into the room and, without switching on the light, entered the single bed. We resumed our sleep somewhat relieved at the reduced cost!

Our room-mate turned out to be Sergeant Milton Turner of the US Army, a quiet and likeable man. Many British people regard the Yank as loud-mouthed and brash, but my experience of the US soldier during the war did not substantiate this view. Milton, who was a little older than we were, joined us to see a bit of Washington on the Sunday. We visited the Capitol and the White House and, somewhere on the way, I bought a cheap camera which took away almost all my money. Regrettably, I did not know how to use a camera and took snapshots of Milton and Robert in the park area behind the White House where they are so far away as to be unrecognisable. Milton had to leave us before Robert and I visited the Pan American Building.

Our visit to the Pan American Building led to an amusing incident. The ground floor of the building consisted of a spacious area where a parrot sat on a very high perch which raised it almost to the level of the balcony above. Separated from Robert and in civilian clothes, I had mounted the stairs to the balcony and, together with a small group of people, found myself looking at the colourful bird. A girl of about my own age asked me something about it and, when I answered this, a man of about forty asked what kind of bird it was. I turned to look him straight in the eye as I thought he was having me on, but, as it appeared he was not, I told him it was a parrot. He then asked if it had come from Africa whereupon I said that, as we were in the Pan-American Building, I considered it to be a native of the Amazon Region of South America. His next question almost floored me. 'Is that where you come from?' he asked. I told him it was not and that I came from Scotland and so we got into conversation. When he learned that I was a radio officer in the British 'Merchant Marine' (the name used by the US for their equivalent Service) he told me that he had been offered the rank of major in the US Army and that he and his wife were visiting Washington from Texas. They were well dressed, had a very large car and he was in the oil business. But I have always wondered that such a man did not recognise a parrot!

My newfound Texan acquaintance asked me if I would like to accompany him and his wife on their tour of Washington. I gratefully accepted their hospitality if Robert, who was somewhere else in the building, could be included in the invitation. He readily agreed and so I found myself climbing into the largest car I have, even sixty-seven years later, ever been in.

During our tour of Washington, we sped past the Pentagon and went as far as the US Military Cemetery, across the Potomac River, in Arlington, Virginia, where I was impressed by the smartness of the two soldiers who stood guard over the tomb of the 'unknown warrior'. I have since stood beside similar tombs in other cities and have wept for them all. Anyone who does not weep, does not understand. On leaving our hosts at the airport, I wandered around rather aimlessly as, having spent so much on my camera, I could not buy anything in the large cafeteria.

Robert and I also visited the Smithsonian Institution, Washington Monument and Lincoln Memorial. Of these, I was most impressed by the Lincoln Memorial where the elevated and larger-than-life stone image of Lincoln sits sprawling in its chair. I then held the simplistic view, which I had been taught at school, that Lincoln had been the great emancipator of the Negro slaves. It was many years later that I learned that his main aim was to preserve the union of the States and that the freedom of the slave was incidental. Having made full use of the day, we made our way to the clean and spacious railway station to catch a train back to Baltimore.

We were scarcely in the station when it was announced over the public address system that a train was leaving for Baltimore. As we had no knowledge of the train times, we thought this was fortunate, but were soon told that we could not travel on that particular train as it was not a train of the Baltimore and Ohio Railroad. We had travelled to Washington by that railroad and as we held return tickets, had to make the return journey on one of their trains. This came as a surprise to me. I had never heard of two railway companies competing on the same route. I got into conversation with a middle-aged lady on the subject and, because she recognised my accent as British, she invited Robert and me to have a milkshake with her in the station buffet. Her name was Judith Robles, a Jewish lady born and brought up in the East End of London whose family had emigrated to the States when she was fourteen. I was embarrassed that I did not even have enough to buy a milkshake, but Judith easily got back the price of the milkshake as I corresponded with her for many years during which she was to spend holidays with my parents and with me and my family.

We made the return journey in a Pullman-type carriage on an almost empty train. It seemed a long journey, was certainly a monotonous one and we arrived very late and very tired. We had only enough small change to allow us to take a tramcar to Robert's home in William Street and later to convey me by tram to its terminus at the docks as we had vacated the hotels. This was the only time I was in Robert's home. His parents were asleep as we quietly drank iced-tea in the kitchen. I then walked through deserted streets and stood alone at a tram stop before boarding the empty tram.

Liberty Ship D had become the SS *Samite* and when I mounted the gangway, as I had not sought out the name on the bow or stern and there were so many identical Liberties in the docks, I confirmed with the watchman that I was boarding the right ship. This so amused the watchman that he recounted it to someone in the crew and the following day they joked about me returning so drunk that I didn't know which vessel I was boarding! It had indeed been a memorable day. My father wrote a letter of thanks to the Washington address of Mr and Mrs Brooks, who had taken us around Washington, but received no reply.

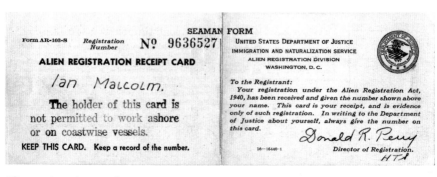

Alien registration receipt.

CHAPTER 5

THE SHIP AND DEPARTURE FROM BALTIMORE

The Liberty Ship was based on a design taken to the USA in 1940 by representatives of the Sunderland shipbuilding firm of Joseph L. Thompson & Sons, but the man whose name became synonymous with the Liberty was the US industrialist Henry J. Kaiser. Due to the heavy losses at sea, ships were required in a hurry and Kaiser used prefabrication and assembly line methods to build ships faster than ever before in history. 2,610 Liberty Ships were built at various yards throughout the USA. The average construction/assembly time was about a month, but one was launched within ten days of the keel being laid and completed only four days later. The first Liberty Ship was built in the same Bethlehem-Fairfield Shipyard in which the *Samite* was built. This was the *Patrick Henry* which entered service in January 1942 and, in all, this yard built a total of 385 of these vessels. This was a creditable record, but speed of work was achieved by paying bonuses and there was an occasion when welders were brought to trial and found guilty of deliberate bad workmanship in order to achieve the bonuses. Britain got 200 Liberty Ships under a lease-lend agreement.

Because the names of the British Liberty Ships bore the prefix 'SAM', British seamen referred to them as SAM BOATS. We believed, as many still do, that this was because 'Uncle Sam' had provided them. It was, however, mere coincidence and the prefix came about because the British Ministry of War Transport described this type of vessel as having the 'Superstructure Aft of Midships'. The *Samite* (7,176 grt) was launched as the SS *Holland Thompson*, but the name changed only days later when the ship was transferred to British registry. I imagined this to be an isolated occurrence, but learned later that this happened to many of the newly launched ships handed over to British crews and that this upset the Americans who had an interest in the original names.

A Liberty Ship.

To the experienced sailor, the Liberties were not fine ships with graceful lines, but rather utilitarian boxes with a maximum speed of about 12½ knots and capable of carrying 10,000 tons of cargo. Their expected life span was ten years, but many lasted for over twenty-five and some as many as thirty. In some respects they were in advance of many ships sailing the seas at that time. They were well-equipped, the accommodation was fairly good, and there was hot and cold running water in all the officers' cabins. They even had an ice-water drinking fountain on the main deck, unheard of on British ships. They were all metal ships with not a wooden deck to be seen, and most were all welded. This latter feature was perhaps the main point of criticism, as ships built in Britain had their plates riveted together at a time when welding had not then been perfected enough to be trusted. At the Baltimore Yard, however, the hulls were vertically riveted and only horizontally welded. This made them stronger and the *Samite* certainly proved capable of taking a great deal of punishment. But when we took her over, she already had two black marks chalked up against her as far as the more superstitious members of the crew were concerned. One was that her name had been changed before she had made her maiden voyage and the other was that it was said that a man had been killed by falling down a hold during her construction. By the time I left her some thirteen months later, some of this primitive superstition had rubbed off on me! It is easy to be rational in security, but, even in peacetime, sailors do not have that luxury.

All the *Samites* officers had a cabin to themselves with the exception of the 2nd 'Sparks' (the term commonly used for radio officers) and myself. We shared not only the smallest cabin but the only one on the inboard side of an alleyway (on the port side) with two portholes facing aft. This meant that we did not receive the advantage of a breeze in hot weather, yet always experienced additional heat from the galley on the deck below. Being a greenhorn, I accepted the accommodation I was given although this cabin sharing was entirely unnecessary as a larger double-berth cabin was left empty next to that of the 1st R/O on the deck above. Opposite our cabin was a somewhat larger one which had been given to the ship's carpenter who, although similar to an engineer and a skilled tradesman, was accorded only the rank of Petty Officer. The *Samite* was the only ship I was on where the carpenter lived among the officers (although he did not eat in the officers' saloon). Perhaps Captain Eccles felt that the Merchant Navy treated its carpenters unfairly. If an uncertificated engineer is given officer status then why not a carpenter?

Our cabin also lacked the small desk which was fitted in every other room yet, although cramped, it was reasonably comfortable. There were our two wide bunks – one above the other – fitted with interior-sprung mattresses and strip reading lights. There was one desk-type chair with curved wooden arms, a fitted wardrobe, a small washbasin with mirror and strip light and a settee covered in the same green Rexine material as the chair. The bunks ran fore and aft while the settee ran athwart ship.

The *Samite* went out into Chesapeake Bay to make a trial run and I stood on the boat deck (the deck above the main deck on which our four lifeboats were situated) on a beautiful afternoon as she sped along at maximum speed. Then days were spent loading our military cargo, which included rolls of newsprint and tins of condensed milk. During the loading, the 2nd Sparks and I had to check the stores in the large rafts which were supplied in addition to lifeboats. This was because the *Samite* carried no midshipmen. (Alfred Holt's apprentice deck officers were called midshipmen while other companies referred to them as apprentices or cadets. Apprentice engineer officers were not carried until long after the war.)

We also loaded a deck cargo which consisted of army trucks so that, when we left Baltimore, both fore and aft main decks could be crossed only by means of specially erected wooden cat-walks. Only the boat deck was clear. The main deck fore and aft of the central accommodation was covered with vehicles held in place by stranded wire.

But to complete our cargo, we moved to isolated Hawkin's Point at some distance from Baltimore to load explosives. We had five holds – numbers one, two and three forward of the accommodation and numbers four and five aft of it. Explosives were loaded into every hold except No. 3, immediately forward of the bridge and central accommodation. So, two months after leaving the UK, we were ready for sea.

My last night ashore was from Hawkin's Point. I had arranged to meet Robert at 7 p.m. in the foyer of the Southern Hotel. I do not recall how I made the journey into Baltimore, but Robert did not turn up. I sat waiting for over an hour in the large foyer, taking little interest in the usual traffic of civilians, servicemen and well-dressed women. Eventually I began the onerous journey back to the ship. A bus took me as far as a police road-block, at some distance from the city, and from there I was given a lift in an already crowded car which deposited me at the end of the quiet country road which led to Hawkin's Point. Fortunately for me, as I did not know the way, two young US Navy sailors, returning to their ship at the Point, disembarked from another car at the same time so that I had their company along the deserted road through the darkness. A letter from Robert, received months later, stated that he had waited for me!

CHAPTER 6

SHIP'S COMPLEMENT

The officers of the *Samite* numbered only eleven. There was the Master in overall command and the 1st, 2nd and 3rd Mates in the Deck Department. The Engine Room Department consisted of the Chief, 2nd, 3rd and 4th Engineers and the Radio Department of the 1st, 2nd and 3rd Radio Officers.

Captain Leonard Eccles, in his fifties, had the rugged weather-beaten features of a man who had done a lot of hard work and had seen everything there was to see. He had almost forty years' experience behind him and we had complete confidence in him. I was never ordered to address senior officers as 'Sir' and, to begin with, although he might not have been aware of it, I never addressed him in this way. This was because I had never used this form of address to my superiors on shore as it is often used only to ingratiate. But if Captain Eccles noticed the omission, it is to his credit that he never said so. He was Mate of the *Protesilaus* when she was lost after striking a mine off the Mumbles Lighthouse in the Bristol Channel near Swansea on 21 January 1940 and his previous ship, the *Rhexenor*, had been torpedoed and sunk on 3 February 1943 when proceeding independently from Freetown, Sierra Leone to Saint John, New Brunswick. These misfortunes had earned him the nickname of 'Unlucky' Eccles. Yet he survived the war and it seems to me the more appropriate epithet would have been 'Lucky' Eccles! He never spoke much to me and, in all the fifteen months we were together, never engaged me in friendly conversation. I think he was a good man who did not know how to relax with a youngster like myself and I was certainly too shy to be familiar with him.

The 1st Mate, Mr W. M. Thomas, was a stocky, heavily built Welshman in his forties. He was always friendly and 'hail fellow well met'. He had been 2nd Mate with Captain Eccles on the *Rhexenor* and had suffered frostbite of the feet during weeks spent in a lifeboat. He was never free of pain and wore heavy boots to alleviate it. His heavy step was particularly noticeable in the early mornings as he tramped the steel decks organising the deckhands.

The 2nd Mate, also a Welshman, was Mr Dai Lewis. Similar to Mr Thomas, he was an experienced seaman in his forties and both held Masters' Certificates.

Ian Smith, the uncertificated 3rd Mate, was a Scot. Although only about two years older than I, he had already been at sea for about three years and had all the self-assurance brought about by experience. He talked of former ships and of being in Singapore before it fell to the Japanese. When he asked me why I had joined the Merchant Navy, I honestly and innocently replied that I was due for call-up and decided on the Merchant Navy. He annoyed me by laughing at this and saying that he'd never heard anyone being so honest about it before. I found it difficult to comprehend why anyone, especially someone in the Merchant Navy, should look upon joining the MN as dodging the column.

Mr R. Ball, the Chief Engineer, was a quiet man of about fifty who had a Chief Engineer's Certificate. The 2nd Engineer was Mr Turnbull, a heavily built man of about the same age who had rather a ferocious look which belied his nature. He too had his Chief's 'Ticket'.

Charlie Duncan, the 3rd Engineer, was uncertificated and, as we carried no electrician, he was also our electrician. He had been born in Glasgow and taken to Australia by his parents when a baby. His home was in the small coastal town of Innisfail in North Queensland and although in his thirties, he had recently married a Glasgow girl only two years older than I was. I learned a lot from Charlie, including Australian slang expressions such as 'fair dinkum', and as he had at one time sailed with the Blue Star Line, I had his word for it that the grub was better on Holt ships. Charlie subscribed to the superstition already mentioned as he had with him the caul in which his head had been encased when born. According to him, no one who possessed a caul was ever lost at sea. Regarding superstition, the Chief Steward later reprimanded me for whistling at sea and although I never came across this one again, it was believed by the superstitious, particularly by those on the earlier sailing ships, that this invited a gale or bad weather.

The 4th Engineer was Harry Gibson who, although only about twenty-four, had his Second Engineer's Certificate and part of his Chief's. Of stocky build, he was a Tynesider who boasted that he wore the same dark brown unwashed shirt for three or four months. I liked Harry a lot and he struck me as being a phlegmatic man who could be relied upon in a crisis.

The Chief Steward, Mr Spears, although a Petty Officer, had a cabin in the officers' accommodation and wore a uniform which sported two sharply wavy gold bands. All Chief Stewards that I ever sailed with lived within the officers' accommodation and I think this was to protect them from the crew if the latter were in their cups and, having decided that the Chief Steward wasn't being generous enough to them, might endeavour to 'sort him out'! Mr Spears was a short, fat, ill-tempered man of about sixty who wore glasses and brushed his few strands of lank grey hair straight back over his otherwise bald pate.

Mr E. S. (Ted) Moore, the 1st Radio Officer/Purser, was a small, considerate and somewhat nervous man in his early thirties whose home was in Liverpool. When we first met, I asked how I should address him. 'Call me what you bloody well like,' he replied, but, although he laughed as he said it, the result was that I always addressed him as Mr Moore.

The 2nd Radio Officer was Neville Caro – an uncommunicative youth of nineteen or twenty, with lank black hair, who came from Blackpool. Like myself, he had only the Special Certificate and, as we were never friends, it was unfortunate that we had to share a cabin. But we never quarrelled; if I said something which annoyed him, only his expression showed disapproval and I never really got to know much about him. Compared with me, he was extremely untidy. When he went to bed, his clothes were just thrown down whereas mine were neatly folded and laid in place.

The crew numbered just over twenty, with many from the Liverpool/Birkenhead area. The Catering Department was composed of the 2nd Steward who was the Captain's tiger or personal steward, two Assistant Stewards who made the officers' beds, cleaned their cabins and served at table, and the Chief Cook, 2nd Cook and Galley Boy. The engine room staff numbered about seven and was composed of Firemen and Greasers plus the Donkeyman in charge. The Deck Department also had about seven ratings: Quartermasters who steered the ship, ABs and Ordinary Seamen (OS) plus the Bosun in charge and the Deck Boy, known as his 'Peggy', who was his shadow. And, of course, there was the Carpenter who really was a department on his own, but who took his orders from the Mate. In addition to the Carpenter and Chief Steward, the Bosun, Donkeyman and Chief Cook were Petty Officers.

Our DEMS gunners numbered about ten: half Royal Navy under a Petty Officer and half Army under a Sergeant, although I believe the RN PO had overall charge. DEMS stood for Defensively Equipped Merchant Ship, an Admiralty Organisation designed originally to provide RN gunners to defend merchant ships against attack. It was apparently at the suggestion of Holts that Army gunners became employed in this duty, as their Naval counterparts were in short supply. So men who joined the Royal Artillery to fight a land war were to find that they had become sailors in khaki in one of the six Maritime Regiments of Royal Artillery. Although members of HM Forces, DEMS gunners signed on Ships' Articles as Deck Hands – RN at 3/6d a week and Army at the usual supernumerary rate of 1s a month – as this gave them civilian status under international law so that they would not be interned if the ship chanced to enter a neutral port. It also had the effect of placing them under the authority of the ship's Master which operated to their advantage as, if they committed a minor offence, they could elect to be tried under the Merchant Shipping Act without it being recorded in their Service Records. DEMS gunners were transferred from ship to ship as necessary and our gunners joined us in Baltimore. Our total complement was in the region of forty-two men.

CHAPTER 7

MY FIRST CONVOY

Convoy UGS 18[1] assembled in Hampton Roads at the southern end of Chesapeake Bay and consisted of sixty-seven ships, including twenty-five which joined from New York. The letters UGS stood for USA to Gibraltar Slow, and as this series of convoys had been initiated at the time of the Allied invasion of North Africa (Operation Torch) in November 1942, we were the eighteenth convoy since that time. Captain Eccles and Mr Moore made the long and hazardous journey ashore by motor launch to attend the Convoy Conference. On their return they brought the news that, due to the rough sea, a pilot had missed his footing when leaving a ship and drowned. Shortly after noon on 15 September 1943, the convoy moved slowly into formation and out into the Atlantic. The *Samite* was at the head of the port column and the convoy speed was 9 knots. Other brand-new 'SAM BOATS' in the convoy were the *Samoa* and *Samwater*, also managed by Holts, and the *Sambrake* and *Samhain*, managed by Ellerman and Bucknall. These five vessels were the first British Liberties produced at the Bethlehem-Fairfield Shipyard. Convoy Commodore, Capt. G. L. Woodruff, USN (Retd) was on the US Liberty Ship *Thomas Pinckney*. Eleven ships of the US Navy provided the escort.

Shortly after we sailed, the USS *Weight* and the Norwegian *Vanja* returned to Norfolk – with steering and engine trouble respectively – and when the USS *John W Garrett* experienced condenser trouble on the 18th, she also detached from the convoy to put in at Bermuda.

Before going to sea, I had heard so much about the U-boats that I expected danger as soon as the ship put to sea. But, fortunately for me, although none of us knew it then, the time when the U-boat had the upper hand had ended when I was at Wireless College earlier in the year. Those who have never experienced a constant threat of danger will read clinical reports of attacks on convoys without appreciating the nervous tension which seamen continually suffered, even when no attack materialised. But, at the age of eighteen, I soon forgot the danger as Convoy UGS 18 proceeded eastwards in relatively calm seas with the sun shining and life assumed an orderly and not unpleasant routine. As 3rd R/O, I had the twelve to four watch, which meant that I was on watch in the Wireless Room from mid-day until four in the afternoon and from midnight until four in the morning. I found that my main problem was not coping with danger, but getting enough sleep. Those on the four to eight and eight to twelve watches can get at least seven hours sleep at a stretch, but those on the twelve to four cannot. Yet I experienced satisfaction from sitting there on my own in the quiet hours of the night when the only person I saw was the standby quartermaster who brought me a slice of buttered toast and a mug of tea, over-sweetened with condensed or evaporated milk, at 2 a.m. Dai Lewis, the 2nd Mate, was on the bridge and Charlie Duncan, the 3rd Engineer, was in the engine room.

My job was easy. For most of the watch I had only to listen on the medium wave calling and distress frequency of 500 kcs (now khz). We listened for messages from the Commodore, sent only in emergency, and, at set times, to transmissions to the convoy from designated land stations. The Commodore, often a senior naval officer called out of retirement, was in charge of the convoy under the Senior Officer of the Escort.

The controlling land stations also never gave us instructions unless it was imperative to do so. From the USA to halfway across the Atlantic our land station was Washington DC, using the callsign NSS. I would tune in to this station on its long wave frequency at a few minutes before 0200 hours GMT and sit listening to the call letters NSS being transmitted in the Morse code over and over again. Then, on the hour, the station would indicate the messages it had on hand, if any. Each ship had its own callsign (the *Samites* was BFPG), but the convoy had been given a collective callsign and this was the one I listened for. But Washington never had anything for us and I reverted to listening on 500 kcs a few minutes past the hour. Although we generally heard nothing, we kept a radio logbook. We signed 'On Watch', twice every hour we wrote 'Silence Period Observed' and we signed 'Off Watch'. Silence Periods were a feature of peacetime rather than wartime radio and were obligatory listening times on the calling and distress frequency when all working had to cease in order to allow a ship in distress a chance to be heard. The Silence Periods on 500 kcs were from fifteen to eighteen and from forty-five to forty-eight minutes past every hour. Every ship had the same type of circular, brass-encased, clock on the bulkhead of its wireless room with the Silence Periods marked in red. But, although observance of Silence Periods had to be signed for in wartime, they just did not exist. The whole clock dial could have been painted red.

Total silence was imposed as a transmission from any ship could give away the position of a convoy to a U-boat listening with its direction finder.

During the quiet uneventful hours of the night, when I listened and heard nothing, I also read books. The book which, for me, is synonymous with my first experience of the 'death watch', when life is reputed to be at its lowest ebb, is a book lent to me by Charlie. It is *The Last of the Australian Bushrangers* by Jack Bradshaw. In the quiet watches of the night, crossing the Atlantic in a slow convoy, I read of the land-based adventures of the Australian anti-hero, Ned Kelly and others of that ilk which took place in the great Australian outback, far removed in both time and place from the wartime Atlantic. Sailors, in their love/hate relationship with the sea, escape from their environment by reading about the land. Many dream of leaving the sea and earning their living by farming. It is a natural reaction. The soil is the antithesis of the sea and many sailors used to say that they would walk with an oar on a shoulder until someone asked what it was!

I did not find the slow passage across the Atlantic in any way monotonous or unpleasant. As often as not I missed breakfast by preferring to stay in bed after coming off watch at 4 a.m. and so rose, perhaps around 11 a.m., in good time to go to the wireless room again at noon. Sometimes I did rise for breakfast which was sumptuous, not only by British wartime standards, but by any standards. We always had a choice of cereal, which would be preceded by grapefruit or tomato juice, and followed by fish, bacon and egg, light-cakes and syrup, toast and tea or coffee. Not many people in today's hurried world enjoy such a breakfast and many contend that it is too much for them. At sea, breakfast was a meal equal to any other and, as morning was often the coolest and most pleasant part of the day, breakfast was eaten with great relish. Certainly everybody did not go right through the menu as I generally did. My only omission was the fish, which I never cared for at breakfast time.

Neville relieved me from watch for half an hour for lunch and I then sat in the wireless room through the sleepy afternoon until relieved by Ted Moore at 4 p.m. Dinner was at 6 p.m. and I relieved him for half an hour for his dinner before a group of us younger officers gathered in Harry Gibson's cabin to play poker or Monopoly. We played poker only for matchsticks and, as we did not have the standard Monopoly, we made the game (board and money) from memory. We could not remember all the London street names and so substituted them by those of Baltimore. I retired to my cabin at about 7.45 p.m. and, after a wash, was in my top bunk a little after 8 p.m. It was not always easy to get to sleep, but, at a quarter to midnight, a quartermaster knocked on my bunk saying 'One bell, Sparks' and left a mug of that ghastly over-sweetened tea. Feeling like 'death warmed up', I would splash myself at the tiny wash-hand basin, dress and go upstairs to the radio-room where Neville eagerly awaited my presence so that he could retire to his bunk. The ether would be dead quiet. I would read my book and perhaps rummage the filing cabinet where I learned from the crew accounts, kept by Mr Moore, that only the Deck Boy was paid less than I was! I was in a silent world of my own. Sometimes sleep lay heavily upon me so that I had to rise from my chair and pace the floor to keep awake. When Mr Moore came to relieve me at the end of my watch, I had no thought but to get to bed and, to his credit, he was never late and usually early. And so the days passed as the *Samite*, the leader of the port column of Convoy UGS18, headed slowly towards the Mediterranean.

About halfway across the Atlantic, the land station from which any instructions would come to the convoy changed from Washington DC to Rugby in England and so, at a specified hour, I now tuned in to Rugby radio (callsign GBR). But after a few minutes listening when no instructions came, I would revert to listening on 500 kc/s for the remainder of my four-hour watch where nothing could be heard but atmospherics during the night.

I pulled back the covers to get into bed one evening to find a flying fish there. It was rather a startling discovery, but I threw the fish, which must have landed on the deck, into the sea and said nothing to anybody. This rather disappointed the jokers who later made what they considered to be discreet enquiries about how I had slept that night.

During the crossing, and for the first time in my life, I saw beautiful sunsets. I sometimes stood on deck as the sun appeared to remain poised on the horizon and then sank slowly behind the many ships moving slowly eastwards in resolute pattern. It was a sight never to be forgotten and one unlikely be seen again.

Liberty ships had torpedo nets which could be lowered into the sea on both sides, but, as they slowed down their speed, the Commodore ordered them to be lowered only once for practice. We also had a barrage balloon which was also flown only once for practice as it too slowed us down.

During one night watch, radio silence was broken by a ship sending a distress message preceded by the signal SSSS which indicated an attack by submarine. The Morse was clear, but so faint that I realised that she was likely to be far away from us. She gave her position in relation to the Seychelles, which meant that the signals had crossed a thousand miles of the Indian Ocean and the continent of Africa before reaching well out into the Atlantic. This was a tremendous distance for a medium wave transmission and was made possible only by the general radio silence. I believe the vessel in distress to have been the *Banffshire*, which was torpedoed and sunk in position 09°26'N 71°20'E on 29 September 1943.

But as we neared Gibraltar, I began to hear Spanish coastal radio stations working on the calling and distress frequency of 500 kcs. Spain was under the Fascist regime of General Franco that had been helped to power by Hitler's Germany and Mussolini's Italy during the Spanish Civil War (1936-39). Although technically neutral, the Spanish government supported the Axis and it was generally recognised that Spain reported all movements of Allied convoys into and out of the Mediterranean via the Strait of Gibraltar.

Approaching Gibraltar, we came under the protection of RAF Coastal Command. I was at first startled and then delighted when a plane suddenly flew over the convoy. Shortly afterwards, I was sitting in my cabin when the Carpenter passed my door with a handful of letters. When about to enter his cabin and as a supposed after thought, Chippy turned to me and said 'Have you got your mail?' 'What do you mean?' I asked and he then explained that the plane which had passed over the convoy had delivered mail to the Naval Escort for the ships in the convoy. I immediately rushed up to Mr Moore on the deck above to ask if there were any mail for me. He had no idea what I was talking about. Coastal Command did not deliver letters and I was the victim of a rather clever practical joke which did not greatly amuse me at the time!

On Sunday 3 October and after eighteen days at sea, our armada of ships passed through the Strait of Gibraltar but, instead of proceeding directly into the Mediterranean as most seemed to expect, anchored just east of the Rock. Rumours began to fly about that we were part of an invasion force bound for the south of France. But after a short time at anchor within the safety of the Rock, the convoy reformed and headed eastwards into the Mediterranean. It now numbered seventy-seven ships. A ship had joined off Casablanca, four left at Gibraltar and sixteen joined off Europa Point.

The US Navy had provided the escort across the Atlantic and the Royal Navy was to take over that duty and escort us through the Mediterranean. Due to a 'bungling of communications', the words of the Commodore in his report, there was a mix-up as to where the RN escort was to relieve the USN escort. When the USN escort received notification of where the takeover was to take place, the convoy was already east of that position and had to sail back until the RN ships were sighted!

I can only deduce that we had sailed past them during the night. The information concerning the rendezvous had not been received early enough by the USN escort, due to it having been transmitted to them in a code to which they did not have access. I should like to have heard the comments made by some of the merchant skippers about that little episode! The RN escort consisted of the Flower Class corvettes HMS *Lotus, Poppy, Starwort, Dianella* and *Saxifrage* and the *Lulworth,* which bore the name of her class of vessels.

CHAPTER 8

ATTACKED

Monday 4 October was a beautiful day. We were sailing leisurely in the blue Mediterranean, the sea was calm and there was the comforting view of the North African coastline in the starboard distance. Our position in the convoy had been changed and I believe we were now the last ship in the second column on the port side. It is likely to have been the engineers (certainly not the deck officers!) who suggested that we had been relegated to this position because of bad station keeping. But, as the Commodore's report states that station-keeping was above average, the real reason would be that convoys assumed a different pattern in the Mediterranean, with fewer but longer columns than those maintained in the Atlantic. When the convoy was off Oran at 0800 hours, seventeen ships, including the Commodore's, detached themselves to enter the port. Sixty-one ships proceeded eastwards, with Commodore Berry, RNR, now in charge.

The day passed as usual and, as usual after dinner at 6 p.m., we played Monopoly in the 4th Engineer's cabin. About 8 p.m., I repaired to my cabin to get ready for bed and my less than four hours sleep before going on watch. Neville Caro had begun his watch and so I was alone in the cabin. It was almost dark as I stood in trousers and singlet washing myself at the small wash-basin when the tranquillity of routine was startlingly shattered by the loud incessant ringing of the ship's alarm bells. As far as I was concerned, the bells were aptly named! They certainly struck terror into me. Men were shouting and running about and yet, because of nearly three weeks of peaceful routine, I could hardly believe that the danger I had expected before coming to sea was actually upon us. My 'action station' was the wireless room. I did not stop even to put on my uniform jacket, but grabbed my life jacket and ran upstairs to the wireless room. Mr Moore was already there and Neville had departed to his post of assisting a gunner at an Oerlikon on the bridge directly above. Ted Moore and I stood together for only a matter of seconds before the guns of the *Samite* began to fire. As soon as our guns 'opened up', Ted yelled the appropriate cliché, 'Give it to the bastards', and seconds later the *Samite* was hit. The explosion did not seem all that violent to me, but I saw the fear in Ted Moore's eyes as I am certain that, unlike me, he had not forgotten the explosives loaded at Hawkin's Point.

The *Samite* was now out of action. The reassuring throb of the engines had ceased and the ship drifted silently to a stop. The generators were not functioning and we were in total darkness. There was a fire in No. 3 hold. It seemed that we would have to 'abandon ship' and Captain Eccles gave the order to proceed to 'boat stations' so that we lined up on the boat deck beside the lifeboat to which we had been assigned. Ted Moore put the secret code books into the purpose-made perforated lead box and heaved it into the Mediterranean. On our port side a ship was engulfed in flames and I saw silhouetted figures running along her catwalk, similar to ours, over her deck cargo. In the stillness, men's voices carried clearly across the water as they abandoned the stricken ship. The convoy continued on its way. The casualties were left behind in the silent darkness.

The convoy had been attacked by German aircraft and one of our Army gunners told me shortly afterwards that the ship had been hit by an aircraft which they had shot down. It is little wonder that he thought this, as we subsequently learned that we had been struck by a radio-controlled glider bomb delivered from an aircraft which could remain out of range of the ship's guns.

I was frankly disappointed when I learned that the *Samite* was not going to sink. It was more heroic and romantic to be a survivor of a vessel lost at sea! But the *Samite* was in a mess and we were indeed 'survivors' as the glider-bomb had hit No. 3 hold, the only one which did not contain explosives. Had the bomb hit any other hold, the ship would have been blown up. The official war history of Alfred Holt & Co., *A Merchant Fleet in War* by Captain S. W. Roskill, RN, records the incident, but omits the important fact that we were carrying explosives. We were in no way unique in carrying this dangerous cargo as many of the ships were similarly loaded. According to Roskill, the attacking force consisted of twenty-five torpedo bombers and twenty Do. 217s equipped with glider bombs.

The explosion had blown some of our deck cargo into the sea. The steel deck on the port side of No. 3 hold had been ripped up and engine room pipes exposed. The officers' dining saloon was a shambles. The area of damage extended to directly underneath and two decks below the wireless room, yet Ted Moore and I had experienced very little of the explosion although a broadcast receiver had been lifted from the screws which held it in place and our wet batteries, in the small battery room off the wireless room, had been dislodged.

Directly below us was the cabin of Mr Ball, the Chief Engineer. He had left his cabin when the alarm bells rang, but returned for something, perhaps a torch, when the bomb struck. The steel deck of his cabin was given an undulating appearance and Mr Ball received an injury to the lower part of his legs which caused them to swell up. His bunk, however, remained intact and when Charlie and I visited him, he lay cheerful enough, but in pain.

Our casualties were mercifully few and were laid out on the port side of the boat deck, just aft of my cabin. Mattresses and bedding, including mine, were dragged out for them to lie on and a steward arrived on the scene with mugs of tea. I immediately noticed the tea had a peculiar taste and mentioned it to the steward – when he told me it had been laced with rum, I handed it back to him saying that I didn't 'drink'.

Injuries were generally of a minor nature, but Alf Taylor, the Chief Cook, had a fractured skull. Arthur Neil, a thirty-year-old AB from New Ferry on the Wirral, was missing and it took a great deal of searching before he was found dead behind the steel door on the port side which led from the crew's accommodation on the main deck. We surmised that he had been going to his action station when he saw the glider bomb approaching. He had then stepped back into what seemed to be the comparative safety of the doorway so that, when the explosion occurred, the door was blown back against him.

A corvette came alongside and a voice enquired through a megaphone as to how things were with us. Looking down at her crowded decks, I was amazed at the number of men who stood there. She was so much smaller than the *Samite* yet must have had more than twice our complement.

Later in the night, all available hands descended the starboard vertical steel ladder to the foredeck in order to pull on a line fired from the *Saxifrage* which was to take us in tow. On descending the ladder we had to bend down to pass underneath trucks of our deck cargo – which were lying at all angles. As we then waited in the darkness on the foredeck for the line to be fired, Mr Thomas said to me, 'And this is your first trip to sea!' A plane arrived as we waited there and its Morse lamp blinked at us, but as we were unsure of its identity, no answering signal was made.

Liberty Ships were well prepared for emergencies. Each cabin had an old-fashioned style oil lamp which now proved invaluable, and in the wireless room we now used our emergency batteries. It was my job to check and record the specific gravity of these every day and to charge them as necessary. British life jackets were put on over the head and I had already worn one during boat drill on the *Queen Elizabeth*. Our US life jackets were put on like ordinary jackets and had cord ties in front to hold them in place. Each jacket was fitted with a red light at the shoulder which could be turned on to let people see you if you were bobbing about in the sea during darkness. There was also a square-shaped torch with a thin metal handle. By threading a jacket tie through this handle, the torch was held in place in front of you, letting you see where to go, yet leaving your hands free. This was how we were able to find our way about the ship during this period. There was also a knife and a large safety pin attached to each jacket.

The Hunt class destroyer HMS *Cleveland,* which had come out from Oran to assist, now stood by the convoy's casualties and Surgeon Lieut. I. B. MacDonald, RCNVR, and his petty officer assistant boarded to treat our wounded. On completion of this task, they could have returned immediately to their ship, but delayed doing so because, said the young doctor to me with a smile, 'The food is better here.' How he was aware of this so late in the evening I do not know and rather suspect that he wanted to stand by his patients a little longer. The PO saw a bandage on my left wrist and asked if I had been wounded. I had to tell him that I had been ironing clothes when the loose wooden handle of the iron had caused it to slip round and burn me!

I was back on watch in the wireless room when the *Saxifrage* (Lt J. Renwick, RNR) attempted to take us in tow. The first I knew of this was a tremendous and, in the circumstances, rather startling bang on our hull. The *Samite* proved too heavy for the corvette so that she had been pulled back against us. The tow line was cast off and we remained stationary.

The convoy had been attacked about ten miles off Cape Ténez, in position 36° 42′N 01° 17′E: between Oran and Algiers and approximately ninety miles west of Algiers. The burning ship on our port side was the *Fort Fitzgerald*. She had been struck by an aerial torpedo and was so badly damaged that the Royal Navy subsequently sank her by gunfire. The Norwegian ship *Selvik*, which joined the convoy at Oran, and the USS *Hiram S. Maxim* were also damaged. We learned that the crew of the *Hiram S. Maxim* abandoned her, but returned when it became obvious that she was not going to sink. This caused some amusement on board the *Samite*. Typical Yank! Not like the stoical British! But perhaps her master was just a bit more prudent. She had no explosives in her cargo, but her engine room was flooded. The *Hiram S. Maxim* made Algiers under tow. The *Selvik* proceeded with the convoy.

5 October was again a beautiful day, and we now lay on our own in a calm sea awaiting the tug from Algiers. There was no sign of either the *Fort Fitzgerald* or the *Hiram S. Maxim*. It amused my shipmates that I was now dressed in my best, but my reasoning was that this made good sense if we

had to abandon ship. In my pockets were the silk stockings I had bought in Baltimore for my mother and a wallet for Eric containing $10. Even more amusing, however, was the anxiety of Charlie Duncan concerning the repossession of a Gladstone-type leather bag containing presents for his 'wee' wife, as he always referred to her. Charlie had deposited the bag in the lifeboat to which he was assigned and that lifeboat had been lowered to within a few feet of the water. Although it was decided that we were not to leave the ship, the lifeboat was left in that position all night. So Charlie had a problem which was not resolved until the boat was returned to its davits the following day. The Mate refused Charlie's request to retrieve the bag earlier and nobody else had any sympathy for his predicament either. Amusingly one of the sailors, who had been caught naked in the showers when the alarm bells sounded, swore to me that he would never take another shower at sea.

The RN tug *Charon* eventually arrived about midday and the long silent haul to Algiers began. It was a relief to be moving again, although there was now only the swish of water instead of the throb of the engines. During my afternoon watch I kept looking out of the porthole towards the north, where the south coast of France lay and where the German planes had their bases. I had no bunk to go to and would have had to make do with lying on our smallish and not very comfortable settee, but Charlie suggested that I use the longer one in his cabin and even took a turn of sleeping there himself to allow me to have his bunk. As the saloon was in a mess, meals were now brought to our cabins and the RN Petty Officer Gunner did a first-rate job as substitute Chief Cook. The refrigerator was out of operation and large steaks were on the menu, as the meat had to be eaten up before it went bad. During my afternoon watch on 6 October, the body of Arthur Neil was committed to the deep. By the morning of the 7th, the battered *Samite* was safely at anchor in Algiers' harbour.[2]

CHAPTER 9

ALGIERS

It was again a beautiful morning and we were safe. There was an air of happiness and relief on board the *Samite*. At a distance the white buildings of the town looked beautiful and an aeroplane flew about pulling a target at which shore guns fired practice shots. On the main deck aft, the galley boy, helped by a number of the crew, was peeling potatoes. I had got to know this lad of about my own age during the Atlantic crossing and had sat on our deck cargo with him when he had told me that he came from Liverpool and that his father, a fireman in the Merchant Navy, had lost a leg in a Russian convoy.

In our emergency, when officers and men had been pulling on ropes together, there had been no class distinction and I descended from the boat deck and joined the circle of potato peelers. I was happily engaged in this when the Mate called to me from the boat deck that Captain Eccles wanted to see me. Captain Eccles stood on the small deck above the boat deck and in view of the assembled crew I climbed the ladders to where he was standing. He 'reminded' me that I was an officer and said that, if I wanted something to do, I was to tell Mr Thomas. The men on the main deck could not hear what was said, but they certainly understood that he was telling me off for mixing with them. I felt embarrassed, but from then on was held in great esteem by the crew! I had not intended to win popularity by peeling potatoes and although upset by Captain Eccles' disapproval, I later came to realise that he was right.

After dinner that evening, some of the crew went for a swim and on seeing them in the water, I decided to join them. The ship was well out from the shore, the sky was overcast and there was a swell running. I was the only officer who swam on that rather chilly evening when the whole crew lined the decks watching the swimmers.

Algiers was a very overcrowded port so that ships were tied up three abreast at the quays. This meant that if you were on the third ship tied up at a quay, you had to cross two other ships to reach it. Because of our damaged condition, we were taken directly alongside the day after our arrival and began to discharge our cargo. I could go ashore in my first real foreign port and, although we did not know it then, we were to be there for over two months. I got to know the town well and settled down to a different routine which, in my case, did not involve work. The majority of the officers had no interest at all in Algiers and seldom, if ever, went ashore. I wanted to see everything and went almost every day. That first day I went ashore, I felt elated as I walked past RN ships where sailors were whistling happily as they swabbed the decks in the bright clear air of the morning. After the recent dramatic events, it was great to be in such surroundings. This was the life!

Algiers stands on the side of a hill and, on leaving the docks, steps have to be climbed to reach the high-walled promenade which fronts the town. There were always young Arabs at the top of these steps who pounced on all sailors asking if they had cigarettes to sell. I did not smoke and so, to begin with, did not have any cigarettes, but I learned the drill very quickly and began purchasing my weekly ration from the ship's stores. As the ship had been supplied in the United States, we could buy only the American brands of Lucky Strike, Camel and Pieter Stuyvesant which came, duty free, in cartons of 200 costing 2/6d (12½ new pence). The market value, however, was 30 francs or 3s (15p) for a packet of twenty (the rate of exchange was 200 Algerian francs to the pound) so that we sold the cigarettes for twelve times more than we paid for them. I drew money from my pay only on our arrival and after that purchased my weekly ration of 200 cigarettes. The transactions with the black market Arabs were done furtively as the trade was illicit. The young Arabs made their living by it and the profit I made covered my very modest expenditure. The contrast with the United States was striking and the shops contained almost nothing which could be bought to take home as presents. Only leather articles such as handbags were available and most of these were so highly priced as to be almost beyond my pocket.

I would go to the cinema with Charlie. He worked in the engine room during the day so that it was left to me to purchase the tickets. Cinema seats had to be booked in the same way as seats in the theatre. The lady at the ticket office had the seat plan in front of her and I would choose the seats I wanted. She then crossed them out with a blue pencil and I would pay for and be given the tickets. When we entered the cinema an usherette dressed in black (the colour also worn by shop assistants and waitresses) would show us to our seats and, in the continental fashion, expect a tip.

We felt this service to be quite unnecessary as the rows were numbered and we were shown to the lettered seats before the lights went out. While waiting for the performance to begin, we would watch the arrival of others. Always noticeable was the soldier who had a French-Algerian girlfriend. According to custom, he could not bring her alone and so her family came too. Audiences always clapped when the flag of the Free French with its cross of Lorraine appeared on the screen and the flag of Turkey received a somewhat similar reception. I accepted as normal that the dialogue was in English, with subtitles in French, but came to realise that English-speaking people were fortunate that the majority of films were made in the USA.

On a Sunday afternoon shortly after our arrival, Charlie and I hitched a lift to a local beach. We were given a lift, there and back, in a private car driven by a Frenchman and in which his married daughter and small granddaughter were passengers. The man asked which ship we were from and it turned out that he was the pilot who had brought the *Samite* into the port. Although the beach was not at all attractive as it had dirty-looking sand, there were many people there.

Cinema ticket, Algiers.

Sté DES CHEMINS DE FER SUR ROUTES D'ALGÉRIE				
RO	Deux-Moulins	St-Eugène Mairie	Nelson	Place du Gouvernement
05913			1.	
Agha ou Champ de Manœuvre	Jardin d'Essai Musée Nat.	Caroubier ou Kouba	Maison-Carrée Place	2me CLASSE

Tram ticket, Algiers.

I went on a Cook's Tour of the infamous Casbah. The name means 'citadel' and there is a fort at the top of the hill, but the term applied to the whole seedy area adjacent to the fort. We were taken to the latter by coach then walked the whole way down through the steeply descending ribbon of streets to the town. It was an area of poverty, prostitution and violence, an area you dare not venture into alone and was otherwise 'off limits' to the Forces. The streets were extremely narrow and included many steps. Only pedestrians (and perhaps their donkeys) could negotiate them as it was almost possible at times to touch the buildings on either side with outstretched arms. At the conclusion of the tour, the French guide placed himself strategically at the exit from the last narrow street in order to receive tips from the 'tourists'.

Going to the public toilet was a memorable experience. In Britain, an elderly man is usually in charge of a large gentlemen's 'public convenience', where his duties are to keep the place clean and, nowadays, to prevent vandalism. But the day I descended the steps to a large 'public convenience' in Algiers, I found myself witnessing a thriving business. The place was full of US servicemen and in the care of a man and his wife. The lady was behind the desk of a kiosk similar to that of a theatre. The customer paid the 5 francs charge to her and was issued with a number of sheets neatly cut from a newspaper. This was my first experience of seeing a woman in a gent's toilet.

I had become acquainted with Phil Ayres, the DEMS Gunner (Maritime Regiment) who had told me that it was the plane they had shot down which hit the ship. He was a clean-looking, strongly built young farm worker

Phil Ayres.

from Sandown on the Isle of Wight. In his early twenties, he was only a few years older than I was and we began to go ashore together. But this too may have met the disapproval of Captain Eccles as Mr Moore called me into his room to tell me that I should not be friendly with an Army private. I had not enough experience and confidence to tell Ted Moore to 'go to hell' as I ought to have done, but continued to go ashore with Phil, merely arranging to meet him at some distance from the ship. Charlie did not care for this petty snobbery either and the three of us sometimes went ashore together.

No. 3 hold, which had been struck by the glider bomb, contained a large quantity of cans of evaporated milk. So many had been damaged without being broken open that Charlie and I collected them and, for weeks, drank evaporated milk while playing Coon-Can, an earlier form of Rummy, in his cabin during the evenings.

I normally went ashore in the afternoons. There was always a young British soldier on duty at the dock entrance and, to my embarrassment, he always saluted. On the afternoon of 1 November, I was approaching the sentry when I passed a young officer proceeding into the docks. The young man was dressed in naval battledress and I vaguely noticed that he was wearing the cap badge of the Royal Fleet Auxiliary (RFA). I had gone only a short distance past him when he called out to me, 'You're not Ian Malcolm are you?' and I was amazed and delighted that this was Fergus Duncan who lived just across the road from me in Dundee and who had been in a class ahead of me at school.

Fergus was 2nd R/O on the *Empire Scout,* which was berthed not far from the *Samite*. He had been away from home for ten months and at sea since 1940. In the days which followed, he visited me on board the *Samite* and I visited him on the *Empire Scout*. The *Empire Scout* (2,229 tons) was much smaller than the *Samite* and was the ex-German *Eilbek* which had been captured off Iceland by HMS *Scotstoun* in November 1939 when attempting to reach home under the Swedish flag. As she was of 1936 vintage, she did not have the 'mod cons' of the *Samite*, but I took to her right away – she had a character that the clinical Liberty Ship lacked. Fergus shared a small cabin with the bespectacled and youthful 3rd Sparks (many of us were easily identified by these characteristics!) who kept referring to the Arabs as Airabs. When I asked him why he did this, he said he thought it sounded better! The *Empire Scout* was bound for the UK so I asked Fergus to visit my parents, but not to mention that we had been in any danger.

After the war, Fergus became a commercial traveller and was president of the Dundee branch of their association when, on 19 February 1965, he took ill at a function in Dundee and died the following morning. He was only forty and I suspect that, similar to other such sudden deaths which occurred long after the war, the strain of wartime experiences was perhaps a contributing factor.

Every day we were looking for mail and there was great speculation as to whose fault it was when the weeks passed without news from home. But, at last, on 16 November, the long awaited mail arrived and the ship dissolved into silence as we sat in the privacy of our cabins devouring our letters. Few of us received any momentous news and did not expect any. I learned only that my parents and grandparents were well, that things were much the same at the Office and ARP Report Centre, that David Cathro was still undergoing his RAF training in Canada and what the weather had been like in Dundee. It was all very mundane stuff yet, like everyone else, I read the letters over and over again. The important thing was that we were remembered by those who mattered to us and had received tangible evidence of this. The *Samite* was a happy ship in the port of Algiers on the 16 November 1943.

News which arrived that day was that Captain Eccles and Mr Thomas had both been awarded decorations for their courage and leadership following the torpedoing of the *Rhexenor* in the Atlantic, when each had commanded a lifeboat and sailed over 1,000 miles to the West Indies. Captain Eccles was given the OBE and Mr Thomas the MBE. Due to their courage, seamanship and navigational skills, they had saved the lives of the occupants of their lifeboats, yet, because they were in the civilian Merchant Navy, they were given the same awards as those given to civilians in peacetime. I never read the Monarch's Honours Lists without thinking of Eccles and Thomas and the men in the lifeboats, without whose courage and fortitude the West Indies would never have been reached. It seems odd too that Mr Thomas was not considered to be worthy of the same decoration as Captain Eccles when both had shared the same responsibility in the same situation. Obviously the decorations were given according to rank, although it would seem to most of us that a higher decoration should reflect a greater endeavour.

Towards the beginning of our stay, a Frenchwoman came on board looking for business for a laundry. I gave her my washing, but when it was returned, one of my new white shirts was missing. Because of this, I gave her no more and when she came on board on subsequent occasions, continued to press for the return of the shirt. Eventually, I had to give up. I did not get the shirt back and was offered no compensation. I suspected that it had not just been 'lost', as articles of clothing were valuable and almost unobtainable. Shirts which some of the crew had bought in the States for 50¢ (12p) were sold in Algiers for £1. From then on, I did my own dhobi in the small washbasin in the cabin and ironed on a small wooden board which I placed on the settee, the only surface available. The settee was so low that I sat on the chair to iron. Charlie provided the electric iron which had been adapted to function from the ship's 110v DC supply. He showed me how to iron shirts which, at that time, were not of the coat type which button up the entire front. Our shirts had to be put on over the head and had only two buttons below the neck at the front which had to be undone to allow the head to enter. The collar was separate and starched so that it was stiff and glossy. After the shirt was on, the collar was put round the neck and attached to the shirt by a stud at the back. The tie was then inserted into the collar, which was secured by another stud at the front before the tie was tied. The coat type shirt was already in use in the States and shirts which I bought in Canada and States came to be part of my wardrobe, but the over-head type shirt continued to be sold in Britain until the early 1960s.

Charlie also showed me how to darn my socks which, at that time, were all woollen. Holes were not closed up by merely drawing the wool together. The wool which had been worn away was replaced by a carefully woven warp and weft. Charlie maintained that socks should be darned before washing as washing then helped to conceal the darn. In today's wasteful world of synthetic fibres, socks are often discarded when holes appear and darning is almost a lost art. Yet I continue to darn my socks, although the old familiar cards of darning wool seem to be unobtainable and woollen socks become increasingly expensive.

The Mediterranean region receives rain only in winter, when the prevailing wind changes direction with the movement of the sun and approaches from the Atlantic. It was coming down in buckets on the afternoon of 11 November when I had gone ashore to book cinema seats and came, quite by accident, upon the Armistice Day Parade. The pouring rain did not deter the crowd from showing their support for the Free French Forces as they passed. I was particularly impressed by the mounted Spahis and by the soldiers of the French Foreign Legion, so romanticised by P. C. Wren. The Foreign Legion had headquarters in Algiers and I would gaze at the legionnaire on sentry duty at the entrance. I was aware that these men had a knowledge of a North Africa which I would never know. General Giraud was the commander of the Free French Forces in North Africa. He was a very tall man and I saw him extricate himself from a car prior to entering a building.

One evening, towards the beginning of December, Charlie, Phil and I had quite an exciting experience. The ship had been moved from her quayside berth as soon as discharging was complete and was then at anchor in the harbour so that we had to go ashore by motor launch. We had been to a cinema and returned to the quayside wondering how we were going to get back to the ship. It was dark and rather late, so that we thought that we had missed the last US Liberty Boat which conveyed sailors back to their ships. It seemed we were stranded ashore for the night when we spied a coble tied up beside steps leading down to the water. It was more than just tied up; the oars had been removed and a heavy padlock and chain secured it against predators. Somehow or other I had a large safety pin in the pocket of my trench coat and when Charlie prodded the pin into the padlock, it miraculously snapped open. We now had a boat, but no oars. But, at that late hour and only a few hundred yards from us, a US Liberty Ship was bathed in light and discharging cargo. What interested us was that there was a great deal of her wooden dunnage lying around and we selected planks to serve as oars. Men from other ships who were in the same predicament as ourselves had joined us and we set off across the dark harbour in a slow and cumbersome fashion. But, when we were about halfway to the ship, the Liberty Boat, which we thought we had missed, passed us on its way to the ships at anchor! Its bow wave rocked our boat violently and its occupants, seeing what we were up to, shouted derisive remarks! When we eventually reached the *Samite*, we transferred to the ship's motor lifeboat, tied to the gangway. A rope was made fast to the coble and we set off again, with the coble in tow, to deliver our passengers to their ships before taking the coble back to its berth at the quay. The padlock was snapped on again and the owner would never know that his boat had been borrowed. It had turned out to be an unnecessary trip and very hard work propelling the heavy coble with planks of wood. But I enjoyed the escapade and found the pleasure enhanced because we returned the coble and not left it drifting about the harbour as most would have done.

The days passed pleasantly enough and I was quite content to be out of the war and in the safety of the port. Only a few weeks earlier, I couldn't have said where Algiers was: now I felt as if I had always known it. Almost everyone else moaned about being stuck there and most of the officers remained continuously on the ship. I could not understand this. Nobody had very much to do and we were out of danger, yet they were not content.

The only thing that bothered me was the lack of mail. Every day someone, sometimes me, presented his authority to collect mail for the ship at the Fleet Mail Office. This often entailed setting off in the ship's motor lifeboat and I used to enjoy making these trips across the harbour, particularly when I was at the tiller. But every day the answer was the same and every day someone would be at the ship's rail as the boat returned from the shore when a shake of the head conveyed the usual message. We remained in Algiers until the 23 December, but received only the one batch of mail in all that time.

I wrote many letters home. We were allowed only one Air Letter form per week, but could write as many ordinary letters as we wanted. The postage on Air Letters was 3*d* and ordinary British adhesive stamps were used. The letters generally arrived home with Maritime Mail stamped on them although some were stamped From HM Ship, and carried the signature of the Censor. All letters both to and from the ship were censored and all letters from home arrived resealed with a white adhesive label which identified the censor by a number. On the white label in large black letters it read, for example, OPENED BY EXAMINER 7005. We were all very careful what we said in letters, but the occasional letter which I wrote or received arrived at its destination with a piece cut out. This in practice meant that two items of news were deleted as both sides of the paper were written on.

I never saw the airgraph used in the Mediterranean other than at Christmas. Towards Christmas, Forces were provided with copies of a special one, in lieu of Christmas cards, and which was obviously designed to show a harmony which did not always exist between the Americans, French and British. Because I could get only one or two of these Christmas airgraphs, I made one of my own by getting a blank form and tracing the Arab on an Algerian 200 franc note which I thought was an improvement on the standard design, but have an idea that it failed to reach its destination. Although many numbered their letters to see if they all arrived, I did not follow this practice.

The *Samite* did not have a ship's library, as these were supplied by the Seafarers' Education Service of Endsleigh Street, London, to vessels sailing from the United Kingdom. A library consisted of a number of books which came packed in a large wooden box with leather straps and carrying handle, and I later became acquainted with this service as a 'librarian'. Ships could exchange libraries abroad, but if you did not have one in the first place, there was no hope of acquiring one overseas. But, like many seafarers, I read a great deal and my reading during that time included Steinbeck's *Grapes of Wrath* and Howard Spring's *Fame is the Spur*, both lent to me. Somehow I acquired a few pre-war National Geographic Magazines which contained adverts for Mediterranean cruises which the better-off had enjoyed under enemy-free skies while my father and millions of others had been unemployed. The same Mediterranean was now available to people such as me.

Although I had no work to do in the Radio Department, I acquired the job of junior electrician under Charlie. We did not have the luxury of air conditioning and every cabin was supplied with an electric fan which moved within an arc of about 180 degrees as it blew air about the cabin. Charlie showed me how to service the fans which meant

Forces airgraph, Christmas 1943.

cleaning the commutator and adjusting or replacing the carbon brushes. I enjoyed this work very much and soon became the 'expert' so that faulty fans were brought directly to me for repair. I was often in the engine room and sometimes worked on the fans in its store-room/ workshop.

Nobody had a personal wireless set as their use was forbidden while vessels were at sea. This was because receivers at that time contained valves and valves were prone to oscillate. Oscillations were irritating squealing noises which not only prevented the listener hearing the programme, but meant that the receiver was acting as a transmitter, transmitting electromagnetic waves which could be detected by an enemy vessel. A seaman could take a wireless to sea, but it was the responsibility of the 1st R/O to take possession of the valves while the vessel was at sea. There was not much use then in possessing a set which could be used only in port.

There was, however, a master receiver in the chart room which was connected to speakers in the Captain's and Chief Engineer's cabins, the saloon and the crew's mess. (The word 'crew' has two meanings. It may apply to the whole ship's company or, specifically, to the ratings.) As the saloon was in ruins, we now ate in the Chief Engineer's cabin which, with its undulating floor, suffered temporary conversion and was to be used as a saloon for several months. I would sometimes sit listening to the American Expeditionary Station broadcasting from Algiers. As the station invited requests, I wrote asking them to play Tchaikovsky's No. 1 Piano Concerto and sat alone when my request was played. The announcer introduced it by saying 'and here is a request all the way from Bonnie Scotland'. I had said in my letter that I came from Scotland and, no doubt in his haste to get through his mail he had only skimmed the letter and got the facts wrong.

Although Algiers was removed from the war, there was ample evidence of the war in the damaged ships which entered the harbour. Other evidence was the sound of exploding depth charges heard at intervals throughout every night. The depth charges were dropped near the harbour entrance in order to deter enemy submarines, particularly those of the midget variety, from attempting to enter the port. And, occasionally, and almost always during the evening, I would suddenly become aware of the acrid smell of the smoke screen which was the precursor of an air-raid warning. There was never an air raid, but a warning seemed to be associated with a battleship being in port and was perhaps sounded when a convoy was under attack in the vicinity.

The town was full of servicemen and Forces newspapers were on sale daily. The US newspaper was *The Stars and Stripes* and the British one the

ALLIES IN FRANCE

Mass Paratroops and Thousands of Ships: Fierce Battles Reported Last Night

General Eisenhower talks over plans with General Montgomery.

BRITISH, Canadian and American forces began to land in France early yesterday morning.

Mass attacks were made by paratroops and glider-troops in Normandy, while thousands of ships carried other great forces to the beaches of north-west France.

By last night, said a battlefield despatch to the German-controlled Paris radio, a fierce battle was raging north of Rouen between the Allied airborne troops and the Nazis, behind the Atlantic Wall defences.

Other German reports said that between Le Havre and Cherbourg the Allies had continued to land all day under constant fire, and tanks had been landed in the area of Arromanches les Bains, between the two ports.

At some points it was admitted that the Allies had made progress some miles to the south.

Reuter last night said one spearhead had

Premier Gives News In Commons

Union Jack.

THE STARS AND STRIPES
ALGIERS DAILY

Vol. 2, No. 38, Wednesday, June 7, 1944   For U. S. Armed Forces   ONE FRANC

Allies Press Inland

Troops Crack Nazi Beach Defenses

5th Army Spreads In All Directions From Eternal City

Germans Reported Retreating Wildly In Several Places

By Sgt. LEN SMITH

Churchill Announces Seven-Mile Advance

Germans Report More Allied Landings At Guernsey, Jersey

By Sgt. ROY WILLIAMS
(Stars and Stripes Staff Writer)

SUPREME HEADQUARTERS, ALLIED EXPEDITIONARY FORCE, June 6—Allied troops, heavily supported by the British and United States Navies and covered by the greatest armada of planes ever thrown into the air, landed from the sea and the sky on the Normandy coast of France early this morning.

By sundown, the liberation forces, comprising American, British and Canadian troops, were reported to have cracked German beach defenses at several points between the great seaports of Le Havre and Cherbourg and to have penetrated several miles inland.

Prime Minister Winston Churchill, in his second report

The Stars and Stripes.

Union Jack. The weekday *Union Jack* consisted of a single double page sheet and cost 1 franc. On Saturday, there was a double sheet, but the price remained at 1 franc. The paper was sold to British Forces everywhere, but there was an Algiers *Daily Edition*.

There was also an Algiers Daily Edition of *The Stars and Stripes* which consisted of one or two sheets and cost 1 franc. The Africa Edition, published on Saturday, had four sheets (eight pages) and cost 2 francs.

These newspapers adequately conveyed to us that we were winning the war, but played down setbacks experienced by the Allies. The front-page headline of the *Union Jack* on 15 October was 'Volturno Crossed' and on 1 November 'Closing in Swiftly on Crimea'. On 8 November, the front-page headline of *The Stars and Stripes* was 'Russians Sweep In to Kiev' while on the 13th, it was 'Fifth Is Bogged Down In Mud Before New Nazi Line'. (This referred to the US Fifth Army in Italy.) On 1 November, the *Union Jack* carried a front-page article which read 'Red Cross Ship Sunk – A Portuguese freighter carrying 11,000 bags of Red Cross mail for Allied war prisoners in Germany is reported to have been sunk by a floating mine off Marseilles'. There were no references to convoy losses off the North African coast.

Both the *Union Jack* and *The Stars and Stripes* had their lighter side and the *Union Jack* carried the strip cartoon 'Jane', which first appeared in the Daily Mirror and, subsequently, in almost every Service newspaper. On 22 October, the *Union Jack* announced that 'In *Union Jack* her present adventures are running to a close. Do you want Jane to stay with us?' This sparked off correspondence on this important issue and as Jane was retained in the paper, I presume it was by popular request. On 10 November, there was an article which began 'London charwomen today are earning £4 a week – and there are often tips in addition.' In the same issue a letter signed George, Trevor, Terry asked the Editor to settle an argument: 'Is this year (1943) in the nineteenth or twentieth century?' An item of a more sardonic nature was printed in the *Union Jack* on 14 December when reporting a speech by Ernest Bevin. This article began 'Mr Bevin tells the House of Commons that, after the war, Britain will be unable to afford an unemployed man for fifty years.'

The Monday edition of the *Union Jack* gave the previous Saturday's 'Football Results and League Leaders' while a double page issue of *The Stars and Stripes* carried a much bigger section of 'Sports News'. Both papers published poems, submitted by service personnel, in their other than single sheet editions. I enjoyed these poems very much. They increased my interest in poetry and even inspired me to concoct an effort which I did not submit. I believe that their incorporation into an anthology would be a worthwhile project which would give pleasure to the reader and an insight into the feelings of both men and women far from home and with a very uncertain future. The following poem is an example which appeared in *The Stars and Stripes* of Saturday 13 November 1943:

2000 HRS.

At night soon after ten
My heart slips out of bed
And hurries half around the world
To be with you instead.
And then soon after ten,
When taps are ringing through,
My dreams and I track down my heart
So we can be there, too.
And though from dawn 'til after nine
My heart curls up to doze,
And all my dreams stay right in line,
My memory still knows
That night, soon after ten,
My heart will wake again,
To be with you 'til reveille,
From night soon after ten.

A Wave

WAVES (Women Accepted for Voluntary Emergency Service) were members of the women's reserve of the US Navy, and the writer of that sensitive poem must have groaned when she read the incorrectly published title.

A news item on the front page of *The Stars and Stripes* of 13 November is worth recording and read as follows: 'DALLAS – 1st Lt Maurice M. Hall, chaplain of a prisoner of war camp at Huntsville, Texas, said this week that "60 per cent of the prisoners are confirmed Nazis. And you might as well preach Christianity to a wall as to these Hitlerites, ... Unless we evangelise these men," Chaplain Hall asserted, "they will return to Germany after the war with nothing but contempt for our ideals and more than eager to fight another war."' It would appear that all were suitably evangelised!

The same newspaper had an article captioned 'The Cigarette Problem', which was somewhat different from the cigarette problem of today when smoking has become antisocial. An excerpt from the article read: 'America is using 780 million pounds of tobacco this year and is sharing 42 per cent of its cigarette supply with other nations. Next year, however, American manufacturers will be allotted only 463 million pounds of the weed and one cigarette company official predicted a shortage of smokes within twenty months.'

A major concern was the opening of what was called a 'Second Front', i.e. an invasion of the west coast of Europe by the Allies to take the pressure off the Soviet Forces in the East. On 8 December the Algiers evening paper *Les Dernières Nouvelles* had as its front page headline 'L'OVERTURE D'UN SECOND FRONT dans l'Ouest de l'Europe AURAIT ETE DECIDEE' (the headline referred to a decision taken by Stalin, Roosevelt and Churchill at the conference in Teheran). The newspaper related also how, at the conclusion of the conference, Mr Churchill presented Stalin with an inscribed and decorated sword from King George VI and the people of Britain to the defenders of Stalingrad. Stalin was then seen as a good guy, but the city which bore his name was renamed Volgograd some years after his death when he became discredited in the Soviet Union.

As the length of our stay in Algiers increased, the meals served on board deteriorated. Real potatoes disappeared from the menu and were replaced by a dehydrated substitute which was served in tasteless stringy lengths, while the only eggs we saw were similarly dehydrated and tasteless. By December, however, citrus fruits had become plentiful and cheap in the shops.

An incident occurred which was certainly not funny, but which nevertheless led to a considerable amount of humour. It was always a bit dangerous to walk on your own through the docks when it was dark. I tried to avoid doing so, but when I did, felt nervous and had my hand on an old scout knife given to me by my grandfather, although uncertain if I would use it if put to the test. Our Bosun was assaulted in the dock area and his assailants took his soft hat, spectacles and false teeth! As the unfortunate man went about for some time after the incident displaying his toothless gums, the question 'Where's the Bosun's teeth?' became a standing joke on the ship. The Bosun was a slim, pleasant Liverpudlian in his fifties. He was an enthusiastic Freemason, but I declined his offer to put me up for membership. I remember him well although his name escapes me. I believe it may have been Evans.

I was never on a ship which did not have at least one cat and thousands of moggies sailed the oceans of the world at that time. When a sailor brought one on board, Charlie and I washed it and it had found a home.

Mr White had come out from home to replace Mr Ball, who had been taken to hospital upon arrival in Algiers and was subsequently invalided home. Alf Taylor had returned to the ship after a spell in a military hospital under canvas on the outskirts of the town where I had visited him when the hospital grounds were a sea of mud.

Eventually, however, temporary repairs to the ship were completed and during the dull, miserable late afternoon of Sunday 19 December, we sailed out of Algiers to join Convoy MKS 34.

CHAPTER 10

THE FESTIVE SEASON

The majority of the ships in Convoy MKS 34 were bound for the United Kingdom, but we were to take advantage of its security only as far as Oran. Ships constantly joined and left Mediterranean convoys and although I now know that the letters MKS stood for Mediterranean United Kingdom Slow, we had no knowledge of convoy titles at the time. Generally we had only a vague idea of our destination, but, on this occasion, we knew it.

A glance at the map of the North African coast will show that Oran is only about 200 miles west of Algiers, yet it took us three days to get there. A popular misconception (promoted by holiday companies) that the Mediterranean Sea is always calm under blue skies is far from the truth. In winter, the weather can be very bad indeed and, on that occasion, was so bad that we lost the convoy. One of the ships which had been close to us in the convoy was the *Antonio*, and the *Samite* was on her own when one of the mates told me that he was on the bridge when Captain Eccles expressed the opinion that the old *Antonio* would be in Oran by now just at the moment when she loomed out of the murk! The mates were so unsure of our position that, when a town was seen, we went in close and signalled by lamp to the shore 'Is this Oran?' 'No', came the reply, 'this is Mostaganem'. Members of other departments 'roll about laughing' on such occasions. It is great to score off the other fellow, but mighty embarrassing when it happens to you! But, on Wednesday 22 December, we arrived at the outer harbour of Oran where we swung at anchor for two nights until taken into the port on the morning of Christmas Eve.

We entered Oran in pouring rain and I was drenched at my position of answering the telephone on the poop. The answering of the telephones fore and aft was normally the job of midshipmen, but, as we carried none, this job had fallen to the 2nd Sparks and me. Neville answered the telephone at the bow and passed on orders from the pilot on the bridge to the Mate, in charge of the group of seamen at the bow. I did the same at the stern where the 2nd Mate was in charge. By the time we entered Oran, I was accustomed to this duty as it was performed every time we moved ship and this had been a frequent occurrence in Algiers. The orders which we passed on concerned the tying up or casting off of the lines which secured the ship and I found this minor occupation quite interesting as it was always a slow business and Mr Lewis would chat to me about the shipping in the vicinity. Although ships all wore grey wartime livery, his experienced eye identified types of vessel and he could often tell to which companies they belonged. On this occasion, we tied up to buoys in the harbour.

I was to spend a few more Christmases away from home, but that Christmas of 1943 was the only miserable one. There was no festive spirit on board the *Samite* and Christmas dinner consisted of a poor salad. Charlie insisted that I stayed up till midnight on Christmas Eve in order to drink his 'wee' wife's health in champagne – where he got that brew I cannot recall – and I made him a present of 400 cigarettes as he was hoarding this commodity to take home. Being tied up to buoys, we required a boat to get us ashore and Phil Ayres and I had a walk through the town in the afternoon when the streets were crowded with Arabs lounging about as there was no work in progress that day. And why the ship had called at Oran at all is a mystery to me as we sailed independently for Beni Saf the following day.

Beni Saf lies midway between Oran and the Moroccan border and was little more than a fishing village with a population in the region of 11,000. The sailing distance was only fifty-six miles and five to six hours sailing for the *Samite*. As we lay at anchor in the bay under a clear blue sky and on a flat calm sea the morning after our arrival, I was taken by the beauty of the place at the foot of hills which come right down to the sea. Captain Eccles must have made some social contact with the shore as a messenger presented me with 'Captain's compliments' and would I like to go for a row with some young ladies? It was the only social gesture that Captain Eccles made to me and I declined the invitation. It was not so much that I did not want to go, but I was somewhat socially inept and could appear rather boorish as a result. I stood at the rail watching the ship's boat as Neville and Ian Smith rowed three young French girls around the bay in that idyllic setting. It was a contrived situation to give the young bloods some pleasure and I often wondered why Captain Eccles was prepared to lower a boat for such a frivolous purpose when he so often denied us one when at anchor in Algiers.

There was an iron ore mine beside the harbour and the *Samite* had been sent to load the commodity. I vaguely considered this as a safe cargo until the merchants of doom informed me that a ship with such a cargo would go to the bottom in minutes if torpedoed! When eventually taken alongside, we were the only ship in port.

The atmosphere in Beni Saf was very different from that of Algiers and Oran. The village had the same mixed population of French, Spanish and Arab (I continue to refer to the indigenous peoples as Arab because that is what we called them although many were Berber or of mixed race), but there were no service personnel at all. The Arabs, although generally poor, seemed better off than those in the large towns and most were engaged in fishing. Every evening there was a large gathering at the fish market when the fish were being sold and a number of donkeys could be seen tethered to the railings of the enclosure. The donkey was commonly used as a form of transport and a beast of burden and one evening when a group of us were in the village, an Arab was tethering his donkey prior to entering a shop. But, when one of our number called out 'How much?', as if wishing to buy the animal, the man pulled the beast into the shop after him. This, of course, raised a laugh, but the donkey would be of considerable value to the Arab who was unable to assess the character of the approaching group. Beni Saf was primitive. Hens walked about its centre and veiled women carried vases on their heads.

As we thought that we might be returning to the UK from Beni Saf, I wanted to take home as much of the local produce as possible. There were no dock gates and when we went ashore there were often Arab youngsters eager to help and accompany us. Carrying a locally made straw shopping bag and heading for town, I was accosted by a boy and two or three of his companions. These lads were not the nuisances regularly found in the big towns and, as I was in need of a guide and he spoke some words of English, I accepted his offer of assistance. Although I had not seen dates in the village shops, I told the boy that this was what I was after and, having taken my bag to establish his position as my guide, he said he knew where I could get some.

When he led me out of the main part of the village and we started to climb a steep, narrow, path on the hill behind it, I began to realise that I was being taken into the Arab quarter and wondered if it were wise to undertake such a journey on my own. About halfway up, I was suddenly confronted by two descending Arabs one of whom immediately asked if I had any cigarettes to sell. He was a big man with an extremely florid face and wearing a beautifully clean white robe. As I was in an extremely isolated and vulnerable position and he could have flattened me without any bother, I said 'No' although I had a packet of twenty Camel in my breast pocket. But when he smiled and tapped the bulge in my pocket, I gave them to him. He paid me the going rate of 30 francs and we moved on. My youthful guide pronounced 'thirty' as 'toity' and, when I corrected him, he said, 'Americano, he say toity.'

My guide knew exactly where he was going and took me to a shop which sold dates. The shop, which didn't have a great deal of anything to sell, stood in a line of poor dwellings on a terrace in the hillside. It had an earthen floor and a boy was in charge behind the wooden counter. I had a gathering of children with me now; all interested in witnessing the transaction. I asked for three kilos of dates and the young shopkeeper then took handfuls from a container behind him and placed them on scales on the counter. When he turned his back, little hands went out and snatched dates from the scales and, when he turned round again, everybody stood looking at him so innocently that his suspicions were aroused. After picking up more dates, he whipped round, but was still too late to catch anybody. But everybody burst out laughing and he laughed with the rest. On a future occasion, I was standing talking to my boy-guide near the ship when a big fisherman approached and introduced himself as his father. From our conversation, I got the impression that his son liked me and I most certainly had formed a good opinion of him and the Arabs of Beni Saf.

There was a small beach close to where the ship was berthed and a teenage Arab boy and a younger boy came and sat beside me as I prepared to go for a swim from the otherwise deserted beach. The teenager asked me how old I was and found it hilarious that I was younger than his brother who was fighting in Italy. I abandoned my swim because I didn't trust them enough to leave my clothes which were of such value in the area. They thought that I was well off and I suspected that they might steal my clothes. They were right in their assessment of me as, compared to them, I was well off, but I believe I was wrong in my assessment of them.

One evening, Charlie came to my cabin with the news that clothes were being sold in the nearby iron ore mine. The only thing that I was prepared to sell was a pair of trousers which Robert had given me as a present in Baltimore. These were light grey trousers which I liked very much until I sprayed them with acid from the hydrometer while checking the emergency batteries. Little holes had appeared and I had darned them, but couldn't really wear the trousers any more. Anyway, they fetched a good price at the bottom of a mineshaft in Beni Saf that night!

Unknown to me, all was not well on the *Samite* in that idyllic situation and the first I learned of any trouble was when a young New Zealand fireman joined me on the beach one afternoon. Unlike me, he had not walked to the beach, but had jumped from the deck of the ship and swum to it. He told me that he had been involved in an incident with other firemen and had jumped overboard to avoid being beaten up. The New

Zealander was a strong, clean-looking and presentable young man in his early twenties. I knew that there were some rough characters among the firemen, but didn't realise then how serious the situation was.

The trouble came to a head at New Year and was very serious indeed. In most merchant ships at that time, only the officers' accommodation was amidships, but, in Liberty Ships, all accommodation was amidships so that the crew's accommodation was on the main deck directly below that of the officers'. Early on the evening of Hogmanay, I heard voices raised in anger on the deck below. I thought it was going to be a drunken night with the crew, but it was more than that. It turned out to be a very bad night and came close to mutiny.

Three strong and aggressive firemen had been terrorising the crew. When they returned to the ship late after an evening ashore, they had made Alf turn out to make them a meal. One of the trio was a man whose surname was Stanley. He had red hair, was built like an ox and had served a sentence for manslaughter. He was not a man to tangle with, but the consensus of opinion was that the other two 'made the bullets for him to fire'. The crew were sick to death of this bullying and had decided to put an end to it. And they did just that. When the trio returned from the shore in the early hours of New Year's Day, the crew were waiting for them and now it was the bullies who were terrorised. They were so terrified by the reception they met that they were hiding behind winches in the dark and one of them managed to reach Captain Eccles to plead for protection. The DEMS gunners were issued with rifles and the situation brought under control by breakfast-time. The trio were locked up, but the crew refused to sail unless they were removed from the ship.

I left Beni Saf with 7 lbs of dates, 4½ lbs of figs, 14 lbs of oranges and 9 lbs of onions. Others had invested their ill-gotten gains in caged birds. Harry had bought a bullfinch and the PO Gunner had bought a canary for 500 francs. Another fellow had got one for 300 francs, but the PO justified his exploitation by insisting that he had a much better bird! Harry and the PO allowed their birds to fly about their cabins and the PO demonstrated how to catch them to return them to their cages when it was dark. You fixed your eyes on the spot where the bird was sitting, put out the light and grabbed it. The birds were pampered; not only did Harry put a swing in the cage, but he wrapped string round it to keep its feet warm. I left with an affection for the place, but regret the memory of seeing poor Arab women, living in a mud dwelling on a hillside, fighting to purchase a bar of soap being sold at twelve times the price which the vendor had paid for it.

With our cargo of iron ore, we returned independently to Oran. On the way, a case was prepared against the bullies and, as I did the typing, I learned that Mr Turnbull had earlier been threatened in the engine room. We were back in Oran by the evening of 3 January. The bullies were put ashore to be tried by a Naval Court, but I have no knowledge of what happened to them.

Towards 8 p.m. on the evening of our arrival, mail was delivered to the ship and I received four letters, all over four months old.

CHAPTER 11

GUS 26

In the company of six US ships and the Norwegian tanker *Haakon Hauan*, we sailed from Oran on 6 January 1944 to join Convoy GUS 26 (Gibraltar United States Slow). Our hopes of going home were dashed. The *Samite* was returning to the States to undergo permanent repairs.

Convoy GUS 26 had originated at Port Said on 26 December and been joined by vessels from Augusta, Sicily and various North African ports. Others were to join from Gibraltar and Casablanca and, the British tanker *Luculus*, from Ponta del Gada in the Azores. Commodore Hubbard, RNR, on the Norwegian *Fernbank*, had been in charge of the convoy through the Mediterranean and was to be disembarked at Rosia Bay, Gibraltar. Captain G. L. Woodruff, USN, who had been commodore of UGS 18 as far as Oran and who was now on the US cargo ship *Abangarez*, which sailed with us from Oran, assumed the post of responsibility. GUS 26 was escorted through the Mediterranean to Gibraltar by the Royal Navy, where the Ocean Escort of USN ships took over. In the convoy was the first ever Liberty Ship, the *Patrick Henry*, which had joined from Bizerta in Tunisia. The total number of ships was fifty-three. Convoy speed was 9 knots and, although not evident, air escort was provided from 6 to 11 January inclusive and again from 20 January until the ships arrived in the USA.

It was back to the routine of watches, sleeping, eating and brief period of socialising between dinner and going to bed. Then there was the ever-present chore of doing your washing, which was always referred to as 'dhobying'. Perhaps the Captain's dhobi was done by his 'tiger', but every other officer did his own and I clearly remember starching collars on the wild, dark night the convoy entered the Strait of Gibraltar, when only plunging shadowy ships could be made out and the lights of Ceuta in Spanish Morocco blinked feebly from the distant North African shore.

The passage to the States was uneventful and the weather, although the wind blew stronger and the sea was rougher than during our eastward crossing, was good for January. Because of my inexperience, I was in no position to pass judgment on this, but the more experienced seamen said it was the best crossing for the time of year that they could remember. Oddly enough, the Commodore did not agree as in his report he stated that the average speed of the convoy was 9.3 knots and that the speed of advance was 'lowered due to adverse weather'. This is difficult to comprehend when the designated speed of the convoy was only 9 knots! He also stated that the *Patrick Henry*, the *Francis Walker* and the *Thomas Todd* (all US) were 'consistently bad stragglers' due to having foul bottoms and recommended that the tanker *British Engineer* be barred from further convoys until 'his (not 'her') incessant smoking' was rectified by the owners.

The disappointment of not going home was soon forgotten by the younger unmarried men and we looked forward to going back to the States and, perhaps, to Baltimore. My large glass jar of dates was placed on the floor of the cabin and eager hands reached out for them. Figs and oranges went the same way and my strings of onions went to the ship's kitchen at Alf's request when there were no onions left in his store. We were totally ignorant of the deployment and exact destination of the convoy and didn't care all that much anyway.

My watches were as quiet as ever, with only the Spanish coast stations to be heard on 500 kcs when we were within their limited range of a few hundred miles. Then, as we headed westwards into the Atlantic, there was the total silence to which so many ears were listening and hoping to hear nothing. At the designated times I would listen for messages to the convoy from Rugbyradio (GBR) then to Washington DC (NSS) when we reached a given position in mid Atlantic. During the night watch I often read the transmitter instruction manual and schooled myself on how to start up and operate the transmitter in case I became the key man in an emergency. It was a simple enough procedure, but there was never the opportunity to practise. I also studied our replacement copy of the secret BAMS (British Admiralty Merchant Signals) Code Book which had been delivered to the ship before we sailed from Algiers. This book contained the information necessary to decode the messages which might come from Rugby or Washington and which we referred to as BAMS Messages. In order to brighten the dry contents of the book, it was liberally illustrated with amusing cartoon drawings showing members of my profession at work.

At a point close to the American coast, the convoy split into two sections: a New York section consisting of nineteen ships and a Baltimore/Chesapeake section of thirty-four ships. We were in the latter section and dropped anchor in Hampton Roads (Virginia) late in the afternoon of 24 January. The New York section reached its destination at roughly the same time.

CHAPTER 12

VIRGINIA

There is always an excitement of arriving in port although, strictly speaking, we were not yet 'in port'. The long haul from North Africa was over and we could relax in the safety of the USA. The sea watches were over, there was no longer any danger and the lights of Norfolk VA welcomed us from the shore. After almost three weeks at sea when we could not show a light, portholes were hooked open and lights shown on deck. An anchor watch still had to be kept by the deck and engineering departments, but most of us could look forward to a night in bed. But the main benefit was safety.

There was a cheerful atmosphere on the *Samite* that evening and after dinner, although it was rather chilly, it seemed that everybody was on deck enjoying the sights. Then, suddenly, a vessel was seen heading directly towards us and although an anchor was dropped in an attempt to take the weight off her, the cable snapped almost immediately and she maintained her collision course. Luckily she came under control, a second anchor was dropped and the danger was over.

A medical officer boarded and we were subjected to what is delicately described as a 'short arm' inspection to see if anyone showed signs of venereal disease. This was my only experience of such an inspection.

When we dropped anchor in Hampton Roads, we still did not know our destination, but the following day entered Norfolk and tied up alongside. Our first thought was for mail and there was great disappointment when none awaited our arrival. Mail was always a problem on the *Samite*. We understood why it had taken so long to reach us in Algiers, as we had originally been bound for Alexandria when the Luftwaffe had redirected us to Algiers. But it was difficult to understand the great and regular gaps of three and four months during which we received no letters at all. On the following evening, however, mail did arrive and two days later I received my first 1943 Christmas Card. I also received the news that my maternal grandfather, whom I didn't know well, had died.

In letters from Norfolk, I informed my parents that I was now a rich man as I had £101 1s 2d to my credit on the ship in addition to the £5 monthly allotment I had left. I also told them that I had drawn the extravagant sum of $50 (£12 10s) and what I spent the money on. Many of today's teenagers would consider the list 'boring' and perhaps form the opinion that I was 'a mummy's boy', but I was a child of the thirties when every penny was needed to keep our heads above water. Although our economic situation had improved during the wartime years before I went to sea, the very necessities of life were rationed in wartime Britain. In those days, the majority of families pulled together in adversity and children contributed to the home. I had missed not having a mouth organ since leaving my fine instrument on the *Queen Elizabeth* and my first purchase was a mouth organ made in Switzerland as Hohner instruments, made in Germany, were no longer available. It cost $6 (30s or £1.50) and although I never liked it as much as other mouth organs I'd possessed, it was the best I could get and gave me a great deal of pleasure. My other purchases were two pairs of shoes, several shirts with collars attached, a blouse, bars of soap, handkerchiefs, toothpaste, shaving cream, potholders, Vaseline, white shoe cleaner, a nailbrush and two bottles of glycerin and rose water. I had no idea of the size of blouse my mother required, but resorted to the usual sailor's trick of looking for a lady sales assistant of similar build. The glycerin and rose water was also for my mother as she regularly applied this to her hands before going to bed. The shoes were for me and, as shoes were rationed in the States, I went with two of my shipmates to the British Consulate where we were given forms to take to the rationing centre to get coupons to present at a shop. The shaving cream was bought in anticipation as, although I regularly clipped the hairs of my upper lip and side whiskers, I had, at eighteen years and nine months, been able to stave off beginning that lifetime chore.

We docked in Norfolk on Tuesday 25 January and on the Sunday, 30 January, Captain Eccles put back breakfast to 8.30 a.m. to give us half an hour extra in bed. As I have always been a sleepyhead, this was not enough for me and I decided to lie-in and skip breakfast. My shipmates, however, decided that I should get up. My first caller was Alf, the Chief Cook, who came in about 8 a.m. and hammered on my bunk, telling me that breakfast was at 8.30 a.m. I ignored his call, but my steward came a few minutes later with the same information and was equally ignored. Alf came in again and gave another hammer, then Harry tried to get me up and he was closely followed by Ian Smith and Neville. There was no longer any escape and I had to give up, but just when I had pronounced myself awake, Phil Ayres, who was a good friend by this time, came in to oversee the operation. But I missed breakfast that morning. Phil was keen that I learned to play the march of the Hampshire Regiment on my new mouth organ and sat on the settee repeatedly whistling it for me to master.

We discharged our iron ore in Norfolk and my memories of the place include buying a trouser belt when the kindly elderly male shop assistant engaged me in conversation for some time, and of Charlie and I going into a rather cheap shop because we were interested in the suits on display. We did not buy a suit, but spent a pleasant hour sitting in the back shop in conversation with the lady owner. Occasionally, in the States, we came across people who had no time for the British, but they were far outweighed by those who were friendly towards us.

I had always to borrow Charlie's electric iron and wanted to get one of my own. I also wanted a portable gramophone, or phonograph as the Americans called them, and when I saw an auction sale advertised in the local newspaper, I asked Phil to come along to the sale with me. He was down for sabotage watch, but the RN Petty Officer agreed to a change of duties and we went together. By the time we arrived, however, the sale was almost over and seemed to consist almost exclusively of furniture. But we didn't waste the day and crossed Hampton Roads by paddle steamer to Newport News where we had lunch before going to a cinema. The paddle steamer was reminiscent of Mark Twain and the Mississippi and a very pleasant experience. On the upper deck I met a British seaman who informed me that he was, what today would be described as, 'shacked up' with a woman in Newport News.

We returned to the ship for dinner at 6 p.m. and I had every intention of staying on board until Phil came to my cabin at 7 p.m. to ask if I'd like to go ashore again. We then consulted the entertainment adverts in a newspaper and, on seeing one for the Center Theatre which read 'Now Open to the General Public – On Stage – Patricia Morison – Glamorous Hollywood Star – in person', we set off for the Center.

US stage shows were usually combined with the showing of a film. The price of entrance was 85¢, but servicemen got in for 40¢ and we obtained seats in the front row beside the orchestra. On these occasions, we always went in uniform in order to be admitted as 'servicemen', but I've often wondered if the little silver MN lapel badge, the only 'uniform' of the lower deck merchant seamen, was sufficient to identify them as 'servicemen'. Patricia Morison sang several songs and I felt that she was singing them for me as she appeared to be looking directly at me a great deal of the time. The stage show was excellent, as these shows usually were, and the film was 'Gangway For Tomorrow' with Margo and John Carradine.

Norfolk, VA.

One of the letters received in Norfolk was from my father and dated 5 December. In it he said that he thought that the ship had a queer name and asked about her history. I replied by asking him how he came to know the name of the ship as I had never divulged it and that, as she was a new ship, I knew all her history. All mail was addressed to me c/o Alfred Holt & Co., 54 Ullet Road, Liverpool and it was they who wrote 'S.S. *Samite*' in red ink on the covers. When Admirals, Generals and Air Marshals were keeping detailed diaries with a view to writing their memoirs after the war, here was I withholding the very name of my ship. My secrecy was obviously pointless and perhaps I was the only merchant seaman who didn't give his correspondents the name of his ship! In the same letter, I told my parents of the decorations given to Captain Eccles and Mr Thomas, that the Captain's wife had been on the radio relating their exploits in the lifeboats and how Mr Thomas had been telling me that his wife had been buying new clothes and was excited at the prospect of accompanying him to Buckingham Palace to receive his MBE.

On the morning of Saturday 5 February, the *Samite* left Norfolk and moved across Hampton Roads to go into dry dock at Newport News, on the northern shore, where the damage done by the glider bomb could be assessed. During our time there, Charlie and I washed a cat and a dog which had come, or more likely been brought, on board in Norfolk and took them to Harry's cabin to see his two birds! Phil and I went to a roller skating rink, where Phil refused to put on skates, but enjoyed himself laughing at my performance. For my father's collection, I bought two identical sets of stamps; each stamp showing the flag of a country occupied by the Axis powers. I kept one set to take home and used the other set on letters home so that he would have an unfranked and a franked set. Somehow or other, he finished up with one stamp missing from the franked set, but many years after the war obtained the missing stamp from a collector in Aberdeen.

By Tuesday 8 February we were again at anchor in the Roads and, although we still did not know our destination on Thursday, we weighed anchor and headed for our 'home' port of Baltimore the following day.

Chesapeake Bay is one of the great inland waterways of the world and the largest estuary on the east coast of North America. It is almost 200 miles long and varies in width from four to thirty miles. Many rivers, including the Potomac, on which stands Washington DC, and the Patapsco, on which Baltimore stands, flow into it. Its southern reaches are in Virginia and its northern in Maryland. Early Spanish explorers called it the 'Bay of the Mother of God' and Captain John Smith, who led the first permanent English settlement to Jamestown in 1607, explored and mapped it. The name 'Chesapeack', which he used, comes from an Indian word meaning 'great shellfish bay'. It was a marvellous experience to sail through the Chesapeake, even in winter when the sun shone and the air was clear and crisp. With no watches to keep, I enjoyed it to the full.

Sometimes I would sit in our makeshift dining saloon listening to local radio stations, which were all commercial and advertised the products of their sponsors *ad nauseam*. Although I had already experienced this, it was still a novelty and I remember the jingles. One advertised 'Canteen Chewing Gum' when voices in harmony kept singing the name over and over again. And when the time was given, an announcer never just gave the time, but said it was, say, '11 o'clock Bulova Watch Time'. Even at the age of eighteen, I came quickly to realise the shallowness of US broadcasting and to appreciate the high standard of the BBC which I had previously taken for granted.

The journey north through Chesapeake Bay took a day and a night. We were off Baltimore by the morning of 12 February and entered the port later that day. Contrary to expectations, there had been no snow on the ground in Norfolk and Newport News, but there was in Baltimore. It was cold and in marked contrast to the heat we had experienced on our previous visit.

CHAPTER 13

SECOND VISIT TO BALTIMORE, MARYLAND

We were to remain in Baltimore for over five weeks, which means that it took the Bethlehem-Fairfield Shipyard perhaps longer to repair the *Samite* than it took them to assemble her. Once again everyone had to be placed in accommodation ashore, and this time I was put into a large room on the 8th floor of the Southern Hotel together with Mr White and Mr Lewis. We had our own toilet, bath and shower, a telephone and a desk with a supply of hotel stationery. Towards the beginning of our stay, Mr White returned to the room early in the evening to find me sitting up in bed reading American comics. He expressed surprise at my behaviour. How could anyone of my age go to bed so early and ignore the fleshpots of the United States? A week or two later, he complained vehemently when Charlie, Robert South and I returned briefly to the room at 2 a.m. and went out again!

I often went to the Merchant Navy Club and it was there that I met Shirley Westcott, who became my girlfriend during our stay. Shirley was a serious and pretty girl and still a High School pupil although she worked part-time at a telephone exchange switchboard. When I was walking her home one evening, she asked if Scotland were a part of England. A Scot is shocked by such ignorance, but who can condemn an American teenager for thinking this when England is so often equated with Britain? One day I turned up to meet Shirley in a brand new outfit of which I was extremely proud. Everything was new, right down to the shoes: a beautifully cut, grey single-breasted suit which had cost me $20 (£5), shirt, tie, broad green braces and a grey soft felt hat purchased in Baltimore's best department store, the Hub, and made by J. B. Stetson of Philadelphia. The braces, I knew, were a little 'out of line', but nevertheless added a touch of panache. Charlie had talked me into buying the hat although I never wore one, and I still possess the almost unworn article which has turned out to be worth the extravagant price of $10 (£2.50) as it has brought uncontrolled laughter when I have worn it to amuse family and friends. I expected Shirley to remark on how well I was dressed, but she immediately showed her disappointment by asking me why I had not worn my uniform. Like all of us, Shirley was a product of the time. She wanted to be seen with a man in uniform and especially an 'officer'.

I was required to spend every second night on sabotage watch on board the *Samite*. I felt that this was an imposition on radio officers and those employed by other companies were not asked to do work outwith the scope of their department. I shared the duty with Mr Lewis and we were on duty from 6 p.m. till 9 a.m. the following morning. Mr Lewis decided to split the watch so that one of us was on from 6 p.m. to 2 a.m. and the other from 2 a.m. to 9 a.m. The whole thing was a farce as there were three shore security guards on board until midnight-thirty then six after that. There was also a watchman on duty all night.

A 1st R/O who sat down beside me at the MN Club asked about conditions on Liberty Ships as he was about to join one and I took the opportunity to ask his advice regarding my sabotage duties. He advised me that I should be paid 2/6d (12½p) an hour, but not to do anything about it until we were paying off at the end of the voyage when I should refuse to sign off articles if payment were refused. If this happened, he said, the Radio Officers' Union would soon sort it out. I took his advice not to do anything, but, although I kept details of my sabotage watches and calculated that I was due about £30, I signed off without mentioning the watches. The engineer officers did 24-hour shifts on board, but actually worked only during the day.

As there was no heating on the ship when it was being repaired, it was extremely cold during these sabotage watches and I spent quite a bit of time in the company gathered round a brazier in the region of the ship's refrigerator on the main deck where a security guard regaled us with stories of his time with the US Navy on the China Station before the war. I was still in my bunk one forenoon when the aircraft carrier USS *Shangri-la* was launched nearby.

During the evening of a sabotage watch, a young AB, who had been missing for a week, appeared at the door of my cabin. He said that he had friends in Atlantic City and had gone absent without leave to visit them as he knew that a request for leave would be refused. He told me he'd had a great time and that it was worth the fine which he anticipated would be imposed. He didn't know that the crew were living ashore and was surprised to find everything locked up so that he couldn't get into his cabin. He had no money and asked me to lend him some. I gave him $10 (£2) and, as I had a set of passkeys, was able to give him access to his cabin

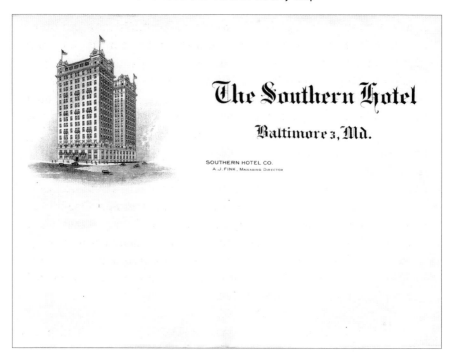

Southern Hotel, Baltimore.

so that he could spend the night there. He took off early in the morning and I never saw him or my $10 again!

One of the security guards admired the now lovely white dog which Charlie and I had washed and looked after and said that his young daughter was distressed because their dog had recently been killed by a car. He was delighted when we said he could have the dog if he wished and so our good-natured pet trotted off with him to its new home.

Our DEMS gunners left the ship in Baltimore. Phil was sent to New York and I received a postcard giving his address as the Seamen's Church Institute. I didn't expect to see him again, but a week or two later he was back in Baltimore to join a new Liberty Ship. This allowed us to spend a few more evenings together, but I heard no more from Phil after that as he was no correspondent, and I was to learn that he neglected writing even to his fiancée. I missed him. He had been a good and generous shipmate who would sometimes bring me a cup of tea when I was on watch.

Baltimore's daily newspaper is the *Baltimore Sun*, and on Monday 28 February the *Evening Sun* carried an article by their reporter Henrietta Leith after an interview with Captain Eccles concerning our experience in the Mediterranean. The column was headed 'of MEN and SHIPS', below which was a drawing of a Liberty Ship and which read:

A British captain paying his second visit to Baltimore in nine months as a "survivor" tells how the crew of a Baltimore-built Liberty ship underwent a mysterious and unpleasant "milk bath" after a bombing attack, but later found out it was a lucky thing they did. The narrator is Capt. Leonard Eccles, who, with a British crew brought over from Liverpool, took command of the S.S. *Samite* when she was launched last August at the Bethlehem-Fairfield yard here. The Liberty ship is now being repaired at the Bethlehem Key Highway yard. The *Samite*'s little show, Capt. Eccles related, began two days out of Gibraltar, after a successful convoyed crossing. Only a half hour after escort planes had turned back, six German planes came over and dropped three bombs. One hit the vessel ahead of the *Samite*, he said, and a short time later a second struck Captain Eccles' ship. The third fell into the sea. The *Samite* was struck in the center with such force that part of the deck cargo was thrown over the top bridge. Captain Eccles and his crew found themselves covered from head to foot with a "hot, slimy liquid."

There was then a sub-heading which read 'Milk Tins Litter Bridge' after which the article continued:

"We didn't know what it was and were guessing that it was from an oil bomb of some sort," he said. "But after about a half hour the liquid resolved into a dry, scaly covering. Then we realised that it was scorched, evaporated milk blown from cans stored in the hold where the bomb hit. There were thousands of bits of the milk tins on the bridge." But the seamen didn't object, for it meant that the bomb had struck in the only place where a hit would not mean an almost certain end to the ship. Every other hold was loaded with ammunition. The next day the *Samite* was towed into port and most of her cargo discharged. After temporary repairs, she began the trip back to her "birthplace" in Baltimore for permanent repairs.

Under another sub-heading, "Good Ship For The Job", the article continued:

Captain Eccles declared he has found the Liberty ship seaworthy in all kinds of weather and a "good ship for the job she was built to do." Referring to the recent cracking up of a Liberty ship in a West Coast port, the British officer said he believed the Liberty ships built in Baltimore are sturdier than those of some other yards because they are "more riveted and less pre-fabricated." [meaning welded – they were all prefabricated] "No matter where you sail today," said Captain Eccles, "you will find that sixty per cent of the shipping is Liberty ships. When you travel in convoy you can look all around you and see nothing but Libertys. It's a novelty for us to see one of our own ships."'

The article then went on to tell of the launching of the *Samite* on 18 August 1943 as the *Holland Thompson* by Mrs Clinton Stinchcomb, the wife of an employee at the yard and to tell the story of Captain Eccles' and Mr Thomas' previous visit to Baltimore as survivors after the *Rhexenor*, had been torpedoed and sunk in the Atlantic.

It has been my experience that newspapers seldom get things right, but Captain Eccles has to bear some responsibility for the wild inaccuracies contained in the article. He could not possibly have known the details of the attacking force, but how he could have said that Convoy UGS 18 was attacked by only six planes which dropped three bombs is beyond my comprehension. Quite obviously many more planes were involved and, as I have already said, Roskill in *A Merchant Fleet in War*, gives the attacking force as 'twenty Do. 217s equipped with the new German glider-bombs, and twenty-five torpedo-bombers.' In any case, four vessels were hit in the attack. It is true that cans of condensed milk were blown about, but nobody was covered with their contents and there were no 'thousands of bits of the milk tins on the bridge' as I was up there shortly after the attack when the bridge was completely clear. Similarly, while trucks in the deck cargo were thrown into the sea, it is an exaggeration to suggest that any deck cargo was 'thrown over the top bridge', as this would have meant that those on the bridge would have had trucks flying at them! Henrietta Leith was exaggerating to sell newspapers while Captain Eccles, in true British style, was playing-down the severity of his experience.

I phoned the 'gents outfitters' where Robert had worked only to find that he was now in the Army. I got word to him that I was again in Baltimore and he sent a telegram by Western Union from Macon, Georgia, saying that he was coming home on leave. After four months in the Army, he had a ten-day leave and returned to Baltimore as a Private First Class and wearing a medal for proficiency in marksmanship to which a bar would be added for every calibre of weapon he became proficient in firing. We had good times together during his leave and continued to meet at weekends after it expired as he had been posted to a camp only seventeen miles away. When I went looking for him one afternoon, I found his house in a working-class area. His stepmother answered the door and, after telling me that Robert wasn't in, said that they were organising a party for his forthcoming nineteenth birthday and that I was invited. I did not attend the party if, indeed, it ever took place. I believe that I was on sabotage duty, but in any case, Robert's stepmother, who appeared to me to be a nice lady, was on a losing wicket in trying to please Robert as it was obvious that he deeply resented her.

Dance halls were always popular and, of course, you went not just to dance, but to meet girls! We sometimes visited a dance hall called Keith's Roof, but the style of dancing in the States was different to that in vogue in Britain and I didn't care for it. Dances which were held at the MN Club, with music supplied by a radiogram, were more enjoyable as the girls who frequented the place had learned to dance the British way.

I went quite a lot to the 'movies' and particularly enjoyed the combined stage and 'movie' shows which were presented at the Hippodrome. Charlie and I went to see Joan Blondell on stage, but it was a 'full house' and we didn't get in. She was one of the 'big' cinema stars of the day. We waited for a while at the stage door to see her, but soon decided we had better things to do. On stage at the Hippodrome, I saw the film stars Virginia Weidler, Edith Fellows and Martha Raye. These stars drew the audiences, but, although they were actresses and not singers, all they did was sing. The other acts in the shows, however, were usually first class.

In comparison to the freezing nights spent on board the ship, the days and nights spent at the Southern Hotel were very pleasant indeed. If you wanted a call in the morning, you had only to lift the phone and tell the girl at the switchboard that you wanted to be called at such and such a time. The American way of telling the time is somewhat different from ours. When we would say five to eight (five minutes to eight), they would say five under eight and when we would say five past eight, they would say five after eight. They didn't at first understand what was meant by half past eight as they said eight-thirty. It caused some amusement when they began to conform with our manner of expression and we to theirs! I often found that the girls wanted to chat and perhaps some of them got 'dates' that way. As during our previous visit when I had stayed at the Biltmore, only accommodation was provided by the hotel. Negro maids cleaned and tidied up our room and I had to chase after one in order to retrieve the comic section of the Sunday Post containing 'Oor Wullie' and 'The Broons' which I had just received from home.

It was now impossible for us to do our own laundry as there was no hot water on the ship, but I gave mine to the hotel laundry only once as it proved much more expensive than one I found nearby. We certainly could not afford to eat in the hotel's restaurant on the $4.50 (£1.50) a day subsistence money paid to us. I found, however, that this payment was adequate to buy meals elsewhere. For breakfast, I went to a small café beside the Southern where I had cornflakes with the additional luxury of cream, bacon and eggs (sunny side up!) and coffee for 60¢ (15p). My other meals cost an average of 80¢ (20p) so that I had enough over to splash out occasionally on a more expensive meal such as chow mein or chop suey in a Chinese restaurant.

On one occasion when I was in this Chinese restaurant, a poor man came in selling needles and I had just bought a packet when a Chinaman approached and ordered him out. The needle seller was angry at being ejected and made a scene when, in a loud voice, he proclaimed that this was his reward for contributing to Madam Chiang Kai-shek's Fund for China! Everyone in the restaurant knew that the man was unlikely to have contributed anything to that fund, but what struck me was that this man was little more than a beggar and although I saw a number of beggars in the United States, begging had been eliminated in Great Britain. On another occasion when I was there with others in the small hours of the morning, a young drunk sailor in the US Navy said to me that he was exhausted so that I suggested that he should return to his ship. 'What?' he said, as if I were mad. 'We're sailing in the morning.' I deduced that he was apprehensive at what lay in store for him 'out there' and wanted to maintain his links with the safety of the shore until the last minute. But he should not have given the information as to when his ship was sailing to anyone. When he rose from his seat to order something from the counter, we talked to the girl who was with him and no doubt Charlie tried to impose his charm on her. Although a bit tipsy, she expressed her loyalty to her escort by saying, 'If a boy shows me a good time, I'll stick by him.' Like myself, the sailor and his loyal, but temporary, girlfriend were teenagers.

During this period, I was struck by the animosity of the US press towards the Soviet Union, which they almost always referred to as Russia. According to the Press, the terms which Russia had meted out to the Finns had been too harsh and was an example of how Russia would treat our present enemies after we had won the war. The newspapers regarded our Soviet ally as our future enemy and it was already being suggested that our next war would be against the USSR. History books state that the Cold War began after the Second World War, but it was already taking shape during it. When I visited Hamburg in the spring of 1946, a former German officer, who had been part of the army of occupation in Denmark, spoke to me as if we had been allies during the war. According to him, the war against Britain had been a mistake when our mutual enemy was the Soviet Union.

In spite of the fact that we asked our correspondents to send their letters directly to us via the ship's agents, Ramsey Scarlet & Co., Keyser Buildings, Baltimore, we went weeks without receiving any mail and I never got a letter less than three weeks old. Letters from home informed me that they hadn't heard from me for a month, they'd had a mild winter, some oranges had appeared in the shops and that my mother had been conscripted to work part-time in a shoe shop. On the 23 February, I sent a Night Letter Telegram via Commercial Cables asking my parents to send a list of articles which they required together with measurements. In order to save them money and because we were going to have such a prolonged stay in Baltimore, I told them to reply by airgraph, but this proved to be a mistake as we left Baltimore without a reply being received. A birthday card posted to my father on 3 March arrived exactly on the morning of 6 April, his birthday.

I was with Charlie at the MN Club one evening when I received a second-hand invitation to the home of a former Dundonian. I didn't, however, like the manner in which the invitation was extended and made the excuse that I was on sabotage duty. I met many fellow Scots at the Club and particularly Glaswegians. In addition to dances, the Club provided table tennis and snooker and, once a week, free cocktails. I was told that they had, at one time, laid on free beer every night, but had to stop this because some abused the privilege and I certainly saw one or two unable to stand towards the end of a free drinks night. The Club had no bar, but there was to be one in the new, larger and more central, premises about to be opened and some people felt that this would spoil the place. Charlie had cause to remember the MN Club because somebody pinched his raincoat there and thoughtfully left an old one in its place. We hoped at first that this had just been a mistake, but Charlie's coat was not returned and a new one cost him $29 (£7.25).

On the afternoon of 20 March, Charlie and I checked out of the Southern Hotel together and stood at the entrance waiting for a taxi to convey us and our luggage back to the ship, which was now ready to accommodate the crew again. When a taxi came along, Charlie signalled the driver to stop and went out into the road to ask him if he could take us. The driver agreed, but, just then, a US Army captain calmly helped his girlfriend into the cab. Charlie was never backward on such occasions. 'Where do you think you're going?' he asked. 'In this taxi,' said the captain. 'Oh no you're not,' said Charlie, but after further argument, we all got in together as we seemed to be going in roughly the same direction anyway. I heard the girl express surprise to her escort and sensed that he too got a surprise to find himself entering the docks and taken to the gangway of a ship. Charlie wasn't in uniform and, while I had mine on, it wasn't visible under my trench coat and I was wearing my Stetson! We derived some amusement from this and felt that the forward captain had shown himself up in front of his girlfriend.

Neville was already in our cabin when I arrived. It was a small room and after the space of the hotel and what with our increased amount of luggage, I felt that it was ridiculous to put up with it when there was an empty room next door to Ted Moore's cabin on the deck above. I said so to Neville and, dumping my luggage on the floor, went immediately up to ask Mr Moore to enquire of Captain Eccles if one of us could have the spare room. We were informed the following day that Captain Eccles had agreed to my request and Neville was given what was the better room on the top deck and I had the cabin to myself. This made a tremendous difference although it was the smallest of the officers' cabins, was inboard with portholes facing aft and had the additional handicap of being above the heat-producing galley. Even for one person it was small, but whereas the floor had always, necessarily, been cluttered by the blackout screens and wind shields for the two portholes, plus a 'dhobi' bucket and a waste paper bin, I was now able to put my luggage and all this clobber on the top bunk and sleep in the bottom one which had previously been Neville's. Incidentally, I had twice fallen out of the top bunk without injury and how I missed hitting the wash-hand basin in my descent is difficult to understand. I now had two wardrobes and four drawers at my disposal as there were two drawers under the bottom bunk and two under the settee and, in addition to all this, had got rid of Neville with whom I had little in common and who was so untidy. I was so delighted to have the cabin to myself that it took me some time to get over it! I would sit there, in the 'new' second-hand patrol jacket which I had bought from my steward for £2, regarding the room with extreme satisfaction!

During this second prolonged stay in Baltimore, I again had little contact with the many Negro citizens other than the elevator attendants and room-maids in the hotel and the 'boy' of about thirty years of age in the hairdresser's who brushed me down so thoroughly after I had a haircut. On one occasion, Charlie and I boarded a tramcar at the terminus near Fort McHenry. The tram was empty and we chose a seat at the back. As the tram proceeded into town, Negroes came and sat beside us and, when we began to be surrounded only by Negroes, it dawned on us that we were in the section of the tram set aside for them. Nobody said anything and we remained seated where we were. Strangely enough, it took a long time for me to realise that there were no Negroes ever present in all the places I visited – the restaurants, the art galleries, the dance halls, the theatres, cinemas and the skating rinks. The reason for this is that at home there were only white people and so I accepted seeing only white people in the places I frequented in the States. Ironically, the Star-Spangled Banner, the US national anthem, with its proud words 'the land of the free and the home of the brave' was composed by Francis Scott Key when he was held prisoner on board a British warship bombarding Fort McHenry in 1814.

Our new complement of DEMS gunners, this time all RN, joined the ship the same day that the crew returned to live on board permanently.

The *Samite* was ready for sea, and the news was that we were going to New York to load. The ship moved out to anchor in the harbour the next day and, looking out of the porthole in the wireless room, I could see part of the shipyard and the top of the Southern Hotel. A barge was alongside, tugs were scuttling about and there was the soporific drone of an aeroplane. It was such a peaceful scene when the war was going on in Europe and the Far East and when convoys were fighting their way to Russia under the most appalling conditions.

Shortly before sailing, Captain Eccles brought mail when he returned from the shore and I received Christmas Cards which had been posted in Dundee on 23 November and 1 December 1943. Ian Smith came into my cabin to show me a Forces Hymn Book which had been sent to him by the minister of his church in Elie and which obviously pleased him a great deal. Seeing Eric's signature on a Christmas Card, he said that he, too, had a younger brother called Eric.

We expected to travel north to take the shorter route, via the Chesapeake and Delaware Canal, but in this we were mistaken. On the evening of 21 March, we weighed anchor and headed south through Chesapeake Bay.

CHAPTER 14

NEW YORK CITY

The *Samite* proceeded south through the Chesapeake during the night and anchored the following morning in Hampton Roads where the towns of Norfolk and Newport News could clearly be seen with the now familiar paddle ferry, *Hampton Roads*, plying between them. Some hours later we sailed for New York, but I cannot recall whether or not we were in the company of other ships although it is likely that we had an escort of some kind. Our course lay close to the shore and looking out of the porthole during the afternoon watch, I could see sandy beaches, and, on occasion, Mr Lewis standing on the port wing of the bridge surveying the shore through his binoculars. Early in the evening of the 24th, we dropped anchor in New York Harbour and the following morning moved to a berth on the Hudson River side of Lower Manhattan.

I stood on the boat deck with Mr Moore, who pointed out the various landmarks as tugs slowly manoeuvred us towards our berth. The focal points were, of course, the island of Manhattan with its skyscrapers – the first in the world to be built, to maximise limited space – and the Statue of Liberty which, someone had told my father, 'had turned its back on America'! But the harbour itself was full of movement and interest with a variety of ships, tugs and other small craft such as the numerous ferries which plied between the islands of New York City.

A few hours after berthing, I received a letter from my folks which mentioned that they had previously sent an airgraph in reply to my cable asking what they required. But that airgraph, which I was always looking for, had still not reached me. I had a letter home ready for posting, but had left it open in order to let them know of the mail I received on arrival. I had difficulty in finishing it, however, as Charlie came along to my cabin with the letters he had received from his 'wee' wife and insisted upon reading them out loud! Today, when communication by telephone and e-mail is available throughout the world, and when letter-writing is almost a lost art, it is perhaps difficult for a younger generation to understand what these, always old, letters meant to us. As we went months without a word from home, we read them again and again.

In my letter I mentioned arriving in New York and, thoughtlessly, enclosed a souvenir book of matches advertising Baltimore's Southern Hotel. This letter arrived without being opened by the censor and I still have the matches which were an irresponsible enclosure. I was now giving my address as c/o Glen Line Ltd., 20 Billiter Street, London, E.C.3. Alfred Holt & Co. owned both the Blue Funnel Line of Liverpool and the Glen Line of London and the *Samite* was a Glen Line ship, registered in London.

We spent a week in New York and, although I saw a great deal, I regret not visiting the Statute of Liberty and going to see Paul Robeson in *Othello*.

Finding your way about Manhattan is easy as the streets and avenues are, generally, numbered. The avenues run north/south and are numbered from east to west while the streets, which run east/west, are numbered from the south. There was an excellent transport service which included a subway system covering the whole extensive metropolitan area and on which you could travel, irrespective of distance, for only 5¢. You had to have a nickel (5¢) coin to place into the slot which released the turnstile to allow entrance to a platform, but, if you required change, an attendant was ready to provide this at a kiosk. Even in these days of almost full employment, there were 'down and outs' who spent their nights going round and round on the subway trains as, for only a nickel, they could stretch out on a seat. The route was of no importance. Nowhere else could they obtain such a cheap 'bed' for the night and, in winter, the subway must have been their means of survival as it is doubtful if anyone can survive sleeping outdoors in the freezing temperatures experienced in winter.

I went to the top of the Empire State Building, then only twelve years old and the highest building in the world, from where the view is tremendous. I went to the NBC (National Broadcasting Company) Studios where, for the first time, I saw television. This was on a guided tour of the building and the 'tourists', which included some RAF lads, were encouraged to present themselves before a television camera while the images could be seen on a screen at the other side of the room. Also in the studios, I sat in the audience witnessing the recording of an episode of the popular radio comedy series *Duffy's Tavern*.

I also visited the Rockefeller Center and RCA (Radio Corporation of America) building, where the only other occupant of the elevator studied my uniform before bluntly asking, 'What are you?' A tall young man wearing a large Stetson, he had come from Texas to join the US Merchant Marine.

Broadway was, of course, a magnet and, on stage, I saw the comedian/pianist Jimmy Durante, nicknamed 'Snozzle' because of his big nose, and Xavier Cugat and his Latin American Band. Jimmy Durante was a pianist who turned to comedy because people laughed at his nose. Cugat was a rather stocky man with a pencil-thin moustache whose gimmick was to hold a Mexican chihuahua while conducting.

Charlie and I 'hit the town' one evening and began by going into a bar in Times Square. It was very busy and two US sailors stood at the counter immediately in front of us when Charlie asked me what I wanted to drink. When I said 'Coca-Cola' one of the sailors, who was half drunk, turned to his mate and repeated my request, more than once, in a sneering fashion. I was never in bars and immediately sensed that my request for a non-alcoholic drink had so upset this guy that there might be trouble. His mate, however, who didn't appear to be so drunk, turned round and saw the British uniforms. He tried to warn his pal who also, eventually, turned towards me. When he, too, saw the uniforms he was all apologies and emphasised that it was 'all right by him' if I wished to drink Coca-Cola – I could drink what I wanted and could he buy me a drink.

We were later in the table tennis section of a large entertainment centre near Times Square when we met two girls, a slim blond and a voluptuous brunette, who, by glances and smiles, indicated their willingness to be 'picked up', and Charlie made the overtures. I cannot recollect what we did before going to a Midnight Movie, but I know that I went there with reluctance as I couldn't see the sense of beginning to watch a film at such a late hour when it left you shattered the following day.

The four of us were sitting having milkshakes in a drug store afterwards when the blonde decided that she desperately needed a packet of wooden nail files. I dutifully bought them, but she had been asking for so much that Charlie lost his temper and asked if she had the 'gimmee gimmees'. He had to explain to me that this meant 'give me this and give me that' – a phrase which I have always found so hilariously apt. But, like gentlemen, we saw her home so that we had to make our way back to the ship from Long Island at 2 a.m.

Due to her 'gold digging' tactics, the blond was eliminated from any future meeting, but Charlie arranged with the brunette that she would meet us again with another companion. But this future meeting showed that, although Charlie was less gullible than I was, he was not so far behind in the gullibility stakes!

Gloria Katz, the girl with us on our first meeting, brought along the tall blond Helen Torgrimsen. We met outside the Hotel Astor, on Broadway at

44th Street, and they caught us in their machinations right away as, while we had already dined on the ship, they immediately informed us that they had not yet eaten and suggested the Astor. One look at the prices on the Astor's menu told us that we were out of our depth so that we sat and drank water while the girls tucked in. When Charlie paid the bill, the cost of which was, of course, shared by me, he included a tip which brought such a derisory remark from the waiter that Charlie asked for the return of the tip!

It was raining when we left the hotel and the girls expressed such abhorrence at this most shocking inconvenience that we were forced into the further expense of taking a taxi to the nearby Radio City Music Hall. We saw the show from seats in the gallery and it was excellent. There was an on-stage display of ballet and a performance by the high-kicking 'Rockettes', followed by the film *Up in Arms* in which Danny Kaye and Dinah Shore had the most wonderful time on a troopship heading towards the war in Europe. During the show, Gloria kept nudging me to put my arm round her, but this I stubbornly refused to do as she had been Charlie's girl during our first meeting and had transferred her affections to me only because Charlie had transferred his to Helen Torgrimsen, whom he considered better-looking! This was the sum total of my acquaintance with New York girls. It brought no pleasure, but only anxiety because of the expense and contributed to a more cynical view of the human race.

As our time spent on the Barbary Coast had aroused my interest in the region, I bought *Filibusters In Barbary* by Wyndham Lewis when I came across it in a second-hand bookshop in the vicinity of Times Square towards midnight on 24 March. Then, although on my own, I walked all the way through the deserted streets of Lower Manhattan to the ship. Once you left brightly-lit Times Square, the place was dead as the skyscrapers contained mainly offices.

On the evening before we sailed, Harry and I went to the Gay Blades Rollerdrome on Broadway at 52nd Street, which advertised itself as 'The Largest and Most Beautiful Roller Skating Rink'. It was open on weekday evenings until 11.30 p.m. and on Saturdays until midnight, but a concession was made to the Sabbath by closing at 11 p.m! It was a huge place and very busy that evening. The procedure was similar to that in a dancehall in that music played and men asked girls to skate with them. Skating in threes with a girl between two men seemed to be the norm. When I skated with a girl called Mary, from the Bronx, the young US sailor completing the trio exhibited his nautical knowledge by stating that we were 'convoying' Mary!

Mail awaited our return to the ship around midnight and at last I received the airgraph in reply to my telegram. Dated 24 February, it was addressed to the ship c/o British Min. of War Transport, Windsor Station, Montreal, Canada and, as this was not in my mother's handwriting, it had been redirected by Holts. But it was now too late to buy the articles asked for.

My 1943 *New York Handy Guide* states that 'No other city in the world has provided more generously for the comfort and entertainment of servicemen [no mention of women] and seamen than New York.' I do not dispute the claim, although the only generosity I experienced was a reduction in the price of theatre/cinema seats. The hostile attitude of the waiter in the Astor and the prices for servicemen (and seamen) in the hotel, plus the mercenary outlook of the girls with whom we associated, did nothing for New York's image as far as I was concerned.

We sailed in the New York Section of Convoy UGS 38 on the morning of 31 March 1944 and, as our destination was Cape Henry and not Norfolk, it would appear that the suggestion of Captain Woodruff, Commodore of UGS 18, to 'have sections rendezvous outside the Chesapeake Bay approaches', had been adopted. We were again loaded with the materials of war, with our decks covered with army vehicles over which wooden catwalks were built to allow access fore and aft. This time, there were no explosives in the cargo and, as usual, we did not know our destination. But we did know that we were returning to the Mediterranean.

CHAPTER 15

UGS 38

The New York section of Convoy UGS 38, consisting of seventeen merchant ships and four US Navy escort vessels, anchored off Cape Henry in the late afternoon of 1 April. On the morning of 3 April, we rendezvoused with the main (Norfolk) section and the whole convoy, comprising eighty-seven merchant ships and an escort of nineteen US warships, moved into formation and stood out into the Atlantic. On the *Samite*, we believed that we were bound for Anzio and I continued to believe this until I learned from now declassified information supplied by the US Department of the Navy that it was for Augusta (Sicily) and Naples. Fourteen of the twenty-two British ships had Augusta as their first Italian port of call while the others were passing through the Mediterranean to Port Said, Alexandria and points east. Of the sixty-three US ships, thirty were for Oran, six for the Azores and Casablanca, one for Bizerta, twelve were to pass through the Mediterranean and fourteen had Augusta as their first port in Italy. Two French ships were for Casablanca, while two Norwegians were for Bizerta and Alexandria. Captain Thos. A. Symington, USN, on the US cargo ship *Carrillo*, was Commodore. Commander R. L. Lovejoy, USN, on the British tanker *Athelchief*, was Vice-Commodore. Convoy speed was set at 9½ knots.

In addition to the young AB who had borrowed $10 from me in Baltimore and was never seen again, a steward had 'jumped ship' in the States. This was a man in his late thirties called Breen and when we lay at anchor prior to sailing from Hampton Roads, some members of the crew said that he was on a US merchantman about to sail with us in the convoy. How he was able do this I do not know, but the reason was not hard to find as the US Merchant Marine was much better paid than the British Merchant Navy. Breen had been my cabin steward and his place was taken by a young Londoner of about eighteen who had been incarcerated on

Ellis Island because he had 'jumped' a previous ship. I quite liked this lad who regaled me with stories of his life in the USA over a period of about eighteen months when he had even attended High School! Ellis Island, near the Statue of Liberty in Upper New York Bay and within a stone's throw of the fleshpots of Manhattan, contained a pool of labour on which shipmasters could draw in emergency. The quality of that labour was, of course, always in doubt and when a deserter returned to the UK, he was immediately apprehended.

The weather was good as the convoy moved eastward in eight columns of ten or eleven ships with 1,000 yards between each column and 500 yards between ships in a column. The majority of the ships were Liberties and it was almost like being part of a slowly moving city, although each vessel was an independent and isolated unit. The *Samite* was the leading ship in the port column.

The routine already described prevailed and at meal times there was the usual banter between departments with the engineers chastising the mates for their 'ridiculous' instructions to increase or reduce speed by one or two revolutions of the engine. (I heard of one engineer who, on receiving such an instruction, merely pressed his thumb against the bulk head!) The job of the mates was not easy. They had to concentrate on maintaining our correct position in the column and also be on the lookout for signals from the Commodore. This was obviously more difficult in bad weather, but it is difficult to remain vigilant when conditions are seductively good and everything goes right 99 per cent of the time. As for my job, I have had it put to me that it must have been boring or stressful, but I found it neither as, while listening, I could do other things. But like everyone else on every ship in the convoy, I had to remain alert and ready to jump in an emergency.

The Commodore's Report states that, 'after seven days out (torpedo) nets were ordered streamed', but that two US ships had not complied with the order. The reason given by the masters of the offending ships was that they were unable to stream the nets 'on account of a green crew'. The Report criticizes the station keeping of the *Empire Archer* (Br) for 'many times going well ahead of the convoy and the *Polarsol* (Nor) which was 'usually way behind'. The British tanker *Empire Cavalier* is reported as having dropped out of sight, with engine trouble, on 12 April. She rejoined the convoy on 15 April, but again fell astern on the evening of 16 April and was ordered to proceed, under escort, to Gibraltar.

Two US ships detached from the convoy at 10 a.m. on 13 April, in Lat. 33° 30'N Long. 30°05'W, for the Azores. During the evening of 17 April, in Lat. 30°24'N Long. 08°44'W, three US and two French ships detached for Casablanca while two US vessels joined from that port.

As we neared the Strait of Gibraltar, the Morse of the Spanish Coast Stations could again be heard. These stations all had three letter call signs beginning with the letters EA. EAC, for example, was Cadiz.

Other signals which I heard in and near the Mediterranean, on this and on our previous crossing, were those sent by British Hospital Ships and Hospital Carriers. These converted merchant vessels were painted white with a broad green band round their hulls broken in the middle to accommodate a large red cross on each side of the ship. They sent radio signals at four-hour intervals and, at night, sailed fully illuminated in order to broadcast their humanitarian work to the enemy. According to the Geneva Convention, this should have guaranteed them safe passage, but several attacks were made on these ships in the Mediterranean where the *Talamba*, *Newfoundland* and *St David* were sunk with considerable loss of life. I remember logging the signals of the *Oxfordshire*, the *Aba* and the *Leinster*.

The convoy passed through the Strait of Gibraltar on 18 April and the British ship *Crackshot*, from Gibraltar, joined off Europa Point at 2.30 p.m. This time, there was no change over to a Royal Navy Escort and the US Navy Ocean Escort continued to shepherd the convoy. In longitude 02°00′W (just east of Melilla in Spanish Morocco), the Escort was joined by the US destroyer *Lansdale*, minesweepers *Speed* and *Sustain* and the Dutch Cruiser *Van Heemskeerck*. By the evening of 19 April we were off Oran and thirty US ships, including the *Mercy Warren* which had joined from Casablanca, entered the port together with the solitary British Liberty Ship *Samaffric*.

The coast of Algeria was in sight to starboard and the weather continued fine, but we on the *Samite* were no longer seduced by these seemingly comforting factors and became more apprehensive as we headed eastward. Cape Ténèz, the scene of our previous encounter with the enemy, was passed without incident and, by late afternoon on the 20 April, we came abreast of Algiers when the *Royal Star* (Br), *Campidoglio* (It), *Cartago* (US) and the tanker *Salt Creek* (Br) joined the convoy at 5.50 p.m. in Lat. 36°54′N Long. 03°12′E.

CHAPTER 16

HITLER'S BIRTHDAY OR THE DAY WE WERE DONE OUT OF THE 'ITALY STAR'[3]

I was on watch in the radio room during the afternoon of Thursday, 20 April 1944, when Mr Moore entered to inform me that we could 'expect some fun tonight' as a message had been received from the Commodore that an enemy plane had been seen shadowing the convoy. Mr Moore was always nervously jovial and his use of the word 'fun' did nothing to reduce either his or my apprehension.

This was now different from the previous occasion when the attack had been so unexpected. This time we had the opportunity to prepare so that I dressed in my best uniform, with small valuables stuffed in the pockets, and lay down on my bunk, fully clothed, at about 8 p.m. Strangely enough, I went directly to sleep.

I awoke, quite refreshed, and looked at my watch to find that I had been asleep only about three quarters of an hour. As dusk was the time of greatest danger, I hoped that it was now dark and removed a porthole ventilation cover to see if this were the case. It was almost totally dark. I thought, and hoped, that the danger was over for the night, replaced the porthole cover, made a trip to the lavatory, returned to bed and lay listening.

In spite of the anticipation, the roar of the aircraft which suddenly passed over the ship, at almost mast height, came as a shock. I swung out of my bunk and began tying my shoelaces while listening attentively. Perhaps the plane was one of ours? Then, from somewhere in the distance, there was the faint sound of gunfire and the *Samite* was struck with such force that I felt that she had been lifted backwards out of the water. I donned my life jacket and cap and was in the alleyway outside my cabin on my way upstairs to the radio room when I heard the Chief Engineer, on his way to the engine room, say 'We've had ours.' The alarm bells were then, rather unnecessarily, sounded.

I have no recollection of the *Samite*'s guns being fired at all and the information which Ted Moore had conveyed to me during my afternoon watch was a précis of the following message sent by the Commodore on advice received from the Escort Commander.

TO ALL SHIPS   4/20/44

TONIGHT EXPECT TORPEDO AND BOMB ATTACK WITH FLARE ILLUMINATION X FLARE MUST SILHOUTTE TARGET TO PROPERLY LOCATE IT X MOST PROBABLE DIRECTION OF ATTACK RECIPROCAL OF BEARING OF FLARE X EARLY USE GUNFIRE WILL DEFINITELY LOCATE THE CONVOY FOR THE ENEMY X DO NOT OPEN FIRE UNLESS ENEMY PLANE PLAINLY VISIBLE AND WELL WITHIN RANGE X

This was why our guns were not firing and why the enemy was allowed to make his initial attack without opposition. But the guns of the convoy did open up, and I witnessed the tremendous display of tracer fire which silhouetted the torpedo bombers as they flew low down the columns at some distance from the *Samite* on the starboard side. I saw also a great pall of black smoke which was all that was left of a ship, either two or three columns away, and a great jagged piece of metal, which had been part of her, lay on our boat deck.

Once again, the convoy continued on its way, leaving damaged ships behind. Our situation, however, was not nearly as serious or uncomfortable as it had been when we were struck by the glider bomb. This time we had collected an aerial torpedo on the starboard side of No. 2 hold. The accommodation was unscathed, the engines (although stopped) were still capable of functioning, the lights in the accommodation remained on, there was no fire, no ammunition on board and no-one was hurt. Ted Moore and I waited in the radio room while the damage was assessed by Mr Thomas and the Carpenter. The decision was that we were unable to proceed. Mr Moore started up the transmitter and sent brief details of our situation to the Commodore followed by 'suggest proceed FFA' (the call sign of Algiers radio station). Within minutes the reply came: 'Proceed FFA.'

No. 2 hold was flooded, the ship was down by the head and the rudder refused to function so that the *Samite* could not be steered. Water ballast was pumped out of the forward deep tanks and the after double bottom tanks flooded to bring the ship into a more or less horizontal position and, about an hour later, the RN tug *Vagrant* took us in tow from a position on the port bow. On watch in the radio room that night, I felt quite happy to be out of the convoy and heading for Algiers although I now know that it continued on its way without further molestation.

During the forenoon of 21 April, and for the second time in just over six months, the *Samite* entered Algiers harbour in damaged condition and assisted by a tug. I was on the boat deck as, well down by the head, we moved slowly past the end of the mole on which stood three British soldiers watching us enter. Suddenly one of them called out excitedly and his voice carried clearly across the water, although he was some distance away, 'It's the *Samite*'. Then he, or one of his mates, shouted, 'Three cheers for the *Samite*' and they gave us three hearty cheers. They must have been associated with the ship during her previous visit to the port and these three squaddies would never know how much we appreciated their spontaneous gesture and how I have remembered it down the years.

Troopship *Paul Hamilton* (Picture taken by USS *Menges*' photographer's Mate 1/c Arthur Green. Picture source: US Coast Guard Historian's office)

CHAPTER 17

ASSESSMENT OF THE ATTACK

If you have to be torpedoed, ours was a comfortable affair. But others were not so lucky. We knew that there were other casualties, but other than that knew nothing, although I heard it rumoured in Algiers that a troopship had been lost. Only in recent years have I learned the extent of the tragedy of that night.

The column of black smoke which I saw reaching to the heavens and the jagged piece of metal on our boat deck were all that remained of the US Liberty Troopship *Paul Hamilton* when all on board perished. *The Atlantic Battle Won (History of United States Naval Operations in World War II*, Volume X) by S. E. Morison states that 580 men, including 498 of the Army Air Force, lost their lives when the ship was 'blown to bits' because she was also carrying high explosives.

British servicemen were generally conveyed in former passenger liners with a reasonable turn of speed. The US lacked such liners so that slow Liberty Ships were converted to troopships where troops were accommodated, in five-tier bunks, in the upper parts of the holds, generally above the waterline. But, because the Liberty was designed as a cargo ship, it was necessary, for the stability of the ship, to have heavy ballast in the holds below the troops. High explosives/ammunition was a convenient ballast providing, of course, that you personally were not travelling on the ship. Five hundred and eighty homes in the United States must have received telegrams following the annihilation of the *Paul Hamilton*. I wonder what these telegrams said – 'Your son/husband has been killed in action'? Whatever they said, I would guarantee that they did not disclose the fact that these, generally very young men away from home for the first time, had been sent to the Mediterranean war zone on a floating bomb by some individual sitting behind the safety of a desk in Washington DC.

The other major loss was that of the US Destroyer *Lansdale* which, according to the official history of the US Navy, was sunk by an aerial torpedo with the loss of 'forty-seven officers and men out of her total complement of 282'. It would appear that, although they were all mothers' sons of the land where all are deemed to be equal, a distinction had, even in death, to be made between officers and other ranks.

The *Royal Star*, which had been in the convoy for only a matter of hours, was struck by a torpedo between the engine room and the stokehold. One man was killed and the ship was abandoned apart from the Master, who remained on board when the tug *Athlete* attempted, unsuccessfully, to tow her the following morning. The tug cast off only minutes before the vessel sank and the Master, who had jumped into the sea, was picked up and carried to Algiers by HM Motor Launch 568. The US Liberty Ship *Stephen F Austin* was damaged and arrived in Algiers under tow.

Since researching nautical matters, I have found that mistakes are commonplace and what has been written about Convoy UGS 38 is no exception.

First of all, the now Declassified Convoy Document has three different spellings of the name of the Commodore's ship; *Carrillo*, *Carbillo* and *Cabrillo*. The same Document lists three different positions where the attack took place; 37°00′N 03°20′E, 36°39′N 03°42′E and 36°59′N 02°42′E. The latter position would put the convoy west of Algiers and strangely enough, the *Blue Star Line at War 1939-1945*, by Taffrail, states that the '*Royal Star* of 8000 tons, sailed from Algiers to join up with a large *west*-bound convoy off that port.' HMSO publication which lists all the British Vessels Lost and Damaged at Sea 1939-1945 states that the *Samite* was struck in position 37°02′N 03°41′E. *The History of US Naval Operations* states that 'this convoy was attacked at a point only three miles off Cape Bengut'.

The incident is recorded in *A Merchant Fleet in War 1939-1945*, the history of Alfred Holt & Co written by the naval historian Captain S. W. Roskill, RN. Roskill says 'the *Samite* herself was hit by a torpedo on the starboard side forward, and a huge column of water deluged her decks. The enemy aircraft which had dropped it (the torpedo) then flew over the ship, just clearing her masts'. This suggests that the aircraft flew over the ship after the torpedo struck which, of course, is impossible. Aircraft dropped their torpedoes about 100 yards from their targets and the plane was well clear of the ship before the torpedo struck.

The number of planes involved in the attack is again a subject of controversy. The Commodore estimates twenty-three, Morison, in the *History of US Naval Operations*, estimates between twenty-five to thirty, while Roskill in his history of the Royal Navy, *The War At Sea*, states that 'some sixty aircraft' were involved. Taffrail plays safe by electing for 'a considerable number of low-flying torpedo-bombers'. One thing is certain – nobody was counting!

CHAPTER 18
ALGIERS AGAIN

We tied up alongside and discharging commenced immediately. The sodden contents of No. 2 hold, which included tool kits, were dumped on open ground about fifty yards from the ship and took the shape of a large untidy pyramid. The following morning, however, the ship's cat played on the small heap which was all that was left of it after being plundered during the night.

As our stores had been replenished in the United States, our food was again excellent and one lunchtime, when discharging was taking place, an RNVR lieutenant sat on my right at the rectangular table on the starboard side of the saloon. The table accommodated four people and we occupied the two seats facing for'ard with a porthole directly in front of us. An Arab docker kept looking through the porthole and, in spite of the lieutenant's verbal injunction to 'bugger off', accompanied by gestures which no-one could fail to understand, he kept coming back to leer at us. But he came back once too often – the lieutenant was ready with the jug of table water, which he received full in the face. I was shocked by the incident. The Arab may have asked for it, but he was vulnerable because he was a second-class citizen in French Algeria when similar action against a London docker could have brought the Port of London to a standstill. There was a humorous saying during the war, regarding the three categories of naval officers: 'The Royal Navy were gentlemen trying to be sailors, the Merchant Navy were sailors trying to be gentlemen while the Royal Naval Volunteer Reserve were neither sailors, nor gentlemen.' No mention was made of the Royal Naval Reserve: the men of the Merchant Navy who transferred into the Royal Navy during the war and without whom the Royal Navy could not have functioned. Going into town one day, I was given a lift in a jeep driven by a Lieutenant Commander, RNR, who said he was a Blue Funnel officer.

In spite of the above incident, I formed the opinion that the British forces got on reasonably well with the Arabs, but did not take too kindly to the French, many of whom were Vichy. But, when a derogatory generalisation was made about any nationality or race by anyone on board any ship on which I sailed, someone always added the ameliorating rider 'but the women are all right!'

Arab workmen were not allowed to use the crew's toilet and a primitive contraption, screened off by canvas, was rigged for them at the stern. As all their deposits fell straight into the harbour from a great height, we always looked up to assess the situation when rounding the stern in a boat!

Most of the films showing in Algiers were war films and only three days after being torpedoed, Charlie and I were in the audience at the Rio Cinema watching Noel Coward's *In Which We Serve* which was advertised in French as *Ceux Qui Servent Sur Mer*. It was pure wartime propaganda with Coward himself playing the part of the gallant and phlegmatic upper-crust English RN captain whose destroyer was sunk under him in the Mediterranean. A scene where the destroyer's guns were blazing away at the enemy was all too close to the experiences of some of the audience so that a young RN rating, who had too much to drink, jumped onto his seat and was shouting 'Give it to the bastards' before his good-humoured mates pulled him down.

Harry and I visited Le Bosphore, a small music hall with a band and a stage show where drinks were served to the customers sitting at tables. Only civilians and officers were admitted and the place had a family atmosphere as French Algerians (no Arabs) were there with their children. We were ushered to seats at a table on the balcony from where we saw only the last (conjuring) act of the stage show, after which a naval lieutenant in his thirties took the stage to sing the French Canadian song 'Alouette' while holding a little girl in his arms. Le Bosphore closed at 9 p.m. which was, nevertheless, later than the closing times of most other civilian establishments. We left before then to go on to a cinema to see Jean Arthur and Cary Grant in *Top of the Town* which I described in a letter home, in the parlance of the day, as being 'sticking out'!

As during our previous visit, spending money came from the sale of cigarettes on the black market. I had no scruples about this as cigarettes, although in great demand, were not a necessity and the young Arabs to whom we sold them made their living by reselling to the French. The ship's stores had been replenished in the States and our weekly ration still consisted of a carton of 200 cigarettes, containing ten packets of twenty, of the brands mentioned earlier. Although one of the few non-smokers on the ship, it never occurred to me to stockpile and I bought my ration only when in Algeria. This gave me a net income of 27/6d (£1.37½p) a week as a carton cost 2/6d (12½p) on board while a packet retailed to the middlemen for 30 francs (15p). We could have bought clothing in the States to sell, but nobody did this although the black market was rife everywhere in the Mediterranean theatre. A shirt, which had cost Charlie $2 (50p) in the States, sold for 250 francs (£1.25p).

I spent pleasant days at a small nearby beach, to which I hitchhiked or took a tram and where French women came with their children. Jacqueline, who was about three, began to come and sit beside me so that I took copies of the *Sunday Post* comic section to the beach and read 'Oor Wullie' and 'The Broons' to her. The fact that I knew no French and she no English did not seem to matter and her mother would always smile in recognition on meeting and departing. One day, from that beach, I suddenly spotted far out at sea, a convoy moving, almost imperceptibly, eastwards. It is likely that this was Convoy UGS 40 which passed Algiers on 11 May and was attacked off Cape Bengut that evening.

The old and rickety single decker trams were usually packed, with straphangers in the open central space and others hanging on the outside at the rear. Some Arab women wore the yashmak, but, as these were transparent, I saw that they also wore powder and lipstick and even had their finger nails painted red, as did some Arab boys.

Heading for the beach one day Charlie and I, out of uniform as we usually were, attempted to board a US Army truck which had stopped to pick up some sailors. As I was climbing on board, a US soldier pushed me back saying 'No Frogs [French] allowed.' When I said we were merchant seamen, he helped us on board and could not apologise enough for his mistake. They were not, he explained, permitted to give lifts to civilians. I was also taken for a Frenchman in a café when the girl at the desk, who had been speaking English to the man before me, addressed me in French.

One day, when we were looking for a lift to the beach and thumbing every army vehicle, Charlie said I was wasting my time when I thumbed a staff car. But it drew up about thirty yards beyond us, so that we ran to it and jumped in. It was a large car and I sat on the bench seat beside the US Army driver and his mate while Charlie went into the back beside two good-looking French girls. It was rather strange to be invited to join this cosy foursome, but the reason soon became obvious. A US checkpoint had to be passed and, before it came in sight, the girls were deposited by the side of the road. We then drove on to the checkpoint where the driver asked one of the guards if it would be OK if he gave our girlfriends a lift. After some discussion, which ended with permission being granted, the car was turned round and we went back for the girls. The car was turned again and proceeded through the checkpoint to the beach where Charlie and I were hastily dismissed. Although the driver, a loudmouth who knew everything, had the social use of the car, he wasn't allowed to take girls in it, but had got round the problem by using us. We, of course, didn't care. We had got our lift to the beach and found the incident amusing. But how did they get the girls back into town?

Merchant Navy personnel could use clubs provided for HM Forces and, on the odd occasion, I would dine at the British Officers' Club. There was also a Merchant Navy Club, an Empire Club, a Malcolm Club for the RAF and a Pinder Club for the 'Other Ranks' of the Army, Navy and Air Force. Charlie and I made frequent use of the Pinder Club by merely discarding evidence of rank. During the summer evenings, dances were held in the open air where the dance floor was the concrete area behind the Club. On four evenings a week, dancing was to recorded music played over loudspeakers located in the trees, but on Wednesdays it was to a 'live' band. There was always a shortage of women and I was there early one evening when only a few soldiers were present and not a woman in sight. Two very tough looking British Tommies then made a show of one asking the other to dance and they took the floor together where they cavorted so as to have the rest of us 'in stitches'. Although, the previous year, I had seen only Wrens (WRNS) who worked in the Fleet Mail Office, I now saw WAAF and ATS girls in the town.

One Sunday afternoon, a 'down at the heel', middle-aged merchant seaman wearing an over-sized black overcoat sat down at the piano in the same open-air area. He played classical music to an audience which sat in total silence and gave him an ovation equal to that given to any concert pianist. This was my introduction to learning that the lower deck of the MN had a number of well-educated and talented men who, generally due to 'drink', had become misfits at home, but had found refuge in the Service.

When going for a haircut, I had to keep telling the barber to take more off as they insisted on giving you little more than a neck trim. Charlie, however, was quite content with this and consequently went once a week. One day, while sitting in a barber shop waiting for him, I sat next to what I thought was a British Tommy to whom I remarked, 'They don't take much off, do they?' 'No compris, me Roosian,' he replied.

On leaving the barbers', we made for the British Army Officers' Shop as we had heard we could buy clothes there. The British Forces had changed into shorts on 24 April and I was anxious to get shorts as I had left home without tropical kit and had been unable to buy any in the States. We were told at the shop that they were not allowed to sell shorts to naval personnel, but I was able to buy two khaki tropical shirts, two pairs of stockings, a pair of garters, a towel, a hairbrush and two sets of collar studs: all for 270 francs (£1 7s). I wrapped everything in the towel and, when we were crossing the road outside the shop, the hairbrush fell to the ground where it was narrowly missed by a passing tram and then by a car which swerved to avoid it.

As it was too late to return to the ship for lunch, we went to in a French restaurant. The meal consisted of a salad made up of a few horseradishes and lettuce followed by a dish of chunks of black beef accompanied by boiled vegetables which we did not recognise. As we were provided with only a fork, we found it impossible to break up the hard pieces of meat so that we left them untouched. We did, however, find the dessert, which looked like some kind of jam, to our liking. Dark brown bread was provided with the meal and, although very hard, was quite good. I noticed an elderly man whittling pieces off with a pocket knife then stuffing the remainder into his pocket when he left.

On returning to the ship, I was told that a Dundee chap named Smith had called to see me, but he never called again and I have no idea who he was. But the great news was that, after so many futile visits to the Fleet Mail Office, a great batch of mail had at last been collected.

I got eleven letters, nine of which were dated late October and early November 1943, and one from my father said that he had been in London during a doodlebug (V-bomb) raid. The censor cut out the part mentioning how long the raid had lasted although I rather think this must have already been known by the Germans!

Charlie took pity on me and gave me a pair of his white shorts and the loan of a white tropical shirt, but shortly afterwards I managed to buy a pair of khaki shorts so that I generally wore khaki. By early May, it was already hot enough to be uncomfortable by the evening on our all-steel Liberty Ship, which absorbed the heat of the day and did not relinquish it until the following morning. When we sat in our cabins during the evenings, portholes and doors were left open while our primitive electric fans stirred the humid air as they moved sluggishly within their limited arc. Tropical kit had not been required during our previously stay as we had arrived late in the year.

On 25 May, I went on board the Blue Funnel Liberty *Samwater* to meet up with fellows who had been in Halifax with us. The following day there was even more of a reunion when Clan Line's *Sambrian* came in with others who had been in Halifax, and whose 3rd R/O was my pal George McPherson. George wasn't long in coming on board and said that he was especially glad to see us as they had heard that the *Samite* had been lost with all hands. He and I then spent some days ashore together, but he wasn't permitted to go every day as his No. 1, who must have been a bundle of fun to sail with, had decreed that either the 2nd or 3rd R/O had always to remain on board. All these fellows had been to Sicily, where many had bought guitars.

I met a 3rd R/O called Petrie in town one day. He had attended evening classes at Dundee Wireless during my time there and, although we arranged to meet, he didn't turn up – as this was not the first time this had happened, Charlie chided me as being naive.

More mail arrived on 3 June, and I received three airgraphs dated early September 1943, which had been addressed to the Gainsboro Hotel in Halifax. I was now suggesting to my correspondents that they should write to the *Samite* c/o GPO London. This was the address of all RN ships and appeared to bring the mail a bit faster. Censorship was becoming more lax as, in my letters home, I was now naming places in Canada, the US and North Africa which were not cut out although, later, in Oran, when I named the Cathedral and gave details of the statue at its door, the censor deleted the information. We were still allowed only one Air Letter form a week, although I sometimes managed to get extras, and they required a British 3*d* stamp. On 22 May, I received a letter written by my mother on 11 May. This was indeed a record, but by 13 June, I was again complaining about the mail service.

I noticed that fifty centimes, 1 and 2 franc bank notes were now in circulation whereas these small denominations had previously been available only in coin. Also in circulation was United States 'invasion' money, which was US notes with a small red or yellow stamp on them. A set of Algerian stamps for my father's collection cost me 112 francs (11/3*d*).

When returning from the beach with Charlie and the 4th Engineer of the *Samwater*, I had my watch stolen. I was a little way behind as we walked through the Arab market, adjacent to the Casbah, when a group of noisy kids began pulling at my arms, making as if they wanted to buy my towel. They then disappeared so abruptly that I instinctively knew that something was wrong and discovered that the wristwatch I had bought in Halifax had disappeared with them into the Casbah.

A sudden commotion on deck one afternoon caused me to investigate. The sky was black with locusts which had been blown out of Africa and, as they could go no farther, were landing on every ship in the harbour where sailors, armed with brushes, were sweeping them into the sea. It was an opportunity not to be missed and, as the creatures were easily gathered up, some of us filled Harry's cabin with them which, of course, brought the desired reaction. The following day, there was a tidemark of dead locusts resembling that of seaweed on the beach.

Crossing a square on my own one evening, I discovered an almighty fight going on in a building. When I stopped to see what was going on, a young US sailor, who could not have known what the fracas was about, said to me 'Hold this', thrust his limp white cap into my hand and shot up the entrance stairs to join the fray. I felt a bit guilty as I flung the cap into the doorway after him, but wish I had kept it as a souvenir.

As we had been put out at anchor as soon as the cargo was discharged, going ashore was sometimes impossible due to Captain Eccles' reluctance to put down a boat. This was the case when we lay only a maddening twenty yards from the quay and all seemed resigned to remain on board for the evening when shouting drew me outside to investigate. A young Scottish seamen, dressed in his best and standing on a makeshift raft, was using a piece of wood as a paddle in a frantic attempt to reach the steps. Water was slopping over his shoes as his mates shouted both encouraging and derisory remarks and nothing would have pleased them more than to see him land in the drink. But he made it and, with a wave, headed for the town with soaking feet.

Although not yet seaworthy, the *Samite* sailed from Algiers on the morning of 18 May. Temporary repairs were to be completed in Oran and we made the 200-mile passage in Convoy MKS 47, arriving the following evening.

Officers' Club ticket.

CHAPTER 19

ORAN

Oran, dominated on its western side by the lofty Abbey of Santa-Cruz, was under US control and organised to make life as comfortable as possible for US personnel. The US Red Cross Empire Club (referred to either as the Empire or the ARC and which we could use) was dedicated to their comfort with a cinema, dance hall, snack-bar, lounge/reading room, games room, two music rooms (one classical) where you could lounge in leather-bound easy chairs listening to records of your choice, put on by grey-uniformed ladies of the US Red Cross. During summer evenings, a Spanish language class was held on the roof from which there was a lovely view of the blue Mediterranean. The class met from 7 to 8 p.m. on Mondays and Thursdays and only two US soldiers and I were regular attenders, although others dropped in and were never seen again. This became such a regular feature that it annoyed us as the teacher was forced to spend time with these guys going over the numerals which had already been mastered. One of my fellow students had worked in a hotel before joining the army. Another, a tall, slim man, was disfigured by severe facial burns. He told me that he received his injuries when the tent in which he was sleeping had caught fire and was concerned that, when he returned home, his family would be distressed by his appearance.

One evening after class, the teacher took me to his home, an upstairs flat in the centre of the town, to meet his wife. I accepted a cognac, but refused a meal as I was aware that I would be eating part of their meat ration. But they insisted that I should come again, for a meal, so that I returned to enjoy a meal of roast beef, chips, tomatoes, brown bread, toast and green grapes, accompanied by a table wine which I liked very much. The teacher's wife also spoke Spanish, but knew no English so that he had to act as interpreter as I knew no French. I deliberately curbed my appetite and, as the teacher smoked cigarettes, took along a few packets in return for their hospitality. He was a Frenchman of Spanish descent whose father had been British Consul in Morocco and I was shown the Consul's Certificate dated 1886.

In retrospect, it was idiotic to study Spanish in French Algeria when I should have been learning French. But there was only a Spanish Department, dealing with South America, in the Dundee jute office to which I believed I would return after the war and that was the reason for my choice of language.

A week or so after our arrival, a ship going to Italy and returning to Oran was short of a 2nd Engineer and Harry was asked to make the round trip on her. I offered to look after 'Oscar', his pet bullfinch, until his return, but he insisted on giving it to me. Mr Turnbull lent Harry 2nd Engineer's epaulettes and Harry later told me that he had, very wisely, allowed the crew of his temporary ship to believe that he held the same position on the *Samite*. 'Oscar', incidentally, made a successful bid for freedom some weeks after I took possession of him. I often allowed him/her to fly about the cabin and he took off one morning when Charlie barged in. Harry and I were always good friends; he had bought a piano accordion in the States and every so often would come into my cabin with the instrument slung round his neck to demonstrate his progress!

To the west of Oran, there are miles and miles of beautiful sandy beach which was divided into sections by the US authorities and designated according to rank and sex. You could eat and drink there, there were dressing huts, showers, deck chairs, coloured sun shades and limejuice free on tap. While you swam or lazed on the beach, the trumpet of Harry James, or the *Bob Hope Programme*, would be coming over loudspeakers. It was all very different from what was happening on another sectioned beach in Normandy to which officers and 'other ranks' had equal access.

To get to the beach, which was about ten miles from the town, you had only to hitch-hike. Usually it was a US truck which picked me up, but sometimes it was a jeep and once an ambulance. Once, too, I got a lift back in a six-seater Ford car driven by a soldier who expressed his view that five Americans were worth one Russian. Then there was the hair-raising experience of returning in a jeep when I had the option of being left alone on the deserted road or sitting on the hard petrol tank with its mere inches of freeboard. I held grimly onto the rail, approximately four inches above the tank on which I sat, while the driver raced his mate round the hairpin bends of the high coastal road with its sheer drops to the sea. There was also the occasion when I stood waiting for a lift together with an RAF chap, a US soldier and two French girls. A US truck came along and pulled up a little way down the road so that the RAF fellow and I ran towards it. As we drew near, however, it moved off again and we stopped running. But, as soon as we stopped running, it stopped again so that we, again, started towards it. This time, though, soldiers already on the truck were waving us away as the truck backed past us to pick up 'les' girls. It was a dirty trick, but we had the consolation of, shortly afterwards, being conveyed to the beach sitting in a jeep which was more comfortable than standing in a crowded truck.

When my young steward informed me that he was to take part in a jitterbugging contest at the Empire Club on the evening of 28 June 1944, I went along to see him perform. The customary red stamp was applied to the back of my hand before admission and the place was packed with GIs (a slang term for enlisted men of the US Army, with the letters standing for Government Issue) and US sailors who had come along to support their buddies. Apart from two WACs, all the girls were French. Competing couples were gradually eliminated until only the steward and his partner remained on the floor with a US sailor and his partner. The steward and his partner were brilliant and there was absolutely no doubt in my mind that they should have won, but, when the final judgment was left to the crowd, their thunderous applause gave the prize to the other couple.

Although the ship was not at the quayside, a large friendly hound appeared at the top of the gangway one morning, having been brought on board by one of the crew the previous evening. It was returned to the shore, but, while waiting for a lift a day or two later, I was amused to see the mutt staring ahead as it sat beside the driver of a US truck.

Charlie was in charge of the engine room at night. His work was not onerous and, for a short trial period, he was able to come up to his cabin for an hour or two until it was found that the ratings failed to work without supervision. Charlie had sandwiches laid out for him because he was a watch-keeper and I usually helped to demolish them!

I regretted not having any practical work to do in the wireless room, but continued to assist Charlie with his electrical work. He slept in the mornings, but was free to go ashore with me in the evenings and sometimes in the afternoons. Harry, like all the others, including the 2nd Sparks and 3rd Mate, who to my knowledge were never at the beach, did not generally want to go ashore. I could not understand the general malaise of the officers and why even the young men preferred to remain on board for weeks and months on end in such interesting surroundings. Mr Thomas had not been off the ship since we had been in New York in March. The crew, I may say, did not suffer from the same malaise, although their interest in the shore largely coincided with their interest in alcohol[4] as there was none on the ship. On an isolated occasion, Ted Moore and Dai Lewis went ashore together and came back saying that it was not such a bad place! I had learned semaphore in the Boys' Brigade, but my semaphore was rusty so that, when I saw US ships communicating by this method, I studied the old set of semaphore cards given to me by my father in order to try to read the fast movements of the flags. US merchantmen carried signallers, proficient in both semaphore and the Morse lamp and whose only job was to signal. On British vessels, the deck officers, in addition to their knowledge of navigation, cargo handling and the general running of the ship, had the burden of using the Morse lamp, although they occasionally called upon the services of the radio officers if the Morse were too fast. When I first had to do this, I found it difficult as it is one thing to read Morse by sound and another to read it by sight. Visual Morse was transmitted either by means of a hand-held Aldis lamp or by the larger lamps secured on the wings of the bridge.

The 1943 Christmas airgraph had shown a Britisher, an American and a Frenchman standing laughing together, but there was not always such camaraderie between the Allies and tension was in the air, leave curtailed and naval and military police out in force when battle wagons of different nationalities were in port. Oran is only a few miles east of Mers-el-Kebir, which was then a naval base and where British warships had fired upon French warships in July 1940 when there was a risk of the latter being used by the Germans after the fall of France. This resulted in great loss of life on board the French vessels and bad feeling between the two navies. The *Richelieu* had, fortunately, been in Dakar at the time of the incident and I saw her more than once in Algiers. While other ships were camouflaged by being painted in one shade of grey, she was painted in two shades which were used to cover her in most distinctive sharp, wavy bands. When a US battlewagon was in port in summer, her band came ashore and played jazz for the boys in the open air. There was a number of South Africans in Oran and, with reference to camaraderie, the British troops used to sing a parody of the South African song 'Sari Marai' which went: 'There's 50,000 bastards in the old Transvaal, but f— all in Mersa Matruh!'

The 4 July was not a holiday on British ships, but when the crew of the US ship lying next to us saw our crew working that morning, they shouted across 'Don't you know this is Independence Day?', 'Scabs', etc. This resulted in Captain Eccles giving the crew the rest of the day off, and it was a mystery to me why there was always so much work to be done on a new ship idling at anchor over such a long period.

Although Algiers was the wartime capital of the Free French and there were many refugees in Algeria, there was no great jubilation at the news of the landings in Normandy. According to *The Stars and Stripes* of 7 June, the occasion was too emotional for many French people who had relatives and friends in France. The newspaper reported that, on hearing the news for the first time, one lady 'excused herself and turned to weep bitter tears.

The waiting had been so long.' I wrote home on 16 August, the day the Allies invaded Southern France, saying that 'I would have liked to have taken part in one of the invasions, but fate settles these things.'

There must have been very few radio receivers in the homes in Oran, as news was broadcast every evening over loudspeakers in the streets and during these summer evenings, the people ceased to stroll in order to listen attentively as the news was read. There were celebrations when Paris fell to the FFI (French Forces of the Interior) on 23 August, but this was nothing to the hysteria on the evening of 24 July when a rumour that the war was over hit the town. The first I heard of this was when the crew of a neighbouring ship were running around in great excitement, claiming that Germany had collapsed. This was confirmed by men returning from the shore and the town was apparently in an uproar, with the strains of the Marseillaise and the Spangled Banner heard everywhere and people shouting 'Fini la guerre!' *The Stars and Stripes* reported that the rumour had started about 7.28 p.m., but towards 9 p.m. subdued crowds began making their way home. Everyone wanted so much to believe that the war was over.

Oran was as busy a port as Algiers and we were usually at anchorages from which it was necessary to get a boat to take us ashore. Captain Eccles did not always place a lifeboat at our disposal and sometimes it was just not possible to go ashore. If we did manage to go, return was usually made by taking the US Liberty Boat which left at 10.30 p.m. so that all were on board their ships before the 11 p.m. curfew. I went down to breakfast one morning to learn that John Richard McDonald, a thirty-one-year-old AB from Port Madoc, was dead. He and two of his mates had missed the Liberty Boat the previous evening and, while his mates had decided to sleep on the quay, he had elected to swim to the ship. It was thought that one of the depth charges, dropped at intervals at the harbour entrance, had exploded when he was in the water so that he had been stunned and drowned. Most of the crew attended his funeral, but Captain Eccles, Mr Lewis and I were the only officers present and we each had a cord. Photographs were taken of the ceremony and sent home, no doubt by the padre who officiated, to the next of kin. We made the journey to and from the cemetery in an army truck and when we returned to the centre of the town, the solemnity of the situation was shattered by crew members hammering on the partition which separated us from the driver to get him to stop at Joe's Joint where they piled out for a drinking session. I am sure, however, that their behaviour would have met with the approval of their deceased shipmate and was in no way disrespectful to his memory.

I experienced nervous tension when returning alone to the docks at night to get the Liberty Boat back to the ship and it wasn't only marauding

Arabs who gave cause for concern. One evening, at the entrance to a short tunnel which gave access to the quay, I was accosted by a group of US merchant seamen, led by a particularly nasty individual, wearing a soft hat set squarely on his head, who demanded to know if I were a Limey. And while I would always reply in the negative to such a question, I was particularly vociferous on that occasion when a brief geography lesson was necessary to establish my innocence. I could see that there was considerable doubt in the minds of the group as to whether the Scots were different from the English when they, reluctantly, allowed me to proceed to the quay.

On another occasion, I was on the quay waiting for the 10.30 p.m. Liberty Boat when a group of young US Navy men, who had been drinking, gathered round and tried to involve me in an argument about the war. Although it was not as threatening a situation as the one mentioned above, it was still unpleasant and caused me to be apprehensive. The sailor directly in front of me was waving his hands to emphasise a point when he caught the corner of my spectacles and sent them flying into the dock. All nervousness left me. 'Right fellow,' I said, 'I'm going up the gangway behind you to report this to your commanding officer.' And, just as my demeanour changed, so did his and he became nervous and apologetic while his shipmates condemned him for his action. He fumbled in the small top breast pocket of his naval blouse and extracted a $10 bill. 'Will this cover the cost?' he asked. As I believed it would and could see no profit in taking the matter further, I took the note which went into the wallet I had for Eric.

When I reported the incident at the US Port Surgeon's Office the following day, they sent me to the 23rd Hospital, about seven miles outside Oran, for an eye test. I was taken by ambulance, but had to hitchhike back. I lost my glasses on the evening of Tuesday 8 August and, on the morning of Saturday 12 August was, without charge, given a pair of the small framed, steel spectacles worn by US personnel. This was certainly fast service and when my optician in Dundee later saw the spectacles, he was impressed. 'These are toric lens', he said and, apparently, in advance of what was available in the UK. When I appeared in the saloon for breakfast the morning after losing my glasses, explanation, predictably, brought only amusement.

It was always, therefore, a relief to meet up with members of the crew when returning to the docks at night as I benefited from their protection. Sitting with them on some boxes on a quay one evening while waiting for the Liberty Boat, a sailor 'in his cups' pronounced that I was the 'best officer on the ship' when his companions, likewise inebriated, expressed agreement. I knew they were talking rubbish, but as flattery to me was of absolutely no advantage to them, they must have liked me well enough.

Sunday 16 August 1944 was one of those red-letter days when mail arrived and I received perhaps the biggest batch ever: fourteen Air Letters, five ordinary letters, three airgraphs, three V-mail (the US equivalent of the British Air Letter) and four postcards. I learned that David Cathro, who had been stationed at East Fortune, Midlothian, on returning from training as observer (navigator)/wireless operator in Canada, had been in Algiers and was now 'somewhere in Italy' although he had previously written that he expected to be sent to Burma. I had been disappointed at not being able to meet David in Canada, now it seemed that we may have been in Algiers at the same time. I learned too that Robert South was in France and that Eric had passed his Junior Secondary Certificate exams and had begun his working life in the office of Thomas Bonar & Co. Ltd. Eric was still attending his vegetable plot in Victoria Park and now had his first pair of long trousers.

Before being shipped to France, Robert was stationed at Yeovil, in Somerset. He had written to my parents from there and on 25 August I received news from them that he had been wounded. He had been in the Army only about six months and I philosophised on the fortunes of war as US troops who had been in Oran for nearly two years had seen no action and some complained about the quality of the ice-cream. British servicemen who were wounded in action received no special decoration, but US servicemen were awarded the Purple Heart. I do not think that Robert was hurt very seriously as he soon made a full recovery.

A letter from my pal John Noble described his cycling holiday in the Highlands. John kept me up to date with news of the Eastern Report Centre of the ARP and the Office, which was something of a transit camp for teenagers in that they entered on leaving school and left when called up – the boys at eighteen and the girls at nineteen. John himself had failed his medical for the Services as he had rheumatic fever when small.

When the ship was silent as we read our mail, two men must have felt the sadness of isolation as they received no letters. I learned this from an AB from London, who was one of these men and obviously depressed as the lack of a letter suggested that nobody cared if he lived or died. We could now write only ordinary letters home as, towards the end of July, the Ministry of War Transport Office had informed us that Air Letter forms would no longer be issued to us.

The US Empire Club was my Mecca and there was a large hall in the building where, for 5 francs, ice cream was dispensed in cans, about 3½ inches high and 3 inches in diameter, which may have originally contained evaporated milk. The hall was generally full of US Servicemen standing and eating the ice cream at long continuous rows of what I can only describe as high 'desks'. One day, when I arrived at the head of the queue, the girl doing the dispensing filled only half my can, saying that there was no charge as that was the last of the ice cream. But I had no sooner found a space at a 'desk' when the US soldier, who had been behind me in the queue, was at my side shouting that 'no Limey was going to have his ice cream'. Although I pushed the can towards him and told him to have it, he continued to rant while all in the hall looked on silently until his wrath dissipated. Incidentally, we now had our hair cut by former Italian POWs at the barbers shop in the Empire where the charge of 5 francs was half that of the French barbers and no tipping allowed.

There was a Spanish quarter in Oran and one of the girls who served in the hall at the Empire Club was Anna Casteliago, a slim dark girl with a pretty face and likely to have been of Spanish extraction. I don't know how I came to know her name and, although I found her attractive, I never spoke to her other than ask for an ice cream. But there must have been mutual interest as, one day when I was on the officers' section of the beach, she arrived with some of her work mates and, when the latter spotted me before she did, I knew by their looks and gestures that they were saying to her, 'I told you he was an officer!'

I have no recollection of how I met Sgt John S. Gill of the US Army, who appeared to be in his late thirties and was part of the medical team on a Victory Ship. We went into town and to the beach together and, as his ship returned to Oran during our stay, we joined up for a second time. Because he introduced himself as Gill, I wasn't aware that this was his surname until he gave me his full name and address in Philadelphia when we finally parted.

Charlie and I often went to the cinema of the Empire Club where we would watch the film while we each consumed a kilo of black grapes from the old newspaper in which they were wrapped. I particularly remember seeing Bing Crosby in *Going My Way* when he played the part of a priest and sang, not only the title song, but a song which extolled the virtues of education by stating that we had the choice of either 'swinging on a star', if we studied, or being like a donkey, fish or pig if we did not. Almost all the films were in black and white although there was the occasional one in Technicolor. Generally, the show consisted of one film and nothing else, but, occasionally, there would be the bonus of a short film in 'The March of Time' series and, on the very rare occasion, a cartoon. When films were shown on the deck of a US Army Hospital Ship lying alongside the *Samite*, many of our crew watched from our deck although we were at liberty to go on board the US ship. I could not be bothered with this as the sound was barely audible and it may have been on board the hospital ship that I saw the film *Song of Bernadette* when I found the American pronunciation of Bernadette rather incongruous. (Because the terms America and American have been incorrectly commandeered by the citizens of the USA, I try to avoid using them.)

One evening, I was mounting the ship's gangway from a crowded Liberty Boat when, as the boat drew away, a US sailor claimed in a loud voice to his companions, 'I bet I can tell you what that fellow is. He's a radio operator.' As I have already said, many of us were easily identified by our spectacles and our youth and, had I been a bit more mature, I would have acknowledged the accuracy of his deduction instead of feeling embarrassed and proceeding without turning my head.

Before the grape harvest, apricots, cherries and plums had been available and melons, at 12 francs a kilo, were plentiful by the end of July. Black grapes were 5 francs and green grapes 20 francs a kilo. Oranges, too, became plentiful and I often returned to the ship with my pockets stuffed full of mandarin oranges. Water must have been a problem for the farmers and fruit growers as it was the very end of August before rain showers brought an end to a drought of four months.

The weather was hot, but it was at night that I found the heat oppressive as, even towards midnight, the air blew so hot from the desert that I slept only in my underpants without even a sheet over me. I always remade my bed after the steward had made it as it was their custom to fold the top sheet and blankets in without tucking them under the mattress which I preferred. I found, too, that if the ship were rolling at sea, this held you in better and so less likely to fall out. Every week we got a change of one sheet, one pillowcase, a face towel and a bath towel, plus a bar of Colgate's soap. I saved my soap to take home as Charlie supplied me with a jelly type available to the engine room staff.

There was great optimism now regarding the war. The Allies were doing well on all fronts and nobody had any doubts about the outcome. But *The Stars and Stripes* expressed reality with its caption 'It's all over bar the fighting.' I wrote home that we hoped to be home soon and, at any rate, I had to be home by 6 January 1945 as we had signed eighteen-month articles. (This was incorrect; we had signed on for two years.) But we were already looking ahead to peacetime and it was rumoured that men of twenty would be required to undergo one year's National Service 'after the war'.

We were given the opportunity of sending cables home. These were of the EFM type where you couldn't say what you really wanted to, but had to choose numbers on the back and which were translated into phrases. There were 189 numbers/phrases under fourteen headings such as Correspondence, Greetings, Money and Congratulations. I chose numbers thirty-three and eighty-seven for my Cable and Wireless 'Via Imperial' cable to my parents, dated 4 August. They received this on the 6 August as 'AM WELL AND FIT ALL MY LOVE' and without an 'office of origin' on the form. We were allowed a maximum of three numbers for the price of 2/6d (12½p), but I chose only two as nothing else seemed appropriate. Some of the crew came to me to send similar messages for them.

The only souvenirs available were leather goods and I was always on the lookout for a handbag which I could afford. Eventually, I bought two. On the road from the docks I was accosted by an Arab peddler who had only rings and wallets and, when I told him it was a handbag I was after, he called a mate over and I was offered the only handbag he had for sale. I examined it and asked the price, whereupon bargaining took its usual course. I was told that a bag of such quality would cost 1,200 francs (£6) in the shops, but that, because I was his 'verry goot friend', he would let me have it for 700 francs (£3.50p). I laughed and offered 300 francs (£1.50p), which he immediately accepted so that I was left with the feeling that I had been done! I did not, however, see a similar handbag in the shops for less than 450 francs (£2.25p).

As I still had 600 francs (£3) in my pocket when I proceeded into town, I thought I might be able to buy another and better handbag, but when I saw one which I liked in a shop window, it was priced at 750 francs (£3.75p). I entered the shop and asked the French shopkeeper if I could see his handbags and that I was willing to pay up to 600 francs for one whereupon he brought out a box of them, each priced at 750 francs, and asked if I could pay a little more. When he saw he could not get any more than 600 francs out of me, he offered me one of the bags for 600, but, as I hung back from buying it, he said I could have any bag in the box for 600. I was still undecided and left the shop to have at look in a nearby shop where I was offered a bag, similar to the one I liked, for 600 francs, but which was not so well finished inside. I returned to the first shop, where two French ladies were looking in the window, when the shopkeeper spotted me and brought the bag out. I asked the ladies for their opinion and, as they gave their approval, I bought the bag. It had been a hard sell for the shopkeeper who was understandably annoyed with me as I am sure he gave me a bargain.

Although the old Spanish fort, known as the Belvédère, stands high on a hill to the west of Oran, the Abbey of Santa-Cruz, surmounted by its statue of the Virgin Mary, and standing on a lower spur of the hill, is nearer the town and more dominant. It was a natural challenge to me and, directly after lunch on Monday 11 September, I set off on my own to make the climb. To reach the hill, I had to walk through the Arab quarter where every building had painted on it, 'This building is off limits to American and British Forces and Merchant Marine' The area was almost deserted but, suddenly, from across the road, I was hailed by the Arab boatman who usually rowed me ashore from the ship and who had been walking in the opposite direction. He crossed to speak to me and, when I asked him if I were on the right road to the Abbey, he insisted upon acting as my guide. A man in perhaps his late thirties, he sported a moustache and always wore a topi, denim jacket, denim trousers and sandshoes. We communicated by means of his broken English, and, during our journey to and from the Abbey, he told me that, when twelve years old, he had gone to sea on a French ship and had visited Dundee and Glasgow. He also told me that, in addition to his native Arabic, he spoke French and Spanish, but could not read or write in any language as he had never gone to school.

Towards the foot of the hill, we passed Arab hovels similar to those I had seen in Beni Saf and, about half way up, came upon Arab women and children gathering firewood near where French troops were building something within a small enclosure. On reaching the old deserted Abbey, which had been built during the sixteenth or seventeenth centuries when the Spaniards had occupied the Maghreb (the region of north-west Africa between the Sahara and the Mediterranean) we found it locked so that we could not enter, but it was a small building and we could see the whole of the interior through the spaces in the iron door which had an inscription in Spanish on it. From the Abbey, we had a superb view of the town and port although, at times, the view was obscured by mist drifting below us. I have extremely poor photographs taken at the Abbey on the cheap camera I had bought in Washington DC and which I had permission to take ashore. There is a number of old Turkish forts around Oran and, on the way down the hill, we passed one which had the date 1753 on its wall.

I did not insult the boatman by offering him a tip when I left him to go to the Empire to see Gloria Jean in the film *Pardon My Rhythm* and then attend the Spanish class, but gave him a couple of packets of cigarettes when he next rowed me ashore.

Notices were displayed at the Empire Club advertising a tour on Sunday 24 September. I put my name down for it and it proved so popular that two trucks were needed to convey the 'tourists', who were all US servicemen except for two or three South Africans and me. Our first stop was Fort Belvédère, above and somewhat to the south-west of the Abbey of Santa-Cruz and accessed by a road cut out of the hillside. The beginning of the road was tarmaced, but it soon became an earthen track where the wheels of the trucks ran too close to the edge for the peace of mind of the passengers. Arriving at a particularly sharp bend, the drivers had to reverse to negotiate it. Almost all the passengers in my truck were already standing up ready to jump off, which they hastily did as the truck reversed to within a foot or two of the sheer drop. But, being British, I was one of the few who stoically remained seated and derived some childish satisfaction when the danger was over and the others climbed back on board. Our visit to the old deserted fort, 1,125 feet above sea level, included an inspection of its dungeons. On the hill opposite, we saw the white dome of a tomb which, the guide explained, was reputed to be that of the son of an Arab king. Below us was the Abbey and although we passed close to it on our descent, we did not visit it. Passing through the squalid Arab quarter on our way back to town, we saw men sitting at tables outside cafés and cobblers working, but most were occupied in peeling the skins off cactus fruit.

The tour concluded with a visit to the mosque which, although a lovely building, was not as elaborate as the one I had visited in Algiers. We had, of course, to remove our shoes before entering and, on leaving, had to donate 5 francs to the man who washed the feet of the faithful before they entered. On our return to the Club, my offer of a gratuity was adamantly refused by the guide. He explained that he was a Belgian refugee and said, 'we are all in this (the war) together.' In a letter written on 26 September, I said 'I went on a tour of Oran' and, as this was not deleted by the censor, it allowed my parents to know exactly where I was.

The *Samite* entered dry dock in August and emerged in September with an ungainly, strengthening metal strap running fore and aft on the outside of her starboard hull at No. 2 hold. On 27 September, we went out on trials and, on 1 October, sailed for Casablanca in Convoy GUS 53.

CHAPTER 20

HOMEWARD BOUND

We arrived in Casablanca on the evening of 3 October but instead of anchoring in the harbour, as we had expected, went directly alongside to commence loading a full cargo of phosphates. A gang of Arab dockers had the dirty and unhealthy job of working down the holds spreading the dusty cargo which would, otherwise, have remained heaped in the centre of each hold. As always, the mates had to supervise the loading which went on throughout the night and until loading was complete. They had also to see to the adjustment of the mooring ropes as our berth was subject to the rise and fall of the Atlantic tides, a task they had been spared when we were alongside in the, almost tideless, Mediterranean.

An RN DEMS gunner and I went ashore together the day after our arrival and were walking into town when an Arab approached with a gent's shining ring for which he wanted several hundred francs. As he gave me only a momentary glimpse of the ring, his manner was so furtive that I immediately thought that it had been stolen. But my companion had seen the trick before and pronounced that it was made only of brass. The Arab was annoyed at being found out, but accepted the 30 francs (15p) I offered him and I still have the ring as a souvenir.

There was much more in the shops than in those of Algiers and Oran. Leather goods were half the price so that I regretted the purchase of the handbags over which I had agonised. There were window displays of clothes not seen in the Algerian ports, although coupons were still required to purchase them. I bought a purse and a wallet before we sat down to a tea of ham and two eggs in the British Union Jack Club. These were the first real eggs we had tasted for a long time as the ship's prolonged stay in North African ports had again reduced us to powered eggs and dehydrated potatoes.

Casablanca was also under US control and, after tea, we discovered the huge US Red Cross Club called the VOX. It contained even more than the

ARC Club in Oran and, in its shop, I bought what I thought was a lovely lady's broad leather belt with a sewn design, but which nobody ever wore. We ended the day at the VOX cinema, sitting in leather-bound easy chairs at the front of the balcony watching a film about Washington DC which I had seen years before. A stage show followed the film, but, as it was poor, we were not reluctant to leave halfway through in order to be back inside the dock gates by 10.30 p.m. It was a pleasant day, and the one and only time when I sat in a leather-bound easy chair in a cinema with a decorated belt round my waist and a brass ring over the tip of my little finger as it was too small to go on. The Yanks sure knew how to look after their Forces.

When walking into town on my own, I was accosted by a mob of Arab youngsters and was surrounded by them when I heard my name called. I looked up to find Captain Eccles leaning out of a taxi. 'Are you all right?' he asked. He drove on when I replied in the affirmative, but his intervention relieved the pressure and I was able to proceed without further hindrance.

On 5 October, my cabin was given to a Master and Mate returning to the UK as DBS (Distressed British Seamen whose ships had usually been lost) who signed on as supernumeraries paid 1s a month, as we had no passenger certificate. I moved in with Caro on the bridge deck, where the drawer space was too limited to accommodate all the extra gear I had acquired and a filled suitcase was relegated to the CO_2 room.

Our cabin was on the port side between Mr Moore's cabin and the Captain's shower room, on the other side of which was the wireless room. It was somewhat larger than the one I vacated, had a small desk and was better located in that it was away from the heat of the galley. Captain Eccles' accommodation was on the starboard side of the deck while, also on the starboard side, directly opposite the wireless room, was the chart room.

Charlie hoped to come ashore with me on our last night in port, but Mr Turnbull said he had to stay to blow out the port boiler so that I went by myself to spend my remaining 150 Moroccan francs. Returning to the docks that night, I was very glad to meet up with some US sailors to have their company into the docks.

The day before we sailed from Casablanca, I received an unexpected letter from Mrs Blow of Crouches Farm, near Sandown, on the Isle of Wight, whose daughter, Peggy, was engaged to Phil Ayres who had left the ship in Baltimore. Mrs Blow had sent on a letter which I had addressed to Phil at the farm and gave me his new address on the *Samlossie*, c/o P. Henderson & Co., 95 Bothwell Street, Glasgow (or GPO London). But her reason for writing to me, on 2 June 1944, was to get some news of Phil as Peggy had received only eight letters in eleven months and Phil's last literary effort of 21 March had contained little more information than his new address. I told Mrs Blow what I knew and corresponded with her for a year or so after that. In that first letter, she said, 'We are getting enough worry here without him, as last week we had an alarming experience and lost some of our cattle'. A subsequent Air Letter from her, in which she expressed her concern for the poor souls farther along the coast (the London area) who were being subjected to V-bomb (flying bomb) attacks, was the most censored letter I received as the back page barely hung together after the censor had cut great holes in it. Then, in a letter written on 10 September, she said that the flying bomb raids had stopped and that Phil's cousin, Leslie, who had joined up the same day as Phil, had, at nineteen and a half, been killed in Italy on 26 June. She also said that it had been a beautiful day and that they had all been to church that morning.

Together with a friend, I visited the Isle of Wight in October 1989 and we drove to Crouches Farm in the hope that I might meet Phil again after all those years. I asked the lady selling vegetables in the small hut/shop beside the farmhouse if Mrs Blow still lived here. 'Yes,' she said, 'I'll get her for you.' But the lady who emerged from the farmhouse was the daughter-in-law of the Mrs Blow who had written to me and who had died in January 1965. Her husband, however, was still alive and living at the farm, but not at home when we called. When I asked the incumbent Mrs Blow if Peggy had married Phil, I was told that she had not. 'But,' she said, 'I'll give Peggy a ring and you can have a word with her.' Although all Mrs Blow's correspondence with me was due to her concern for her daughter, Peggy had no recollection of me and said she had an appointment with the hairdresser. Phil, she said, was living 'over Andover way' and expressed her view that New York had been his downfall.

We sailed from Casablanca on Sunday 8 October 1944 to join Convoy SL (Sierra Leone) 172, bound for the UK and which was to rendezvous with MKS 63 from the Mediterranean. The Commodore of the Mediterranean section, on board the *Pegu*, became Commodore of the combined convoy, while the Commodore of the Sierra Leone Section, on the *Silverlarch*, became Vice-Commodore. The combined convoys totalled twenty-four ships after the *African Prince* joined from Lisbon.

During the passage through the Bay of Biscay, I stood leaning on the port side forward rail of the boat deck when the DBS Master joined me and tried to engage me in conversation. But, because he was a Captain in his fifties and I was only nineteen with limited experience, I was unable to respond as I should have done and never learned why he was travelling DBS.

As the convoy proceeded northwards, the weather deteriorated and became so bad that one evening, when the ship came down on a wave with a tremendous thud, Ted Moore thought we had been torpedoed and dived into his room for his life jacket. Liberty Ships rolled frighteningly in bad weather. They rolled slowly to port before drawing up at an angle of about 40°. Then, at an accelerating and alarming speed, they swung over to starboard.

We were approaching the English Channel, and on the port wing of the convoy, when one of the escorting corvettes came up on our port side and ran parallel with us. The sun was shining, but the wind was strong and both ships plunging in heavy seas as the young corvette commander bawled through a megaphone to enquire as to what charts we had. When he received a reply, his response of 'Crikey' greatly amused Captain Eccles.

The convoy rounded the Lizard and anchored off Falmouth. We could see the town and it was pleasant to see green countryside, but we did not stay long before continuing up the Channel. If anything, the weather was even worse and we lost a lifeboat, together with its davits, over the side before anchoring off Cowes on the Isle of Wight on Sunday, 15 October. I wrote a letter in the hope that a pilot might take it ashore, but there was no pilot and the letter was never posted. We remained for an hour or two before carrying on towards London.

I wanted to go home with everything clean. I had done my dhobying when crossing the Bay of Biscay and now began the difficult job of packing. My now two suitcases, one of which I lined with bars of soap, could not hold all the additional gear and presents, but I was fortunate in being able to procure a large cardboard carton. This was when I first heard of, and was accused of having, 'the Channels', the feeling of elation which sailors, and especially 'first trippers', experience when nearing the end of a voyage.

We docked somewhere in the Royal Group of Docks on Monday 16 October 1944. The final telegraph signal 'Finished with engines' was rung by the bridge to the engine room and voyage one of the *Samite* was over.

CHAPTER 21

HOME

Our arrival coincided with such a pea-souper of a fog, compounded of course by the blackout, that Charlie and I had literally to grope our way out of the docks that evening to send telegrams home. This was done from a phone box and I wired that I would probably be travelling on the night train to arrive in Dundee early in the morning on Thursday 19th. We then found our way into a pub, the first I was ever in, where the landlady smiled indulgently when I asked for a cup of tea. The place was a haven of light and comfort on that dark and dismal night when foghorns moaned on the River.

The Customs men didn't come on board until the Wednesday and we were given a thorough going over. An objectionable searcher ransacked the cabin. He made me turn out everything and pulled drawers right out in order to search the spaces with his torch. Finding that I had 2 oz of tobacco (for my grandfather) over my limit, he gave me a severe dressing down and I have always wished I had told him to go to hell and suffered any consequences. I paid £1 6s 4d duty on the articles I had declared on the manifest. The pink customs' receipt lists: Fourteen Pair Art. [Artificial] Silk Hose Value 30s (13s duty), Two Leather Bags Value £1 (5s duty), Two Art. Silk Articles [one was a blouse] Value 10s (4s/4d duty) and One Pair Shoes [for my father] Value £1 (4s duty). I had an exposed film and this was taken from me to be developed and vetted before it was posted to me.

When my packing was complete, Alf Taylor came up to my cabin with onions to replace those I had given to him ten months previously for ship's use. I told him to keep them as there was no space left in my luggage and did not fancy travelling with a string of onions round my neck! And as I still had that extra 2 oz of tobacco, I gave it to Alf.

I left the *Samite* that same day and, as I didn't want to crush my Stetson, had it in my hand when I went to say goodbye to Mr Thomas. I found him in his cabin with Mr Turnbull and when Mr Turnbull saw the hat, he asked if it was felt. On learning that it was, he took it, punched it out and rolled it up explaining that this would not harm a felt hat. This was a relief to me as I was then able to put it in the pocket of my raincoat. In saying goodbye, Mr Thomas, quite unnecessarily, thanked me for my services so that I stupidly mumbled 'that's all right'. I was fortunate in sailing with such pleasant senior officers.

The taxi driver, conveying me to Kings Cross Station, told me to give him my customs' receipt together with half-a-crown (2/6d or 12½p) for the policeman on the dock gate who would otherwise ransack my luggage to check if I had any dutiable items in addition to those listed on the receipt. When we stopped at the gate, the policeman walked slowly from his hut to the taxi and took the folded receipt, with the half crown inside, proffered by the driver. He then, just as slowly, returned to his hut before re-emerging to hand back the receipt, minus its contents, and telling the driver to proceed. Done in an imperious manner, this was the standard practice of Port of London Authority Police. But taxi drivers were just as much on the fiddle as the Dock Police and I was charged the hefty sum of thirty bob (£1.50) for the journey to Kings Cross. As the Royal Group of Docks was outside the Metropolitan area, the journey was not metered and they charged as much as they could get away with.

I arrived at Kings Cross about an hour before the train was due to leave and gave my heavy luggage into the care of a porter before entering the station café for something to eat. Thinking that I had ample time, I remained there until about fifteen minutes of departure, but, when I went out, the train was not only at the platform, but absolutely packed. I could have kicked myself for my stupidity when I had arrived so early. It was a Pullman-type train and, as I crushed my way through a crowd of servicemen and women standing in the door area, I heard an ATS girl saying, 'I don't know where he thinks he's going.' But about two tables from the door, an RAF greatcoat lay on a seat and when I asked if this were anyone's seat, the coat was lifted and I had a seat!

The long overnight journey into Scotland was tedious, with the geography of the route unknown to most of us. When the train was coming into a station, you would hear someone ask, 'Where's this?' and passengers with window seats would wipe the steamed-up windows to see the name of the station. Even in the middle of the night, there were always people with tea trolleys on the platforms and it was a relief to get out to have a cup of tea and stretch your legs. York, in particular, was a very busy station where there was always another crowd of people waiting to board an already overcrowded train.

I conversed with the RAF man beside me, and it was just as well that he knew that I was going to Dundee as I was asleep on my arms on the table when he shook me saying, 'Isn't this where you get off?' The train was standing in Taybridge Station and I had to rouse myself and dash to the guard's van to collect my luggage before it left for Aberdeen.

Although I had wired home from London that I would probably be home that morning, I had no thought of anyone meeting me as the train arrived about 6 a.m. and my arrival was doubtful anyway. I got a porter to assist with my luggage and we went up in a goods lift to the taxi rank. But when I got to the top of the outside stair of my tenement home, Eric and my mother were entering the house. They had been to meet me and had waited until all the passengers had left by the main door.

Sitting at dinner (the midday meal) that day, I said, 'I suppose you know we were bombed and torpedoed?' There was a startled silence. Fergus had kept his word and Holts had not informed them.

The following day, I was with my mother in our kitchen/living room/master-bedroom, when I turned on the wireless. The valve set took a few seconds to heat up and the first words which we heard of the song 'Long Ago And Far Away – 'you're here at last' – were so appropriate. Incidentally, although I had been so proud to come home with everything clean, my mother washed everything again as she said 'they could dae wi' a guid boil!'

I had left an allotment of £5 per month to my mother. This amounted to a total of £75 and, although she had banked this for me, I told her to keep it to pay for my Wireless College fees and kitting me out. In addition to that, I had paid off with £100, a not inconsiderable sum in those days.

My father confessed to me that he had not told my mother how we had parted at the dock gate on that July morning in Greenock when I had said that I would likely be able to come out to see him again after I had reported in. It had been on his mind all these months that we had not said a proper 'goodbye'.

I signed off the *Samite*, at the Mercantile Marine Office in Dundee on 23 October, but my pink C. R. S. 3. Form, headed 'Merchant Navy Personnel', gives the date of discharge as 17 October 1944. The date of engagement was 6 July 1943.

CHAPTER 22

RECALLED TO DUTY

I had arrived home on Thursday 19 October, and by the middle of November was anticipating the arrival of a telegram. On entering the house late on the evening of 29 November, my parents' eyes directed me to the small orange envelope, with the word PRIORITY writ large across it, on the mantelpiece. The Reply Paid telegram from ODYSSEY (Holts telegraphic address) required me to report for duty at their Liverpool Office at 9 a.m. on the morning of Saturday 2 December and my one and only wartime leave was over. My father once again took it upon himself to do my packing. I now had a sea chest and a second-hand, wind-up portable gramophone, which they had managed to get for me, and records were carefully packed between clothes. I left from the West Station on the evening of Friday 1 December for the overnight train journey to Liverpool with changes at Perth and Preston. My father accompanied me to Perth and left me in the company of a gentleman whom we met on the station platform. This time, we did say a proper 'goodbye'!

The gentleman was Mr Mitchell from Carnoustie and, as he was travelling to Liverpool to board a ship for Bombay where he was Marine Superintendent Engineer with Burma Oil, we made the journey together. Mr Mitchell had worked out East for twenty-five years and, until the outbreak of war, his wife and daughter had been with him. As his last tour of duty had lasted seven years, he had been home on leave for nine months and expected to be away again for another three years. We were lucky enough to have a seat all the way to Preston, but had to stand in the corridor from Preston to Liverpool before breakfasting on haddock, toast and coffee, at the Officers' Club in Lime Street Station. As we parted company, Mr Mitchell said to look him up if I were ever in Bombay.

Holts had now vacated their temporary premises in Ullet Road and returned to their restored offices in India Buildings in Water Street, in the heart of the city. I expected to be sent immediately to a ship, but the still unsmiling Calverley said that I was to stay in India Buildings over the weekend in case any important messages had to be collected. I do not remember exactly what I was supposed to do, but there was a retired Chief Steward on duty as a telephone operator every night and I was to have the company of another 3rd R/O.

The weekend, however, turned out to be quite enjoyable as the other Sparks and I got on well. He was Colin Rigley from Leeds and we yarned into the night from our camp beds somewhere high up in the large, deserted building. He had been on the *Troilus* when she had been torpedoed and sunk in the Indian Ocean three months previously and expressed surprise that I had never been through the Suez Canal. Unfortunately, as one of us had always to be in the building, we could not go into town together. I went dancing at the Rialto on Saturday evening and he went to the pictures (cinema) on Sunday afternoon. But we were free for most of Monday and spent the day in town together. I bought a copy of the *Handbook of Technical Instruction for Wireless Telegraphists* by Dowsett and Walker and a book on Spanish Grammar while Colin bought books on wireless. After lunch, we went to a news cinema before reporting back to Calverley in the late afternoon. And standing at the desk was Neville Caro.

I could have groaned out loud when Calverley said, 'You know Mr Caro. You'll be sailing together again, on the *Samforth*.' Having been given railway vouchers, we were told to travel overnight to Avonmouth. Colin was to join a ship in London and was to board the London portion of the same train.

All my gear was in the building and Colin gave me a hand with it to the taxi which was to take us to the station. But it turned out that he gave me too much of a hand as he brought out an attaché case which he thought was mine and I thought was his and the mistake was not realised until we got to the left-luggage office in Lime Street Station. When I phoned the office and managed to speak to the owner of the case, he said he had already missed it, but that, as he was coming into town anyway, he would collect it from the left-luggage office.

Our train left at midnight so that we had time on our hands and I again went dancing at the Rialto while Colin went to a cinema. At 11 p.m., we rendezvoused in the station, where we were joined by Caro. The three of us then had coffee and sandwiches in the Officers' Club before Colin left us and Caro and I boarded the Bristol section of the train together.

As usual, the train was packed, but we got a seat in a crowded, stuffy, but friendly compartment so that conversation went on into the night under the dimmed lights. After an hour's wait, we caught the train to Avonmouth and arrived about 9.30 a.m. In the afternoon, we signed on the *Samforth*. The date was Tuesday 5 December 1944.

I received a blow when signing the Articles in that my pay had been reduced. I had been paid £12 10s a month (plus £10 a month War Risk Money) on the *Samite*; now it was to be £10 a month. The Chief Sparks tried to convince me that this was correct, but when the Chief Sparks who was leaving the ship heard about it, he said he would inform the Liverpool Office when he got there the next day.

Neville Caro, on the other hand, who had the same qualification that I had, had his pay increased from £14 10s to £16 a month. He, without any more responsibility, received £6 more a month than I did. And he had the more congenial eight to twelve watch with the privilege of wearing two gold wavy bands on his uniform to my one! He was even less useful than I was as he could not type when I could. Additionally, of course, he was not my favourite person!

The *Samforth* carried more officers than there had been on the *Samite* as she had a 5th Engineer and two Midshipmen. This meant that Caro and I had once again to share a cabin. This time it was the cabin on the bridge deck next door to the Chief Sparks, in the same position as the one we had occupied on the *Samite's* home run from Casablanca. It was a pleasant cabin with a desk and I found that I had plenty of drawer and wardrobe space to stow my gear. Still the junior, I, again, had the top bunk.

Wednesday evening was our last opportunity to go ashore and I went up to Bristol with Michael Shaw, one of the middies. In the blackout, we asked a young, helmeted policeman where we could find a dance hall. He told us that all the dance halls were closed that evening, but that there was a dance in the nearby hall of the Shepherds Friendly Society. We were, apparently, approaching an open, circular, area and the policeman impressed me by the precise way he directed us to the hall which was 'You go in [the circular area] at six o'clock and out at two.' We found the hall but, even before entering, knew that the place was 'dead' by the sound of the band reverberating in the somewhat empty space. But we still reckoned it was better than staying on board ship. I had written a letter earlier in the day to send home with my completed allotment form, leaving £10 a month for my mother to put into War Savings for me. But I forgot to take it ashore and was grateful that a Marconi chap posted it for me the next day.

I stood at the rail of the boat deck as we moved away from the quay the following morning. It was miserable and overcast, best described by the Scots word 'dreich', when only a solitary woman sweeper leaned momentarily on her brush to watch our quiet departure – all very different from the musically accompanied departure of ships on wartime films.

We dropped anchor in Milford Haven Bay, in Pembroke, where the Bristol Channel Section of Convoy ON 271 gathered and I wrote my last letter home in the early hours of Saturday morning, having spent the evening in the middies' cabin arguing about Home Rule for India! In the company of the other vessels in our section, we sailed to rendezvous with the main section of the convoy which left the Mersey on Saturday 9 December. Like almost all the ships, we had no cargo so that we were sailing in sand ballast and knew only that we were heading for somewhere on the other side of the Atlantic. We hoped and expected to be in port for Christmas. ON 271 comprised seventy ships, including the *Samite*, and in the escort were the corvettes *Dianella*, *Lotus* and *Poppy* which were escorting UGS 18 when it was attacked off Cape Ténèz.

CHAPTER 23

NEW SHIPMATES

The Master of the *Samforth* was Captain E. A. H. Gepp, a pleasant, stocky built man of only about thirty-six years of age who had his Extra-Masters Certificate. Gepp gave the lie to the saying 'loneliness of command' as he mixed with the ship's officers which, without any loss of discipline, resulted in the *Samforth* being a very happy ship.

The 1st Mate was Mr Guppy, who was a year older than Gepp. He was a tall, slim, auburn-haired man who, I heard, had invented a type of light used on ships in convoy and he too had his Extra-Masters.

I remember the 2nd Mate only vaguely, but he was a well-built man of about thirty whose name may have been Robinson.

Due to the number of Welshmen employed by Holts, the company was apparently referred to as the Welsh Navy although, quite frankly, I never heard the title used during my eight years with the Company. E. H. (Hewell) Davies, the 3rd Mate, was a Welshman from New Quay in Cardiganshire (now Dyfed) who had just completed his apprenticeship and was only eighteen. The stocky son of a tanker captain, he followed his father's example of always blowing out a match and returned it to the box after lighting a cigarette. Hewell, who called himself Hugh, but whom I shall refer to as Huw to give it a Welsh flavour, taught me to sing 'Pwy brynnir benwaig Nefyn...', sung to the tune of the Scots song 'Caller Herrin' and I can still sing it. He died in the 1960s, when he was 1st Mate nearing promotion to Master.

The 1st Radio Officer/Purser was Amos J. W. Parkin, a Scotsman who had a 1st Class PMG Certificate which he had obtained at Leith Nautical College when he was about sixteen. I do not recall seeing him in anything other than a rather untidy battledress which he even wore ashore. He had sailed on Norwegian ships, spoke Norwegian and, during the voyage, made a camera which worked although it had no lens. I addressed him as

Mr Parkin and he addressed me as Mr Malcolm although, when I became No. 1, no junior ever called me Mr, nor did I want them to. Parkin and Caro got on famously and I was an outsider. Yet, although I did not care for Parkin, he was not unpleasant. I was to discover, however, that he had one unforgivable fault. He could never get out of his bunk on time to take over his four to eight morning watch.

Our two midshipmen/apprentice deck officers occupied the farthest aft port side cabin on the boat deck which was the cabin opposite the one over the galley, which I had occupied on the *Samite*. John (known as Ian) Smart, the senior, was seventeen and from Eaglesham in Refrewshire. He was the first person I saw wearing a Second World War campaign medal ribbon and he informed me that it was the 1939-43 Star, which was awarded for six months service overseas. Ian believed he had been accepted by Holts because he had good marks in nautical studies at the technical college he had attended. Although he had gone to sea a week before I did, he had seen no sign of the enemy.

Michael Shaw was very different from Ian and became a pal of mine. Michael was upper class and had undergone pre-sea training at Pangbourne College from where, he said, he could have gone into the RNVR as a midshipman if he had chosen. I formed the impression that Michael had come to sea to travel the world in order to learn the various dances, e.g. jitterbugging in the States and the rhumba in South America! When we argued about Home Rule for India, he and I were for Indian independence while Ian was for keeping India as a colony within the Empire. Michael's parents were friends of Megan Lloyd George, the daughter of the Liberal Prime Minister, and Ian had been a guest in their home. When Michael's back was turned, he whispered to me, 'His girlfriend wears woollen stockings!' There was one thing about the sea, no-one needed to know whether you came from a but-and-ben or a mansion, you were judged for what you were as a person and, during that Atlantic crossing, Ian, Michael, Huw and I spent almost every evening in the middies' cabin arguing about some subject or other.

I cannot recall the name of the Chief Engineer, although it may have been Kneile. He was in his fifties, wore medal ribbons of the First World War and was the oldest officer, and perhaps the oldest man, on board. I have no recollection, at all, of the Second Engineer.

The 3rd Engineer was Eric Cameron, from Inverness, who also became a buddy of mine. Eric was a reticent man in his early thirties, with a rather hangdog expression which hid a pawky sense of humour. There was a framed photograph on the desk in his cabin of the lovely Australian girl to whom he was engaged. Eric had been a pianist in both a dance band and an orchestra in Inverness and had met the actress Anna Neagle, for whom he had a great admiration. (Anna Neagle's real name was Marjorie Robertson and her father was a Master with the New Zealand Shipping Company.) Eric's brother, Ian, also a marine engineer, was a survivor of the *Empress of Britain* when she was sunk off the north-west coast of Ireland in October 1940.

The 4th Engineer was Bill Dawson, a tall, heavily jowled man in his late twenties who spoiled his appearance in uniform by wearing a small-brimmed cap which looked as if it should have belonged to an RN petty officer. Bill, too, became a friend. The 5th Engineer was S. Thompson, a young slim man with sleek blond hair.

The Chief Cook was a stocky man in his fifties, who, every evening, as we left the saloon after dinner, stood at the door in his chef's hat and apron seeking the approbation of Captain Gepp for his endeavours. 'Everything all right, sir?' he would ask and Gepp, who no doubt got a bit fed up with being confronted by the sycophant, signified his approval. The food was good on the *Samforth*. The day after joining the ship, I breakfasted on cornflakes, bacon, egg (real and not the powdered variety) and coffee while my lunch consisted of soup, mutton with vegetables, prunes and custard, and coffee.

The DEMS gunners were all members of a Maritime Regiment of the Royal Artillery. The sergeant in charge was a real old regular in his fifties who had at one time, before the war, been stationed in northern China.

This was only the second voyage of the *Samforth*. She had begun her maiden voyage on 22 January 1944 and, similar to the *Samite*, had been built in Baltimore and was not purchased by Holts after the war. But, unlike the *Samite* and many British Liberties, she had not been launched under another name.

CHAPTER 24

WINTER NORTH ATLANTIC

During the dark evening when the convoy was rounding the south coast of the Republic of Ireland, there was the incessant thud of exploding depth charges, signifying that escort ships had made contact with a U-boat. U-boats were active in the area. The US Liberty Ship *Dan Beard* was torpedoed by U-1202 off the coast of North Wales on 10 December and the *Jonas Lee*, also a US Liberty, fell to U-1055 at the entrance to Bristol Channel, on 9 January 1945. The U-boats no longer operated in wolf packs in mid-ocean, but lay in wait for convoys departing from and approaching ports on both side of the Atlantic. By the following morning, all was quiet and we sailed in fine weather. The letters ONS, in the convoy title, stood for Outward North-Bound Slow and we moved westward at about 9 knots.

There were days of sunshine and the sea remained reasonably calm for the best part of a week so that I was able to use my gramophone. Four records had been broken in transit to Avonmouth. One of these was Ravel's 'Bolero' and, most unfortunately, Tchaikovsky's Piano Concerto No. 1, which was my favourite. All records were of the brittle wax type, played at a speed of seventy-eight revolutions per minute, and came in two sizes. I had a number of older, smaller size, records of songs and dance music, but had bought two or three classical records of the larger type when on leave. The His Master's Voice record of Handel's 'Largo' turned out to be everyone's favourite and Massenet's 'Meditation' on the reverse side also became a favourite of mine. Both pieces were played by the Boston Promenade Orchestra. I had bought the records in Larg's Music Shop, where I sat with a young lady shop assistant, in a soundproof cubicle, listening to the records before deciding to buy them.

I had brought books from home with me and, even before leaving Avonmouth, had read *Sea Green Grocer*. During the crossing, I read Negley Farson's *Way of a Transgressor*, Penguin Short Stories and a book of sea yarns called *Six Bells*. My reading was often accompanied by the eating of sweets. Eric had given me some of his ration and, soon after sailing, the Chief Steward allowed us a dozen bars of Rowntree's Assorted Centres and a 1 lb tin of Silmos Lollies. And there was a ship's library consisting of about 300 books. The Chief and 2nd Sparks were the librarians and the library was open from 3.30 to 4 p.m. on Tuesdays, Thursdays and Saturdays with the time extended for anyone on the twelve to four watch. The Seafarers' Education Service, supported by ship owners, provided not only libraries, but opportunities for seamen to study by correspondence courses with its College of the Sea.

The war was going well, but on 16 December, when we were well out into the Atlantic, there came the distressing news that the Germans had broken through US lines in the Ardennes. This was the beginning of what became known as the Battle of the Bulge and caused us great concern. It meant that the end of the war in Europe was not as near as we had hoped.

About halfway across the Atlantic, the weather began to deteriorate to become what was, perhaps, the worst I was to experience during my time at sea. Seas became mountainous with visibility so poor that, even in daylight, it was difficult to see the nearest ships in the convoy. For days on end, we walked holding on to the hand-rails (similar to those found in retirement homes) in the accommodation area and even sitting was difficult as you had to take your weight first on one leg then the other as the ship rolled. Cabin drawers flew out onto the floor and we slept, fitfully, hanging on in our bunks, which were wider than those on British-built vessels. At meal times, the stewards put up the fiddles round the tables and soaked the tablecloths to try to prevent appointments being thrown to the floor. And there was the incessant noise: the cacophony of the wind screaming in the rigging, the banging of things in the ship and, inevitably, the occasional sound of dishes crashing in the galley. But nobody was seasick and we all went about our work as usual. It was bad for everybody, but the deck department bore the brunt of the storm. The mates sheltered in the wheelhouse, rather than stand watch on the bridge, but they, and the lookouts, still had to go out into the driving, bitter, wind and rain: the ship had to keep station in the blacked-out convoy where each ship displayed only meagre lights. I made up my mind that, if we were torpedoed, I would make for one of the life rafts as no lifeboat could be launched in such weather. But, every evening, I joined Huw, Ian and Michael in the latter's cabin where we, mentally, escaped from the heaving, iconoclastic, world in which we lived by discussing girlfriends, previous ships, what we had done on leave, world problems and what we would do when we arrived in port.

Just when I thought that the weather could not possibly get worse, we hit fog as we approached the Grand Banks so that the mournful sound of the ship's whistle, sounding for four to six seconds every two minutes throughout day and night, added to our discomfort. As we neared North America, a visual signal was sent, during the day, to all ships from the Commodore, that orders were to be transmitted by wireless on our listening frequency of 500 kcs. The message was to come during my midnight to 4 a.m. watch and I remember sitting, in the battledress I had bought during my leave, waiting to receive it. Captain Gepp, wearing his greatcoat and with binoculars slung round his neck, leaned against the open entrance to the wireless room as he waited with me. I clearly remember thinking, with some elation, 'Is this really me, on a ship on the heaving waters of the North Atlantic when, not all that long ago, I had been a clerk in a Dundee jute office?' The message was sent clearly at about twenty words a minute, yet a radio officer on a US vessel requested a repeat which was, of course, extremely dangerous as this gave U-boats more time to DF the convoy. The fact that the message was transmitted, in plain language on 500 kcs, is testimony to the severity of the weather. I do not remember its content. It is likely that it ordered the *Samforth* and another seven ships, including the MAC ship (Merchant Aircraft Carrier) *Empire Mackay*, to proceed to Halifax, NS. At any rate, this is what happened. The *Samforth* became Commodore Ship of the Halifax Section with Captain Gepp as Commodore. The main section headed for New York, which had become the principal terminal port of convoys.

B1 Escort Group, which had shepherded us from the UK, handed over to W3 Group at 1800 hours on 21 December and, I presume, became Escort to an east bound convoy. Corvettes, with their crowded living conditions, were notorious for their behaviour in bad weather, but duty on all escort vessels in the North Atlantic was a very uncomfortable life with a great deal of time spent at sea. St John's, Newfoundland, was their western base where crews enjoyed a brief respite.

It is impossible to celebrate Christmas Day when it is work as usual and your home is being thrown about in a shrieking hell. But, in spite of the weather, everyone was cheerful and there was none of the grumbling which there had been on the *Samite* in Oran the previous Christmas. The Christmas dinner was superb and in no way reflected the conditions under which the catering staff worked. Even with my voracious appetite, I could manage only three of the courses, plus the glass of port wine provided by the Company. And to show my appreciation for the splendid meal, I, and no doubt others, stood the cooks and stewards a glass of wine which they so richly deserved. To produce such a meal, under such appalling conditions, deserved a medal.

Approaching Halifax, W5 Group became escort of our section and, late on Christmas Eve, we learned, I do not remember how, that a corvette in the vicinity had been torpedoed. Our thoughts went out to the men on the unknown ship and, because of the atrocious weather, we thought that there would be no survivors. But we were wrong and she was HMCS *Clayoquot*, a minesweeper and not a corvette. Because the news reached us at night, we thought she had been torpedoed in darkness, but it had been earlier in the day. Eight of her men were lost, but the majority rescued by the corvette HMCS *Fennel* after being in the water for barely ten minutes. Had it been much longer, they would not have survived the cold. The *Clayoquot* was escorting Convoy XB (Halifax to Boston) 139 when she was torpedoed by U-806 off Halifax, and HMCS *Fennel* and HMCS *Transcona*, the other corvette with them, narrowly escaped a similar fate by each catching an acoustic torpedo in her CAT gear.

Five or six U-boats were in the area and operating very close to the shore. On 21 December, the *Samtucky* was part of a convoy forming off Halifax when she was struck by a torpedo and, on 4 January 1945, the *Nipiwan Park* suffered a similar experience near the port.

It was still blowing a full gale when we dropped anchor in Halifax Roads at 3 a.m. on Boxing Day so that I did not have to complete my watch and, thankfully, went to bed in the safety of the port.

CHAPTER 25

HALIFAX/BEDFORD BASIN

Although Boxing Day was overcast and the gale continued unabated, there was a happy atmosphere on board the ship, which was enhanced when representatives of the Navy League, who could have remained in their own warm homes on that raw day, came out in a launch with gifts for every member of the crew. Each of us was given forty cigarettes and a ditty bag filled with presents. My bag contained a pair of black socks, a bright red spotted handkerchief, tooth powder, shaving cream, band-aid plasters, a piece of cake, pins and needles, black and white thread, lighter flints, boot polish, a pencil and a Christmas card. There were cards to show who had provided the gifts and we were asked to send 'thank you' notes, which I did. My cigarettes, which I gave away, came from employees of firms in Winnipeg and the ditty bag was from the Canadian Legion in Blenheim, Ontario. The gifts were useful and appreciated, but, more than that, they represented appreciation of the job being done by the Merchant Service and a warm welcome from the people of Canada.

The town of Dartmouth lies directly opposite Halifax, on the southern shore, and we lay at anchor to the seaward (western) side of both towns, nearer the Dartmouth side. It was after dinner the following evening that I sat with Michael in his cabin when there was a sudden commotion on deck. We ran out to investigate and found that our anchors had dragged and that the ship was ashore by the stern. Looking over the stern we could see that we were high and dry on the stony beach. It was already dark and we were at no great distance from Halifax's signal tower, but, as no amount of lamp signalling could rouse a response, we had to use our transmitter to contact Halifax radio station to alert the authorities as to our predicament.

At high tide the following morning, a tug came to pull us off, but failed in the attempt so that we remained on the beach. The tug returned when the tide was again high and this time was successful. But to make sure that there was no repeat performance, we were taken through the narrows between Halifax and Dartmouth to join a number of ships at anchor in Bedford Basin, which was well known to wartime merchant seamen as a convoy gathering point. At some distance from Halifax, it was desolate and remote and we had been dumped there out of the way. A railway track ran close to the shore, and trains rounding the Basin signalled the 'woo woo' peculiar to the trains of North America. During the night, the 'woo woo' took on an eerie connotation which added to the feeling of desolation.

Although we had arrived in port during the early hours of Boxing Day, we had still not had an opportunity to go ashore by the time the New Year arrived. Bedford Basin may have been desolate and remote, but the Merchant Navy certainly woke it up at the stroke of midnight. Every ship sounded its siren, flares were sent skywards, illuminating all the ships and on every ship there was someone at a Morse lamp wishing everybody a Happy New Year. The 2nd Mate was on the ship's whistle and the middies and I were on the Morse lamps, and one of the middies sounded the traditional sixteen bells: eight for the Old Year and eight for the New. There was plenty of booze on board and drinking had commenced early in the evening, although I do not recall anyone being drunk. The middies had nothing to drink and, in any case, could not have obtained it as the consumption of alcohol was prohibited in their indentures. I had nothing and the majority of the officers were responsible in their consumption, although the Chief and 2nd Sparks were somewhat under the weather on New Year's Day and lay on their bunks between meals. Beer was on ration to the crew, but the officers had unlimited access to beer and spirits. Yet none abused it although it is a wonder that more of the men, who sailed the dangerous seas throughout the war, did not seek the comfort provided by alcohol.

Captain Gepp and Amos Parkin went ashore on the morning of 2 January and as Parkin, in his capacity of Purser, was to bring back cash requested by the crew, the middies and I hoped to go ashore in the evening. I spent the morning writing up wireless notes in my usual faint-hearted attempt at study and, in the afternoon, typed a letter home using the typewriter in the wireless room while listening to music on the radio. Nova Scotian radio stations played a lot of Scottish music and, that afternoon, the band of Freddy Martin played a selection which included Bonnie Dundee, Bonnie Mary of Argyll and Auld Lang Syne. At the finish of the selection, the announcer referred to 'Scotch' music, for which *faux pas* he, no doubt, suffered the admonition of locals of Scottish descent.

Gepp and Parkin returned during the afternoon and we lined up outside Parkin's cabin to sign for the money we had requested which, in my case, was $40. Michael, Ian and I dressed, ready to go ashore after dinner, but there was no boat to take us and we had to remain on board.

When a boat came for Gepp and Parkin at 9 a.m. the following morning, I was able to take advantage of it and make my first trip ashore after twenty-eight days on board, including nine at anchor when official records show the ship as being 'in Halifax'. Such was the consideration shown to sailors and we were angry about being unable to go ashore during these nine days. We knew it was not Gepp's fault and put the blame down to the British Ministry of War Transport. The middies were unable to accompany me as they had to work during the day. The journey by motor launch from Bedford Basin to Halifax was a long and a costly one when I had to pay for it on subsequent occasions.

CHAPTER 26

HALIFAX, NOVA SCOTIA, IN JANUARY

There had been no snow at all on the ground when we arrived on Boxing Day, but a great deal fell during our stay and, on the morning on 8 January, the radio reported an 8 inches fall during the night. The roads were swept clear by cowcatcher type devices on the tramcars, but it was sometimes difficult to make progress along the sidewalks until workmen got around to clearing them.

I blew a hole in my $40 by spending $20 on a watch to replace the one I had stolen from my wrist in Algiers. It was a seventeen jewel, shock-absorber Swiss watch with a luminous dial and an excellent timekeeper. I was delighted with it and it served me for many years. I gave it to my son in the 1970s when he was about ten and thought I was giving him something special because I had bought it in Halifax during the war. But to him it was just an old watch and he was not enamoured with the gift. No doubt he was right. I tend to hang on to things of no monetary value because of their associations and I still have the watch.

Clothes, still not rationed, were available in the shops, but it was extremely difficult to get ladies' fully fashioned stockings. I tried all the department stores without success. At every store I was told that they usually came in during the afternoons, but you had to be on hand when they arrived as they were snapped up right away. When I asked a shop assistant to keep a pair for me, she said this was against their rules. I tried to buy tinned fruit, but on being told that it was rationed, had to be content with a couple of tins of fruit concentrate. There was still plenty to eat in the restaurants, but now three lumps of sugar were given with a cup of coffee whereas, during my previous visit, there had been no such restriction. Anticipating her husband's release from his prison camp in Poland, John Noble's mother had asked me to get a pipe for him and I did.

When I was ashore with Michael, we usually went to dances in clubs. Some were good and others not so good and there was one when we hardly got a dance because there were more fellows than girls. Prior to one of these dances, I took Michael with me to visit the Kenyons who lived at 73 Edward Street. They were pleased to see me, but unfortunately Ron was not at home as he was now working night shift as a proof reader on the local newspaper. They told me I was welcome to come to the house any time and to come back on the Saturday evening when Ron would be there. I said that I would do this, but it turned out that I was unable to as Parkin and Caro decided to go ashore together that evening and there had always to be an R/O on board. I managed to get someone to phone to let them know that I couldn't make it and, perhaps, Ron was as disappointed as I was as he, George McPherson and I had had good times together during that summer of 1943. As Ron was not in the Forces because of very bad eyesight, I wondered how he proof-read.

I had anticipated receiving a letter from Holts, on arrival in Halifax, explaining my decrease in pay, but as there was none, I approached the Chief Sparks again. He said that he would inform the Old Man, but when after a week or two and I still heard nothing, I went to see the Skipper myself. After I explained the situation, Gepp asked why I had not told him about this sooner. Parkin had said nothing to him and Gepp wrote Liverpool that very day.

I do not know why we went into Halifax as we did nothing but hang about there and, even by the day of our arrival, knew that we were destined for Saint John, New Brunswick. Indeed, the US Navy's sailing card for the *Samforth* had Saint John, NB as her destination on leaving the UK. Perhaps the reason was the increased U-boat activity in the area. But we sailed alone and unescorted to Saint John although the sailing card states that we were in Convoy HF 151. We left Halifax on 12 January and the short passage to Saint John took two days. It was the coldest passage I was ever to experience when it was perishing during the night, even in the wireless room with the steam radiator going full blast. God knows what it was like on the bridge and on these hellish convoys to Russia in winter. On January 14, the day we tied up in Saint John, the British tankers *Athelviking* and *British Freedom* and the US Liberty Ship *Martin Van Buren* were torpedoed and sunk off Halifax. The Battle of the Atlantic may have been won by May 1943, but it certainly didn't end until Germany capitulated.

CHAPTER 27

SAINT JOHN, NEW BRUNSWICK

Saint John, New Brunswick and Halifax, Nova Scotia are the eastern termini of the transcontinental Canadian Pacific and Canadian National railways. Open throughout the year, these ports are of major importance when the River St Lawrence is frozen over and the ports on the St Lawrence and the Great Lakes are closed to shipping (The St Lawrence Seaway was not opened until 1959). Saint John, never abbreviated to St John, is commonly confused with St John's, Newfoundland and lies at the mouth of the River Saint John, on the northern shore of the Bay of Fundy. At its head, the Bay of Fundy experiences a tidal rise and fall of up to fifty feet. At Saint John, the tide is little more than half of this, but nevertheless gives rise to the interesting phenomenon of the Reversing Falls where the river enters the Harbour. At low tide, the river falls six feet into the Harbour, but at high tide is pushed back up hill.

On entering the harbour, our attention was drawn to the exposed upper works of a sunken merchant ship which had come to grief on the small rocky outcrop in the middle of the harbour known as Hillyards Reef. This was Canadian Pacific's *Beaverhill*, which had broken loose from a tug within minutes of leaving the loading berth seven weeks previously and she continued to lie there, with her back broken, until disposed of in December, 1946.

All shipping docked in West Saint John and for the first time since leaving Avonmouth, we tied up at a quay and were able to walk ashore. But central Saint John lay on the other side of the harbour and, although a road bridge crossed at the narrowest point, where the river enters the harbour, this was a long way round. To get to the town centre, we used the West Saint John Ferry which operated between Rodney Wharf on the west side and the foot of Princes Street on the east side. The ferry ran every twenty minutes from 6 a.m. to midnight and a book of twenty, single trip, tickets cost 20¢. As I still have a book containing six tickets, I suspect that I was on my second book.

The fierce loyalty of those who fled into Canada from the embryonic United States, in order to remain citizens of the Crown, is displayed in the street names of Saint John. The main street is King Street, the steepest and shortest main street in Canada. At the head of King Street is rectangular King's Square Park, with its paths laid as the crosses of the Union Jack, and overlooking it was the Admiral Beatty Hotel which has since been converted in apartments for senior citizens. There is Union Street, Queen Street, Queen Square, Princess Street, Duke Street, Charlotte Street, William Street, Earl Street, St James Street and Pitt Street.

I can vouch for the fact that the loyalty to Britain had in no way diminished, as the people of Saint John did everything they possibly could for servicemen and women. On our arrival, we were given *The Key To Saint John* booklet, providing us with information on the facilities available to us. In the booklet, there were welcoming messages from the Mayor and from the Canadian Minister of Transport. The Minister's message was headed 'A Message of Welcome and Appreciation to the Officers and Seamen of the Allied Merchant Navies' and the last paragraph read 'A hearty welcome awaits every Merchant Seaman who comes to our Canadian ports. At no place in the Dominion, however, are they assured of a more cordial reception than at the ancient and historic Port of Saint John, N.B.' I came to subscribe to this view and towards the end of our stay, wrote home 'I reckon I've had a better time here than in any other place I've visited. Most of the boys say the same, strangely enough, and if anyone hasn't had a good time it's nobody's fault but his own.'

The streets were not cleared of snow as they had been in Halifax and it was a tiring job walking through it. But it was great to see horse-drawn sleighs and youngsters hauled about on sledges instead of prams. Our 2nd Mate, however, had a nasty accident as he slipped and fell and broke his collarbone. He managed to walk back to the ship, but was later taken to the General Public Hospital where I visited him. In the ward, a bright and cheerful young Canadian army lieutenant, in his early twenties, whizzed about in a wheelchair. He had lost both legs in the fighting in Europe.

Bill Dawson and I made the long walk from the ship to Rockwood Park and trudged through something like two feet of snow to get to Lily Lake. The park was a hive of activity, with skiers and tobogganists flying down slopes and horseback riders galloping about while the frozen lake was being swept clear of snow for skating by means of a horse pulling a large brush.

I never, anywhere else, came across anything like the City Hospitality Centre in Saint John, NB. This was indeed a unique and generous service

In Kings Square, Saint John, NB.

in which many of Saint John's citizens participated and run by Miss Alice L. Fairweather from the foyer of the Capitol (movie) Theatre, next door to the Admiral Beatty Hotel. Bill and I found Miss Fairweather, a pleasant lady of about fifty, sitting at a table behind which hung the Union Jack and, when we told her of our interest in skiing, she made a phone call before saying to present ourselves at a home in Church Street, Fairville the following afternoon. And it was appropriate to loyalist Saint John that, during the conversation which followed, Miss Fairweather revealed that her favourite author was Rudyard Kipling, the doyen of the British Raj! On leaving the Hospitality Centre, we went to Lily Lake to witness the skating before returning on board for dinner.

As all my colleagues seemed to have 'dates' that Saturday night, I decided to go by myself to the dance at the YWCA in Wellington Row, in central Saint John. Dances were held on Tuesday and Saturday nights at the YW and on Saturday night only, there was a nominal charge of 25¢.

The atmosphere at the YW was very homely and the first dance I went up to was a Paul Jones when I found myself dancing with the girl whom I had already selected as being the nicest looking in the hall. After the dance, I sat wondering if I could dance with her again, as she was obviously with a group, when a couple of dances later, she crossed the hall with a Canadian sailor and sat down beside me. You could have knocked me down with a feather when the sailor said to me, 'Barbara was admiring your dancing

Barbara, Digby, NS.

and would very much like another dance with you.' Barbara was blushing at the method of introduction and I rather think I must have been too. She was the odd one in a party of four married couples and I joined the group and had a great time. And although she was not in uniform, as were all the men in the party, Barbara was a Leading Wren on the telephone switchboard of HMCS *Cornwallis*, at Cornwallis, NS on the other side of the Bay of Fundy, and in Saint John only for the weekend. Like the sailor who introduced us, she was from Fort William, Ontario and, although I never saw Barbara after that night, we wrote to each other for two years so that I came to know her very well. Her name was Barbara Rutledge. Her parents were English and, when a flyer in the First World War, her father had been decorated by George V in Buckingham Palace.

I stayed so long at the YW that evening that I missed the last ferry, but, as other fellows were also returning to ships in West Saint John, we decided to share a taxi in order to save money. On reaching our destination, however, the driver insisted that we each pay the full fare because it was after midnight! The Loyalist Ferry was discontinued when the bridge now spanning the harbour was opened.

It was a beautiful Sunday afternoon when Bill and I presented ourselves at the address give to us by Miss Fairweather, a bungalow well out in the suburbs. A lovely lady ushered us in, but, after she had introduced us to her husband and her daughter and another girl who was to accompany us, we were disappointed to be told by the daughter that the ground was too hard for skiing and were to go sledging instead. The sledging area was quite close by and, although our hands and feet were frozen, we had an enjoyable afternoon. The hill we went down was very steep and at first a bit intimidating to us. But after a few goes, we were hurtling down with the best of them. When the daughter was out of earshot, her pal, a nice friendly girl, intimated that she wanted us away by 6 p.m. as her boyfriend was coming that evening. On returning to the house, therefore, we told her father, who was there on his own, that we had to get back to the ship and took our leave. But we were only about 100 yards from the house when we met the mum struggling home with provisions for our tea and who looked absolutely crestfallen at our departure. She had taken it for granted that we were staying for tea and tried her best to coax us back to the house. But knowing her daughter's attitude, we insisted that we had to return to the ship although in fact we would have loved to have stayed as we knew that we had already missed the evening meal. As we walked down the road, Bill laughed as he said, 'I wouldn't had minded going out with the mother.' And I heartily agreed with him. She was indeed a lovely and gracious lady.

The Capitol Theatre, which housed the Hospitality Centre, dated from 1913 and had been called the Imperial before it became a cinema in the

Sledging at Saint John.

With Inez, Lily Lake, Rockwood Park, Saint John, NB.

1920s. After a massive fund raising effort by the people of Saint John, it was totally renovated and reopened its doors as a theatre in May 1994. Again called the Imperial Theatre, it is the finest theatre in eastern Canada where many talented local artists perform.

There was a plethora of service clubs in Saint John. Some, like the Jervis Bay Navy Club for naval ratings, the Air Force Club and the Navy League Merchant Navy Officers' Club were exclusive, while others, like the YWCA, were open to all the Services. The Catholic Sailors' Club was one which was open to all and Huw and I played snooker there, but it was the YW and the Community Hall of the Carleton Branch Canadian Legion which we frequented.

The Community Hall had the great advantage of being in West Saint John and only five minutes walk from the ship. Like the YWCA, the Community Centre had a homely, village hall atmosphere. I generally went with Huw and the Thursday night dance was the highlight of the week when we were up at every dance and even made an attempt at jitterbugging. Admission was free, tea and cakes were served during the interval and the evenings ended with everyone joining hands and singing 'Goodnight Ladies' followed by 'Auld Lang Syne'. There was always a great discussion on a Friday morning as to what had transpired the previous evening. At breakfast one Friday morning, Mr Guppy sat listening to such a discussion, but, when I made a comment, he said to me, 'How do you know? You were in your bunk at 7 p.m. when I came in with a letter.' (Letters were brought to the R/Os for posting.) I had merely been having a lie-down before getting cleaned up and off to the dance!

On Sunday evenings, we attended singsongs in the Community Hall and at the end of one evening a young lady heard Huw singing and asked him to sing at her church. He agreed and because of this I found myself attending both morning and evening services at a Baptist Church the following Sunday. After the morning service, the organist accompanied Huw singing 'Nearer My God To Thee' and, during the evening service, he sang the hymn to the congregation. Although he said afterwards that he was shaking like a leaf, he did a fine job. There were other solos and a duet and, at the conclusion of the service, the lady sitting in front of me turned to shake my hand and said she was glad to see us there. There were girls with us from the Community Hall and we left for the singsong at the Hall where a Scotsman, from Crieff, in the Canadian Army sang 'Just A Wee Doch-an-Doris'.

I had intended to remain on board after attending morning service, but, when I was changing into my battledress after lunch, I thought it too good a day to waste. Huw was unable to accompany me as he had to stand a watch, but I had the phone number of a girl I had met at the YWCA when he and I had attended the Saturday evening dance there the week after I met Barbara. I called Inez at 1.30 p.m. from a phone box in the docks and met her up town an hour later.

Inez Hiltz was a serious-minded girl who lived at 50 Queen Street and worked in an office in Dock Street. We walked to Rockwood Park and I had the requisite bag of boiled sweets in my pocket so that it was reminiscent of the Sunday walks I had with my parents and Eric before the war. It seemed that all Saint John was there that beautiful Sunday afternoon and skaters, in colourful outfits and of all ages, skated to music coming from a loudspeaker rigged up outside the pavilion. This was winter Canada at its best. I had my camera with me and sent copies of the photographs I took to Inez. And, as she was engaged to an English airman, I thought I would never hear from her again, other than perhaps to thank me for the snaps.

The middies had gone into town together after breakfast one day, and I met them in the afternoon and trailed them round the same shops they had been to in the morning. Michael was keen on photography and wanted to upgrade his basic Kodak Bantam. At J. M. Roche & Co's shop in King Street, he found a second-hand Bantam with refinements which his own camera did not have. The price was $21 or $13 against a trade-in. But knowing that I was keen to have his camera, he said I could have it for the $8 offered by the shop. I jumped at the chance and what a beautiful little camera it was. Although a folding camera, it was three quarters of the size of the one I had bought in Washington DC and took far superior pictures. I had bought three or four 127 films in Halifax, but the Bantam took 828 films. Michael also spent another $9 on all the materials needed to do his own developing and printing and it was he who started me on the same lark. Eric Cameron's cabin was directly below mine and he used to say that he knew when I was engaged in photography as he heard jars being knocked over when I was stumbling about in the limited light produced by a red bulb!

Michael and Ian did not have the freedom to go ashore which I did and had always to have the Mate's permission. I sat with them in their cabin one Saturday afternoon and when I suggested going ashore, they said they would like to, but had not asked the Mate. 'Well, go and ask him,' I said, but they were fearful of invoking Mr Guppy's wrath as the ship was quiet and he would likely be having a kip. I thought it unreasonable that they should be confined to the ship during their time off and, as they were prepared to allow me to act as their agent, I went round to see Mr Guppy. He was asleep on his bunk and it took him a few seconds to collect himself. When he saw it was me and heard the request, he blurted out, 'No, they bloody well can't' and that was that. Perhaps his annoyance stemmed, not only from the fact that he was awakened, but also because the middies were in his bad books as they had forgotten to empty the fresh water containers (in case the water froze and burst them) in the lifeboats after being told to do so! Mr Guppy wasn't a bad sort of chap. He was responsible for the young apprentices and would no doubt have given his permission if asked earlier.

Although almost entirely free, there was a brief period towards the end of our stay when I had to supervise the loading of crates of whisky into a large and specially constructed wooden pen in the 'tween deck of No. 3 hold. The reason for this was to prevent pilfering by the dockers and I remember a docker in my presence, drinking from a small bottle which contained a clear substance which I was led to believe was a hair lotion with an alcohol content. The 2nd Sparks also supervised the work and, during intervals between loading, a large padlock secured this precious cargo. Yet, when I was returning along the quay to the ship one Sunday afternoon, dockers were staggering past me.

The important quest for ladies' stockings was continued and towards the beginning of February, Huw and I entered a store at the optimum time and joined a queue of women at the counter. We each managed to buy two pairs of 'sub-standard' stockings and two of the towels which had also 'just come in' and also coveted by the ladies. In addition, I bought a pair of cotton sheets and in a letter home, said that Eric and I would now be allowed to fight in bed as, when we were little, we were frequently reprimanded for doing so in the bed which we shared.

I tried to get a replacement record of Tchaikovsky's Piano Concerto No. 1, but discovered that what I had was only the first movement as the fast revolving 78s did not contain the lengthy recordings obtainable on discs today. There were four records in the set and, as the shopkeeper refused to sell one separately, and wanted $6.50 for the set, I did not get my record. I was also after a record of a song called 'An Hour Never Passes', but the jazzed-up version which the shopkeeper produced was not really to my liking so that I hesitated. The record shop was a small one and the impatient man was likely to have been the owner. 'Well,' he said, 'do you want it or don't you?' The recording was by Jimmy Dorsey and His Orchestra, singer Gladys Tell, and I bought it. On the reverse side was a nondescript song called 'Two Again' as it was the practice of record companies to put a nondescript recording on the opposite side of a popular piece of music. The hit song during our time on the North American coast was 'Don't Fence Me In', recorded by Bing Crosby and the Andrews Sisters.

We had received no mail in Halifax and the first letters arrived on 15 January, in Saint John, when I got one Christmas/New Year airgraph from my parents dated 8 December 1944. Later in the month, I received one letter dated 12 December, from home, but no other mail during our spell on the coast. The Skipper wrote home complaining about the service. It was the story of the *Samite* mail service all over again so that I suspect that all the ships in the Merchant Navy had the same problem.

The attention which my letters home received from the Censor is interesting. In my first letter home from Halifax, I mentioned its name twice and said we were going to Saint John. These place names were obliterated with a pen although the letter was franked CANADA. My next letter, from Halifax, contained the names Halifax and Bedford Basin and was not censored at all; but, in the postmark, the name Halifax was obliterated. I think that letter must have been posted in town and not on the ship; it was not an Air Letter, but sent airmail. In my next letter, I wrote, 'I don't expect to be away nearly as long as I was last time and in fact expect to see you ...' and the latter information was cut out. But it would appear that there was no censor in Saint John as not one of the four Air Letters I wrote to my parents were censored and every one contained the name of the town. And, later, a V-Mail, the US equivalent of the British Airgraph, sent from New York and containing place names in the City, was not censored. The Navy League Merchant Officers' Club, at 188 Princess Street, supplied writing paper and envelopes with Saint John, NB blacked out although it was possible to read the name through the black ink. Before leaving Saint John, I bought a number of Air Letter forms for future use.

When Huw received a letter from his girlfriend describing the good time she had had when out with another bloke, he was very put out by this and asked what he should do. Older and wiser, I now know that is it unwise to give opinions on such matters as the giver gets the blame when things go wrong. But I was young and inexperienced in matters of the heart and, perhaps rather flippantly, told Huw that I would tear up the letter and send it back to her. He did this and, months later, received an abject apology and everything was all right between them again!

In addition to the 'comforts' we received on arriving in Halifax, we had received another lot when lying at anchor in Bedford Basin. These were delivered by the Red Cross and I got a sleeveless pullover, knitted with very thick wool, a pair of mittens and a balaclava helmet. In Saint John, yet another batch was delivered on board and every man received a polo-neck sweater, either blue, grey or brown, a balaclava, two pairs of grey socks, mittens and a pair of sea-boot stockings. Although I gave most of my stuff away, because my work was indoors, this did not mean that I did not appreciate the generosity of those who had knitted and donated the gifts. All the garments were made of rough thick wool and it was, of course, rather optimistic that they should all fit the recipients. My balaclava seemed to have been made for a baby while the polo-neck sweater was too big. I was delighted to get the sweater as all the other fellows wore one because they dispensed with the necessity to dhobi white shirts. But, when I tried to shrink it by soaking it in hot water and it became bigger than ever, Eric Cameron, with his usual dry wit, said 'you should put buttons on that thing and use it as an overcoat!'

We certainly felt it very cold and sometimes ran into shops to allow our ears to warm up. One evening, when I was waiting at a bus or tram stop (both single deckers as in Halifax) with Michael, a man gathered up a handful of snow and rubbed Michael's ears to prevent frostbite as he said your ears could be frozen without you knowing it. Both men and women wore fur coats, with the fur inside. Before the days of animals' rights and when fur coats were fashionable in Britain, they were worn only by women, with the fur side exposed. Although I was later to hear a lecturer in Political Economy cite the wearing of fur coats in Britain as an example of 'conspicuous consumption', this is certainly not the case in Canada.

With loading complete, we sailed for New York on 8 February. We had expected to return to the UK, but now knew that we were bound for Alexandria. In a letter to my parents, when on passage to New York, I wrote 'I can't say I'm disappointed to hear that we're not now [returning to Britain]. I want to see the world and there's no time like the present.' I also said that I had bought 3½ lbs of tea, two tins of tomato juice, a tin of sardines, a small tin of chicken and a tin of Heinz tomato soup. We carried a general cargo for the Forces and, although I do not remember it, it is likely that we had the usual deck cargo with the wooden catwalks over it. We also carried ammunition, although I cannot recall the ship moving to an isolated berth to load it.

As our 2nd Mate was still in hospital, his place was taken by W. Willsteed who came from the Isle of Wight and was married to a girl from Ladybank, in Fife.

CHAPTER 28

INTERLUDE IN NEW YORK CITY

We sailed independently and were routed via the Cape Cod Canal which cuts through the narrow isthmus of Cape Cod in south-east Massachusetts and, including its dredged approaches, is 17½ miles long. This was not only a safer route, but also had the advantage of reducing the distance to New York by some 70 miles. However, when we arrived at the northern end of the Canal on a bitterly cold but sunny morning, we found it closed and had to go the long way round Long Island to New York. Although an icebreaker was present, it was not ice which closed the canal – a blizzard had brought down power lines so that the bridges over it could not be raised.

We dropped anchor in Gravesend Bay, off the south-west shore of Long Island, late in the afternoon of Monday 12 February and Huw and I spent the evening listening to a programme of popular tunes being played by a New York radio station. These included our favourite, 'Don't Fence Me In', which would always remind us of Saint John, and a rising favourite of ours, 'I'm Making Believe', sung by the Ink Spots. As we were keen to get the words of the latter, I copied them down in shorthand. We did not expect to get ashore as we knew the ship had called at New York only to join a convoy. But we were wrong and some of us did manage into the metropolis.

Immigration officers boarded the ship the following morning and each of us had to appear before them. I was asked if I had previously been to the States and had the Identification Card to allow me to go ashore. If I had the card, there was no need for them to issue a new one. I had the card, issued in Baltimore on 7 September 1943, in my cabin but, because I wanted another one as a souvenir, replied that, although I had previously visited the US, I had lost it. My photograph and a print of the index figure of my right hand were then taken for a new card. But, when the new cards had not arrived by the time the opportunity came to go ashore on the morning of Wednesday the 14th, I rapidly *found* my old one!

I went with Huw and Eric and the long and difficult journey into Central New York took over two hours. We left at 9 a.m. on the motor launch which had called for Captain Gepp and which took us to Staten Island. We then took a bus to the Staten Island Ferry which conveyed us across the harbour and past the Statue of Liberty to the Battery, on Manhattan Island. Then, from the Battery, we took a subway train to Times Square. We were in the area of Times Square from 11.15 a.m. till 3.30 p.m. and spent most of the time in Macy's which, with something like eight floors, boasted of being the largest store in the world. As its escalators were a novelty to us, we larked about on them and the only time I had previously seen an escalator was during a wartime holiday in London with my parents. We also had fun assisting Huw to buy lingerie for his girlfriend, but my purchases were made in smaller shops as funds were low and watches were continually referred to as we had to get the launch from Staten Island to the ship at 5 p.m. But, in spite of spending over four hours in travelling, we enjoyed ourselves and it was preferable to remaining on board. On our return to the ship, Neville Caro handed me my new Identification Card. An Immigration official had delivered the cards that afternoon but, when he was told that I was ashore, he wanted to know how I could have gone without one and was returning on Friday for an explanation.

A combination of circumstances prevented many of the crew from making a trip ashore. Firstly, although we arrived on Monday, the new Identification Cards, which, incidentally, were not shore passes, did not reach the ship until Wednesday. Secondly, we were miles from Manhattan and the central area of Times Square. Michael, who had not been to New York before, was desperate to see the City and, when some were going ashore at about 9.30 on Wednesday evening, he was asking my opinion as to whether it was worth it. He did not go, but like it or not, I had to go again the next day and at least did some shopping for him.

When I had sailed from the States on the *Samite*, only the 1st Radio Officer had attended the Convoy Conference with the Master, but all R/Os were required to attend before we sailed from New York. A launch came on the Thursday morning for Captain Gepp, and Parkin, Caro and I went with him. We were taken all the way to the Battery where the conference was held in the building of the Port Director. The R/Os did not attend the same meeting as the Masters and a US Navy officer instructed us as to the convoy communications procedure. I do not believe that he told us anything that we did not already know and we were each given a copy of the following:

Office Of Navy Port Director

17 Battery Place

New York, N. Y.

Instructions To Radio Operators

1. If ashore and you cannot locate your ship, please phone:
   COMMUNICATIONS DUTY OFFICER – Bowling Green 9-6220 – Extension 42.
   DO NOT MENTION THE NAME OF YOUR SHIP – Talk slowly and distinctly giving your own name only. Officer on duty will be able to inform you how to make ship. Be patient – it will take a few minutes. Always use a PHONE IN A BOOTH - Try to have a pencil ready – Use the back of this notice to write on.

2. The Master of your vessel will receive your communication plan. When he comes aboard, BE SURE TO ASK HIM FOR IT. YOU ARE TO HAVE THE COMMUNICATION PLAN IN RADIO SHACK THROUGHOUT THE VOYAGE. IT IS TO BE GIVEN TO MASTER UPON REACHING DESTINATION.

3. You will have Master instruct all Watch Standers to keep you informed immediately when:
   (a) you are in fog or cannot see Visual Signals from Commodore.
   (b) When emergency exists, as in the presence of the enemy.

4. You will obtain from the Master – WIMS III – and retain possession in shack while at sea.

5. Obtain from the Master the latest BAMS Lettered & Numbered messages of interest to you. They are marked "TO BE GIVEN TO RADIO OPERATOR" and the Master receives them from the New York Port Director.

6. The Radio Officer shall survey each private broadcast receiver aboard his vessel. Any receiver not listed as approved in WIMS III Appendix "D" is to be made inoperative by <u>removing</u> vital parts.
   This order applies to receivers owned by ALL SHIPS OFFICERS as well as CREW. You are responsible to Naval Authorities for the execution of this order, the Master will support you in this.

7. Keeping Radio Log – Conform with instructions in WIMS III – Art.45

8. General regulations for testing in U.S. inland waters *was given your Master upon arrival in New York. Obtain these regulations from him. Testing of transmitters between conference time and ships departure is PROHIBITED unless permission is granted by Port Director as shown below:
   Freq. _____ kcs – Time _____ EWT – Approved _____

9. BE ALERT – SAVE YOUR LIFE AND THE LIVES OF YOUR SHIPMATES – DON'T TALK – DON'T TALK – THE ENEMY IS

ALWAYS LISTENING – YOU CAN TRUST YOURSELF – BUT NOT
THE MAN NEXT TO YOU – JUST DON'T TALK.

21 Dec. 1944.   F. G. REINICKE, Commodore, U.S.N
*Grammar and layout as on original sheet.   Port Director - New
York.

The conference lasted little more than an hour and we were then free to
spend the rest of the day as we wished. I went off on my own to the Times
Square area where I bought the things which Michael had requested before
'taking in' a show at the Capitol Theatre, on Broadway at 51st Street.
Ralph Edwards, the 'star' of the popular radio quiz *Truth or Consequences*
appeared in person as did Gloria Jean who, although billed as Hollywood's
Charming Young Singing Beauty, had only a mediocre voice enhanced by
the backing of Sonny Dunham and His Orchestra. Following the stage
show was Hunt Stromberg's *Guest In The House*, starring Anne Baxter
and Ralph Bellamy, a miserable film which did nothing to uplift the spirits.
The doors of the Capitol opened at 10 a.m. and it was in the same theatre
that I had seen Jimmy Durante, 'in person', the previous March.

What made that day memorable for me was my return to the ship by
a US Navy launch from the Battery. It was late in the evening and dark
and, when the launch set out, it was crowded with US Navy personnel
returning to ships in the harbour. In the darkness, the helmsman
had difficulty in locating the ships of his passengers and called at ship
after ship, depositing sailors, until I was the only one left on board.
I stood at the stern watching the lights of Manhattan recede in the
distance. It was a beautiful and unforgettable way to bid farewell to
New York and a sight which few can have been fortunate enough to
witness.

I was greatly relieved when we weighed anchor the following morning
and escaped an embarrassing interview with the Immigration official.
I still have the two Identification Cards. According to the first one, my
occupation was that of Radio Officer, my height 5 feet 10 inches and I had
black hair. According to the one issued in New York, my occupation was
that of Mariner, my height 5 foot 9½ inches and I had brown hair. The
first card shows me wearing glasses, but I was told to take them off for the
second one and the number 57B was held in front of me. I have an Alien
Registration Number on the first, but the second card is merely stamped
ALIEN SEAMAN.

CHAPTER 29

MY LAST CONVOY

The New York Section of Convoy UGS 75 consisted of twenty-four ships, sailing in four columns of six, six, seven and five ships, which makes one wonder why it did not sail in four columns of six. The Commodore, Cdr. L.W. Mills, was on board the US merchant ship *A. Mitchell Palmer* and the escort consisted of three vessels of the US Navy. The cargo ships with ammunition/explosives on board were the British vessels *Hardingham*, *Samforth*, *Fort Fork* and the Norwegian *Granville*. None of the fifteen US cargo ships carried this cargo. The tankers were the *British Athelchief* and *Empire Cavalier*, the Norwegian *Norheim* and the US *American Trader*. With the south of France now in Allied hands, several ships were bound for Marseilles. The *Thomas Pinckney*, which had been Commodore ship of UGS 18 as far as Oran, was bound for Piraeus and Odessa.

The New York Section sailed at 8.24 p.m. hours on 16 February and rendezvoused with the main, Norfolk, Section in position 36°54′N 74°28′W at 1600 hours on the 17 February. The Norfolk Section sailed at 1100 hours on 17 February and consisted of thirty-three ships escorted by three naval vessels. When the two sections combined, Convoy UGS 75 consisted of fifty-seven merchant ships with an escort of six naval ships. One of the escorts was the *Annapolis*, which was a ship of the US Coast Guard and it is interesting to note that the work of Coast Guard ships was not confined to the coast of the US. The Commodore was Cdr. S. A. Maher on board the US merchant ship *Joseph N Teal*, and the Commodore of the New York Section became Vice-Commodore. As was the norm, both Commodore and Vice-Commodore were retired naval officers who had, voluntarily, come out of retirement to perform this duty. The average speed maintained by the convoy was 9.45 knots.

The passage to Gibraltar took over two weeks and was uneventful. I was happy in the familiar routine and although we who were off watch after dinner played neither monopoly nor cards, we yarned a lot in each others' cabins when the good times we had experienced and the girls we had met in Saint John were remembered. I never found a long passage tedious if the weather were reasonable, as it was on that occasion. I believe that people everywhere are influenced by the weather, but never more so than at sea. This is most noticeable after a spell of bad weather, during which life can be so uncomfortable. When, often quite suddenly, the sea has gone down and it is a fine morning with the sun shining, you can sense spirits rise with, as often as not, the feeling being tangibly expressed by the whistling of a sailor as he undertakes some task on deck.

Caro and I now had a new steward, as our young steward, who had been on the *Samite* for a spell, had 'jumped ship' in New York. The new steward was Arthur Hardaker, one of the DEMS gunners, who was delighted to find himself picking up the wages of a MN steward in addition to his Maritime Regiment pay as it came in very handy to support the family he had back in Manchester. Arthur was a bespectacled man in his thirties who called a spade a spade and I became very friendly with him so that we sometimes went ashore together. I may say that this did not compromise my position on board ship and indeed believe he deliberately addressed me as 'sir' when others were present, although no-one could accuse Arthur of being subservient. I remember him holding his own in a discussion about commissions in the Armed Services when he pointed out that it had not been so very long ago since commissions had been bought for £30. Arthur was of the same mould as the Royal Navy PO in charge of the DEMS gunners on the *Samite*. They were clean and smart, dependable men whose demeanour reflected their military training. Although I could never subscribe to what was generally referred to as the 'bullshit' of the Armed Services, there was surely a middle road. In the Merchant Service, all that was demanded was that a man did his work – the cabin in which he lived could be an absolute 'pigsty' and he could go ashore in such a state that I would want to disown him as being from 'my' ship. Certainly, Masters were required to make a weekly inspection of crews' quarters, but even the best Masters with whom I sailed chose to gloss over the unsavoury condition of some cabins. Arthur remained our steward until the end of the voyage.

The, now Declassified, Confidential Report of Commodore Maher makes interesting reading. Under the heading 'Exercises' he states:'Emergency turns – Feb. 20 and 23. Sound signals Feb. 21 and 23.' Under 'Contacts' he reported the following:

(1) 1944Q Feb. 20 in Lat. 35 08 N Long. 60 02 W At request of SOE (Senior Officer Escort) went Emergency 45° Right. Resumed base course at 2000.

(2) Feb. 22 at 2020P in Lat. 36 40 N Long. 50 48 W.

(3) 1850P Feb. 24 in Lat. 37 16 N Long. 41 39 W. Depth charges dropped. Resumed base course at 1924.

(4) 1010N March 1 at request of SOE went Emergency 45° Right to avoid 4 masted schooner in Lat. 35 50 N Long. 20 22 W. Resumed base course at 1030.

Under the heading 'General report on station-keeping of convoy' the Commodore stated that this was 'Good to Fair', but went on to list six ships which were 'Bad Station keepers': three US, one Greek and two British. One of the latter was the *Fort Paskoyac*, K. L. Jones Master, of which he said, 'This ship could not make more than 9.3 knots most of the time and for days was 2000-4000 yards behind.'

Under 'Name of any vessel in the convoy in which the flag-hoisting arrangements could be improved' his comments were scathing in that he blanketed 'All Liberty Ships in convoy'. And, when he was asked to 'Report on the suitability of Commodore's ship', he said, 'satisfactory except flaghoisting and Xmas Tree facilities have the usual well known defects common to all Liberty Ships.'

Although the crossing was an unmemorable one for me, it could not have been so for the 3rd Mate of the brand-new US Liberty Ship *William Terry Howell* (P. Rogis, Master), as the Commodore, under the heading 'Details of any favorable or unfavorable behaviour by vessels in convoy (Name of Master to be noted against each ship reported on.)', wrote:

This ship was a column leader next to, and on starboard side of Commodore's ship. Just before 1010 on a clear morning of March 1 in response to a request of the Escort Commander, Commodore made customary signal by flaghoist and whistle for convoy to make an emergency turn of 45° to starboard to get clear of a 4 masted schooner. Even tho all other adjacent ships repeated signal, this ship did not do so until repeatedly called by flashing light. The person who may not avoid responsibility for this inexcusable inattention and delay is the watch officer, Joseph H. Prince – 3rd Mate, license number 79669. Convoy had been thoroughly exercised at this maneuver [*sic*] previously. When asked for a statement the master answered that there was no excuse and that steps had been taken to prevent a recurrence. In all other respects this ships performance was satisfactory.

In position 35°46′N 07°07′W, at 0830 on 4 March, four ships departed for Casablanca under local escort. At 4.30 p.m. the convoy passed Convoy GUS (Gibraltar to United States) 75 in the Strait of Gibraltar and, at 5.58 p.m. it dispersed south of Europa Point. There was no longer any great danger in the Mediterranean and all ships proceeded independently to their destinations. When the *Samforth* arrived in Alexandria on 11 March, I wrote home saying, 'Yes, I've made it (through the Mediterranean) this time. Third time lucky.' But I never sailed past the Algerian coast without recalling my experiences in Convoys UGS 18 and UGS 38. Even when I left the sea in 1951, wrecks of German ships could still be seen at Cape Bon where remnants of the Afrika Corps had desperately attempted to escape to Italy in May 1943.

CHAPTER 30
ALEXANDRIA, EGYPT

Alexandria, situated at the western edge of the Nile Delta and on a strip of land between Lake Maryut and the sea, was the chief seaport of Egypt and the main naval base in the Eastern Mediterranean. It was consequently a busy place with the Royal Navy much in evidence. Although there are two harbours, only the western one could be used by ships of any size and it was there that we dropped anchor in the early morning of Sunday 11 March 1945.

The anchor barely had time to settle on the bottom before I was on the bridge beside Huw when he called up the Fleet Mail Office by Aldis lamp to ask if there were any mail for the *Samforth*. We held our breaths waiting for the answer and, when it came back 'yes', we did some spontaneous jitterbugging and looked forward to going for the mail after lunch when the ship had berthed alongside.

As soon as the ship had anchored and obtained pratique from the port doctor, we were boarded by Egyptian harbour police and a swarm of Arabs, from bumboats, who wanted not only to sell us things, but to give haircuts and collect laundry. In no time, the ship resembled a bear garden, but it didn't last long as they were soon driven back into their boats.

When we berthed later in the morning, it was decided to lower a motorised lifeboat to take us to the Fleet Mail Office, about a mile away at the other side of the harbour. As the boat was being lowered, Huw was forced into taking his first swim when his wallet fell into the water. Rapidly divesting himself of shoes and upper garments, he dived in and retrieved it.

Collecting the mail turned out to a bit of a pantomime and rather more difficult than anticipated. Everybody was anxious to get the mail and, after lunch, Huw, the two Middies, the 5th Engineer, the Sgt Gunner and I had an audience when we cast off in the lifeboat. We set off at a

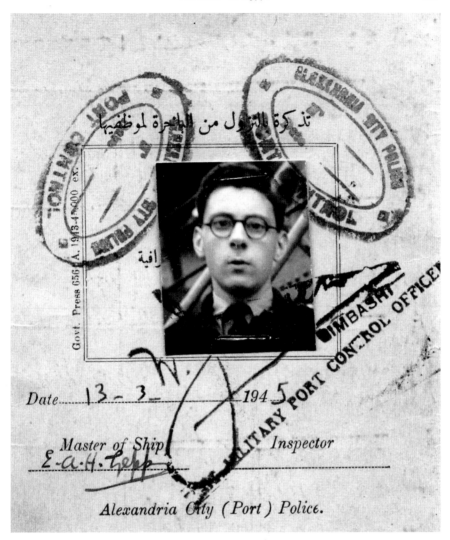

تذكرة بالتزول من الباخرة لموظفيها

Date...13 - 3 - ...194 5

Master of Ship
E·a·H·Gepp

Inspector

Alexandria City (Port) Police.

Shore Pass, Alexandria.

great rate but, in seconds, the engine conked out and we had to return to the ship. All the 'experts', including the Old Man, then descended the gangway to offer advice, but the boat remained immobile for hours with Eric later complaining that Gepp had been a blasted nuisance! It was about 3.30 p.m., and I was still in the boat, when I saw a boat with some British fellows in it, messing about nearby. I waved to them and, when they came over, I asked if they would take me to the FMO. 'Sure,' they said. 'Hop in.'

Michael came with me, and the Wren who gave us the pile of mail was surprised to hear that this was our first in over two months. We were greeted like heroes as we returned to the ship with all the lads out on deck waving to us as the boat drew near. But, in spite of the quantity of mail collected, almost all our December and January mail was missing. I got seven letters and, apart from one dated 21 January, all carried a February date. And not one referred to any of the letters I had sent from Canada and New York. When I wrote home the following day, I think I expressed the sentiment of all on board when I said, 'These fellows who handle the mail ought to be shot for making such a hash of it.' But I also said that I'd had a great day and that my face was already red with sunburn.

Central Alexandria was very European and attractive with beautiful buildings, wide thoroughfares and excellent shops. Mohammed Aly Square, renamed Liberation Square after the revolution of 1952, was the city centre and in the square was the equestrian statue of Mohammed Aly, the great great grandfather of King Farouk, who became the Ottoman Viceroy and Pasha of Egypt in 1805. Mohammed Aly had brought order to the country and was less ruthless than most Turks of his time, which is illustrated by an edict of his which made it illegal, on pain of death, for any village sheikh to beat anyone to death unless provoked!

Alexandria was more cosmopolitan than any other city I had visited and people who looked as if they had jumped out of the Bible walked the streets with women who would have looked at home on New York's 5th Avenue. The single-deck electric trams all converged on Mohammed Aly Square. On my first trip into town, the empty tram which I boarded at the dock terminus filled up with Arabs as it proceeded on its way. Having just drawn money from the ship, I had only notes in my pocket, well in excess of the 2 piastres required for the fare. When the conductor came to me, he could not cash the note I gave him and asked other passengers if they could change it. Everyone tried to help. They were poor people of a different race and culture, but people are the same everywhere. What I did not know on that first journey was that the trams were divided into different sections. The better-off Egyptian, in his European suit and red fez, did not ride with the labouring class. I never availed myself of the alternative means of transport, the horse-drawn gharri, although one gharri driver did his best to get my custom. When I was walking just outside the docks one day, this driver had his horse mount the pavement in front of me so as to block my passage while he shouted invitations to engage his services. I crossed to the other side of the street and continued on my way.

My main objective on that first visit into town was to have a haircut and in a barber's shop in Mohammed Aly Square, I met with the same annoying procedure I had experienced in Algeria. In spite of my protestations, the barber took too little off, was pathetically slow while continually smothering my neck with talcum powder; all part of the act to have you give a good tip and return again soon.

Tram Ticket, Alexandria.

Only the Royal Cinema had air conditioning, but the weather was only pleasantly warm and Eric and I chose to go to the Mohammed Aly Cinema one evening to see Kay Kyser in *Swing Fever* rather than *Broadway Rhythm* showing at the Royal. *Swing Fever* turned out to be an awful film, but we derived some entertainment by criticising it from our seats in the balcony. When Kay Kyser left the room, a broken man after his girlfriend had ditched him, I said to Eric, 'He's away to shoot himself', to which Eric replied, 'It's the best thing that could happen to him.' The dialogue was in English with subtitles in French while, on a separate small screen at the side, the subtitles were shown in Arabic. At the end of the performance, we stood for the Egyptian National Anthem when the rude words which the British troops put to the Anthem, 'King Farouk, King Farouk caught his bollocks on a hook. Queen Farida won't play, 'cause she's in the family way', kept going through my mind.

The British Army version of the National Anthem would not have offended many Egyptians as King Farouk, a puppet of Britain and, incidentally, the first of his line to speak Arabic, was very unpopular. This was brought home to me when I called on ship's business at the Passport Office within the docks. I was being dealt with by a young Egyptian policeman, who had a reasonable command of English, when a colleague brought him a small bowl of food which he told me was called ashoura. He invited me to taste it and, when he saw that I liked it, insisted that I eat the lot. The dish consisted of a white jelly-like substance with maize mixed through it and topped with almonds and raisins. On completion of my business, I was invited to come into the room behind the counter, where I spent some time engaged in conversation with

Cinema ticket, Alexandria.

the policemen. One of them expressed his derogatory opinion of Farouk, his admiration for Russia and how monarchy was no good. He spoke openly before his colleagues and, considering that this seemed to be the general opinion of the Egyptian Police, Egypt was ripe for revolution. The same man asked me to spend the evening in town with him, but, as I suspected that his idea of entertainment might be rather different from mine, I declined the invitation.

On a visit to the Merchant Navy Club, I was given a pass which gave me admission to the Alexandria Fleet Club. The Fleet Club produced a pamphlet which gave a potted history of the club and of the city. The potted history of Alexandria made reference to the Arabi Rebellion of 1882, when 'the forts were bombarded by the *British* Fleet. Arabi was defeated by Lord Wolseley and the *British* Army at Tel-El-Kebir and the *English* occupation of Egypt began'. [Italics are mine.]

Today's merchant seafarers, subjected to the container system which allows them little time in port, will envy our method of discharging. There were no cranes available so that all our cargo was landed, by means of the ship's winches and derricks, onto small narrow carts hauled by small horses and mules. It was a slow business accompanied by a great deal of noise: the rattling of the winches, the shouting of the Arabs and the banging of cases as they landed on the carts. And it went on day and night.

A few more letters reached us on 21 March, and while the bulk of our December and January mail had still did not turned up, I received a letter from home dated 7 March. This was a record: only a fortnight for an airmail letter to reach Egypt! Although postage had to be paid on letters from Algeria in 1943/44, all mail to Britain and the Dominions went free and, as my reference to Alexandria went undeleted in a letter home, censorship appeared to have been abandoned. Letters from my parents oddly intimated that they thought we had been making for South America, but I had no idea where they got such a notion.

The Palace of Ras-El-Tin, meaning Cape of Figs, was the most prominent building at the western harbour and we passed it on our boat trips to the Fleet Mail Office. It is a long, low, light-coloured building, built by Mohammed Aly, and it was there that the court came in summer to enjoy the Mediterranean breezes and escape from the heat of Cairo. The final scene in the demise of the Mohammed Aly Dynasty took place in Ras-El-Tin in July 1952, when the military junta forced King Farouk to abdicate in favour of his infant son, Ahmed Fuad. Farouk sailed for Naples on the royal yacht *Mahroussa* the next day, taking with him his wife, Narriman, (he had divorced Farida) and their son. The following year, the junta abolished the monarchy. But Fuad was the last King of Egypt and not Farouk as most people believe. Rather ironically, Egypt declared war on Germany and Japan only a week or two before our arrival and did so because it was agreed at the Yalta Conference that any nation which joined the Allies before 1 March would be accepted as a founder member of the United Nations Organisation. The decision taken at Yalta caused a number of countries to hastily join the winning side, but some Egyptians did not welcome the news and when Prime Minister Ahmed Maher left the Chamber of Deputies after the Declaration, he was shot dead.

Having discharged the part of our cargo, we sailed for Port Tewfik on 22 March and as we slowly moved out of the harbour, a British destroyer dipped her flag in friendly salute.

CHAPTER 31

PORT SAID AND THE SUEZ MARITIME CANAL

Port Said stands on the western shore at the northern end of the Suez Canal, which had taken over ten years to build and opened in 1869. The Canal, jointly owned by Britain and France, was built by Ferdinand de Lesseps, assisted by some 20,000 conscripted labourers encouraged by the hippopotamus hide lash known as the courbash. Before it was destroyed by Egyptian nationalists during the Suez Crisis in 1956, a statue of de Lesseps stood on the entrance breakwater with its right arm extended towards the Canal. Ships leaving and entering the Mediterranean passed close to that sign, which indicated that ships of all nations were welcome to use the waterway.

We arrived in Port Said in the morning of 23 March and although I cannot remember the details of that first visit, or the passage through the Canal, I clearly remember the usual sequence of events, as I was later to negotiate the Canal on many occasions. All ships for Canal transit had to anchor in Port Said harbour and you were generally within a stone's throw of palm-lined Sultan Hussein Quay, which housed the renowned department store of Simon Artz. As ships which had transited the Canal from the south had also to anchor in the harbour before proceeding into the Mediterranean, there were usually many ships at anchor. The *Samforth* had already obtained pratique in Alexandria, but when Port Said was a ship's first Egyptian port and even if no-one were going ashore, she entered the port flying the yellow quarantine flag and the Port Medical Officer had to clear the ship before anyone could board. He did this as soon as the ship anchored and, while he was on board, the eyes of the occupants of the bumboats, gathered at the gangway, were fixed on the yellow flag. And as soon as they saw the flag begin its descent, they swarmed up the gangway to spread their wares on deck.

As the majority of those who transited the Canal never had the opportunity to visit the town, the bumboat men were their only contact with its citizens. They sold mainly leather articles, but also a variety of merchandise which included watches, shoes and Turkish delight. Some professed Scottish names, such as Jock McGregor and could mimic Scots' accents. And there was always a barber and a gulli-gulli man who produced white mice from the sleeve of his coat and performed other conjuring tricks.

In the days when the *Samforth* transited the Canal, ships proceeded independently. A British or French pilot boarded at Port Said and an Arab was hoisted on board in his rowing boat. And, if transit were at night, a large searchlight, capable of lighting up the Canal 1,300 metres ahead, was fitted at the bow of the ship. The searchlight was operated by a ship's Electrical Officer or, in the absence of an electrician, by the 3rd Engineer Officer. The Canal Company hired out searchlights, but all Holt ships which regularly used the Canal carried their own. When preparations were completed, the ship weighed anchor and proceeded slowly, past the imposing office building of the Suez Canal Company, into the Canal. I stood on deck as the *Samforth* entered the Canal in the fading light when a solitary Arab, on his camel, watched us pass.

Ships could not pass each other when under way in the Canal so that, if two ships met, the one heading south had to tie up to bollards on the western bank. This was the reason for taking the Arab and his boat on board. He sat in the boat as it was lowered then rowed to the shore, looped the hawsers round bollards and the ship drew herself into the side by means of her winches. In the late 1940s, a convoy system was introduced in order to speed up transit through the Canal, which is just over 100 miles long. Morning and evening convoys leave from both Port Said and Suez and pass each other in the Bitter Lakes. There are no locks, but passage is always slow as speed is restricted to a maximum of 7½ knots in order to limit erosion of the banks by a ship's wash. In convoy, a night passage has an eerie yet aesthetic atmosphere. The Canal is not always absolutely straight and, at times, you can see the searchlights and mast head lights of ships which are following, but not directly behind, while there is only the shadowy desert on both sides. Overhead, the stars twinkle in a clear sky. Before the introduction of the convoy system, and when transit was in daylight, it would irritate a Master to suffer the delay of tying up to allow a ship coming from the south to pass. But this was an amusement for the crew, who would line the port side to witness the event. If the crews of both ships were British, the sailors called out to each other in friendly repartee and although it was beneath the dignity of the officers to participate, they equally enjoyed the fun. It was a diversion when you saw nothing but the desert sands. The only points of interest are the isolated Suez Canal Defence Monument and Ismailia, on Lake Timsah, where you get a brief glimpse of vegetation. During transit, a ship's wireless station was at the disposal of the pilot in order to communicate in Morse on medium wave with the Canal radio station, callsign SUQ. But in my experience this was seldom used and we did not keep a listening watch, as a flag or a light at a Canal station would tell the pilot if the passage were clear or if it were necessary to tie up in order to allow another ship to pass. The pilot always knew beforehand if we had to tie up: it was not a case of meeting another vessel unexpectedly and, when we had to tie up, we always had to wait for the other ship to appear.

The Suez Canal became familiar to me, but I never ceased to marvel at this tremendous feat of civil engineering which shortens the sea route from Britain to India by about 7,600 miles. And, although perhaps understandable, the Egyptian nationalists were wrong in destroying the statue of de Lesseps at Port Said, consequent to President Nasser nationalising the Canal in 1956. If it were not for de Lesseps, who incidentally was not a civil engineer, the Canal, of such value to the world and particularly to the economy of Egypt, would not have been built.

It is commonly believed that the town of Suez stands at the southern end of the Canal. This is not so and the town which stands there is Port Tewfik with Suez, 'round the corner', some two miles to the west. It is odd that Tewfik should be ignored. It is seldom shown on maps, and even the US Navy got it wrong as the sailing card of the *Samforth* states that she was in Suez from 23 March until 4 April. We tied up alongside in Port Tewfik on Saturday, 24 March to discharge another part of our military cargo.

CHAPTER 32

PORT TEWFIK AND CAIRO

While the poor flats of the native quarter could not be described as salubrious, Port Tewfik was reasonably attractive. A notable feature was the Abbas Mosque, from the decorated minaret of which the muezzin called the faithful to prayer, but there was also a Roman Catholic church. We remained in blue uniform with white covers over our caps, but it was warm enough to sit at tables outside the Casino Café and to stroll in Main Street, running parallel to the Canal, where slowly moving ships passed close to you as they entered or left the Canal.

The day after our arrival, a great deal of our missing mail caught up with us and I received fifteen letters. That same evening, Captain Gepp came to my cabin to tell me that he had still not had a reply from Holts about my reduction in salary. None of the letters I wrote was censored.

An Army medic came on board on Monday to ask if we wanted to be vaccinated against smallpox. Along with others, I said 'yes' and after being vaccinated in a nearby building the next afternoon, I was given a slip of paper which read: 'This if to certify that 3rd R/Off Malcolm was vaccinated on 27/3/45 with the following result 'Taken Accelarated[7] (Signed) DB'. This was the first time I had been vaccinated since a baby when, although vaccinated twice, it had not taken and left no mark on my arm.

I was sitting in the middies' cabin playing the mouth organ that evening when the Carpenter looked in to say that he'd learned that a dance was being held, but didn't know where it was. The 5th Engineer and I went ashore together, but, after locating the dance at an Army Sergeants' Mess, the sergeant at the door refused admission as it was private. He said that it was unfortunate that we had chosen to come on a 'bad' night as the club was open to us any other evening. But, when I asked what went on during other evenings, he replied, 'Nothing!' We took our leave and went along to the Empire Cinema.

Poor person's house, Port Tewfik.

The decorated frontage of the Empire belied its primitive interior. It was almost full and we were shown to wicker seats by an Arab dressed in flowing robes. I was given a seat in the back row while the 5th had to sit along from me in the row in front. As it was drafty and somewhat noisy, I looked round and was surprised to see, within the confines of the theatre and separated from the back seats by only about thirty yards, an area where Arabs sat eating and drinking at long tables running at right angles to the rows of cinema seats. Caterers stood frying the food, other Arabs wandered about and, as none of them had the least interest in the film, the constant chatter sometimes made it difficult for me to catch all the words spoken on the screen. The cinema was an open-air one with posts round it and in the centre so that a canvas roof could be put in place when it rained, as it had done that morning. The 5th found himself under canvas which still held rain water and, throughout the performance, was subjected to a constant drip. A couple of nights later, Eric and I went to see *Now Voyager* which features the song 'It Can't Be Wrong' and in which, a plain, well-off, innocent Bette Davis falls for the ship's radio officer who lets her down so that she is left a hard, embittered woman.

Our cargo was discharged by the British Army and I learned from one of the soldiers on the night shift that it was possible to visit Cairo as a bus, in the shape of a truck, left from their camp at 7 a.m. every Friday morning. I conveyed the information to Michael. He was keen to accompany me

Hitch-hiking to Cairo.

At the Pyramids.

and I went to ask Captain Gepp's permission for both of us to go for the weekend. Gepp's answer was that he would not mind me being away for the weekend, but that he could not grant the same privilege to Michael because he was a midshipman. We could, however, go for the day and I was put in charge of the 'expedition'. I understood and reluctantly accepted the decision. The 77-mile journey to Cairo seemed a long way to go for the day, but it was better than nothing.

We rose at 4.20 a.m. on the morning of Friday 30 March and, having had a cup of tea and a raw egg switched up in evaporated milk, went to board the truck which took the army stevedores back to their camp. But the truck turned out to be so full that it could not take us so that there was no chance of us catching the 'bus' from the camp to Cairo. Within minutes, however, we were relieved from our predicament. Another army truck came along. It was going to a different camp, just west of Suez, and the driver said he would drop us on the road to Cairo where he turned off to the camp. We gratefully accepted the offer and it was barely daylight when we alighted from the truck at about 6 a.m., to hitchhike to Cairo. There was no traffic at that time in the morning although many Arabs were walking towards Suez to begin their day's labour. After waiting for about half an hour, the first vehicle which came along was a small truck driven by a South African sergeant major with a another Southern African soldier sitting beside him. The driver responded to our signal. They were going all the way to Cairo and we were told to climb in the back of the truck, which was under a canvas cover.

When we got in, we found that there were wooden bench seats on both sides and two civilians already in residence. Dressed in neat lounge suits, they turned out to be pleasant Greek gentlemen who engaged us in conversation throughout the journey. They told us that the bumpy road on which we were travelling had been built only about fifteen years previously and that, before the building of the road, the journey across the desert had been an absolute ordeal. Twice during the journey, we saw a Bedouin with his flock of sheep and a few camels and, after passing through Heliopolis, arrived in Cairo at 8.30 a.m. One of the Greek gentlemen had already left the truck before we alighted from it in Cairo with the other one, who took us to a café for breakfast. It was very pleasant sitting at a table on the pavement in the cool of the morning eating bacon and eggs, although the butter had a strange taste which suggested that it may have been made from either goats or sheeps milk. As we sat there, an Arab came along with a fairly large ape, on a length of rope, which he made do backward somersaults for our amusement. Although we recognised the treatment of the animal as being somewhat cruel, we accepted it as part of the local scene and gave the man a few coins. Our Greek friend insisted on paying for the meal and we left him to seek out Service clubs to find out about tours of the city.

With Michael Shaw, Cairo.

Pyramids and the Sphinx.

We arrived at the YMCA to learn that we had just missed a tour to the Pyramids. Our disappointment was quickly overcome, however, when an Egyptian guide said that he had a car at our disposal and that he could catch up with the main party if we were prepared to pay 70 piastres each although the normal price, when there were five in a car, was only 28. We readily agreed and were driven to the Pyramids of Giza, about ten miles west of the city, in style. In was a pleasant run, during which we crossed the Nile. We left the car at the foot of the hill in front of the Pyramids and climbed it in time to join the main party for a tour of the Pyramids and the Sphinx. The tour was excellent. We were taken up the stairs into the large empty chamber in the heart of the Great Pyramid of Cheops, where we were shown the way by an Arab holding a lighted candle. Inside the Temple of the Sphinx, we had to pay an Arab 5 piastres to light a piece of phosphorus, which he waved around while he tried to impress us by calling out 'All alabaster'. When the light went out, he said, 'You wanna see some more?' to encourage us to pay another 5 piastres.

It is possible to climb the Great Pyramid, but, even at the age of nineteen, I baulked at climbing up those great stone blocks although we saw others doing so. We had our pictures taken on camels, but I forgot to wind on the spool in my camera so that I have only a fuzzy, useless snapshot. We had lunch in the Pyramids Restaurant for Allied personnel and where a sign said 'alcoholic drinks strictly prohibited', before returning to Cairo.

Cairo trams.

Gharries, Cairo.

On the way to the YM, we called at the army barracks of Kasr-el-Nil to enquire about transport back to Port Tewfik and were told that a 'bus' was leaving at 9.30 p.m.

In the afternoon, we went on another YM tour. This included a visit to the Mohammed Aly Mosque where the servicemen and women 'tourists' were asked to pay a few piastres to have the electric lights switched on. The interior was otherwise lit only by subdued daylight and when the many lights, suspended at great length from the high ceiling, illuminated the chamber, the beautiful decoration was exposed. The tour took us throughout Cairo. We saw the Citadel (built from the limestone casing which once covered the Pyramid of Cheops), had a walk through a bazaar, and returned to the YM at 4.30 p.m. where we had tea in the garden at the rear of the building. I noted, in a letter home, that, altogether I had eaten seven eggs that day! As there was time to kill before heading for the 'bus', we went to see Dorothy Lamour in *The Angels Sing* before going to Kasr-el-Nil barracks, where we had peaches in the canteen prior to boarding the large army truck. It had been so warm during the day that I had carried my doeskin jacket, but it was not sufficient to keep me warm during the ride across the desert on that clear, starry night when I sat beside a major from Edinburgh who quizzed me about the UK Customs as he was shortly to be returning home and had collected various articles to take home.

Citadel and Mohammed Aly Mosque, Cairo.

The 'bus' dropped Michael and me at the dock gate at 1 a.m. It had been a long and wonderful day and we had seen the Pyramids of Giza, one of the Seven Wonders of the Ancient World and the only one extant.

Britain had had a National (coalition) Government throughout the war and a general election was now looming. The election was scheduled for early July and those of us who would be twenty-one or over on the election date were given forms of proxy to complete. This meant, of course, that I and a number of others were excluded as it was not until 1969 that the voting age was lowered to eighteen. I doubt if anyone who completed a form could name a prospective candidate in the election although this, I suppose, was no great handicap as we almost always vote for parties rather than individuals. The completed forms were sent to the UK in a batch.

Towing two small, rocket-firing craft, we sailed for Bombay on 4 April (The LCT (R) – Landing Craft Tank with the R standing for rocket – carried as many as 500 rockets and had a crew of about twenty).

CHAPTER 33

PASSAGE TO INDIA

As we headed south through the Gulf of Suez, the sickly smell of oil reached us from the oilfield on the western shore, and we could see the flame from burning gas in the darkness.

We now had on board a few British soldiers under a tall, bespectacled captain. The LCT (R)s were manned by the Royal Navy and we communicated with them by means of a radio telephony transmitter and receiver which had been given us in Tewfik. They were referred to as Sammy 1 and Sammy 2 and, although I did not know it, I was sometimes talking to Neil Soars of Wolverhampton, a cousin of my future wife.

The effects of vaccination began to hit some of us shortly after we sailed from Tewfik. Neville Caro took to his bunk, although I suspected that he was no more ill than I was as I had a bit of a temperature, felt sick and listless and there was such a swelling under my left arm that I could not put it to my side. Parkin and I had to cover Caro's watch, and we did this by working four hours on and four hours off during the day and a six-hour watch at night. By this change in circumstances, I saw dawn creep over the Red Sea shortly after five in the morning. It was now hot and on 6 April we changed into tropical uniform which, in most cases, was khaki. When I looked out my shorts, I found that my mother had ironed them with the creases at the sides so that I had to re-iron them before making an appearance! Clocks were advanced an hour on the 6 April so that Parkin and I had half an hour cut off our night watch, but lost half an hour's sleep. By 7 April, I began to feel better although I still could not put my arm to my side, and a couple of days later Caro took over his watch again.

We called at Aden on 13 April to bunker and I got my first sight of the 'barren rocks' of that arid place. As there were no docks, all ships lay at anchor off Steamer Point and bunkering was done by connecting up to the pipes which conveyed the oil from the shore and terminated at buoys.

Aden was a bunkering port for ships going to and coming from the East, East Africa and Australia via Suez, although Aden itself had neither oil nor coal. The oil was brought by tankers from the Persian Gulf while much of the coal came from South Wales.

Michael had been looking forward to seeing his sister who, was stationed there with the WRNS. But he experienced disappointment as, having been in Aden for eighteen months, his sister had sailed for home only ten days previously, which meant that they had passed each other somewhere in the Canal area. As we stayed overnight, I got a night in bed.

The heat was intense in the Arabian Sea. The all-steel Liberty Ship retained the heat of the day throughout most of the night and I found it nigh impossible to get to sleep, despite only wearing underpants, with the both portholes open and the electric fan stirring the air. The answer seemed to be to sleep on deck and, as the gunners had hammocks, Eric and I asked one if he could get a couple for us. With his usual humour, Eric said that he would sling his outside the Chief Engineer's cabin with one end through the porthole and round the Chief's neck! The gunner had promised his to the 5th Engineer, but got one for me from one of his pals. The hammock, however, had no rope attached to it. I asked the Bosun for rope, but was told that he could supply it only with the Mate's permission. Mr Guppy obliged and I got a quantity of rope yarn plus a stout piece of rope for each end. The rope yarn had to be fed through the eyelets in the hammock and spliced

Hospital ship *Tairea* leaving Aden.

in order to support the weight. Huw showed me how to do this and after some hours of work on deck during time off watch, with others giving me a hand, the hammock was ready for use. I slung it across the corner of the small open area of the bridge-deck behind the accommodation and, to make myself as comfortable as possible, laid a blanket and pillows on it together with a sheet to cover and protect me from the morning dew. Wearing only pyjama bottoms, I clambered carefully in at 8 p.m. and, as the knots were somewhat slack, the hammock immediately dropped a bit so that I lay only inches from the deck. It was a beautiful starry night, but as I had not slept in a hammock before and it was so marvellous to lie in the cool air looking at the stars, I never slept a wink. Only the standby quartermaster, clattering his way to and from the bridge, disturbed me before Caro made a hasty trip from the wireless room to tell me it was 'one bell' and time to go on watch.

I was so tired that my watch dragged that night. I ate the sandwiches provided only a half-hour into the watch and an apple shortly afterwards. The quartermaster brought a mug of the ghastly over-sweetened tea and a slice of toast at 2 a.m. and I rose from my chair to pace the deck in order to keep awake. By the time 4 a.m. arrived, I was ready for my hammock. Parkin, as usual, ignored the 'one bell' of the quartermaster and I had, as usual, to nip along to his cabin to rouse him before he relieved me ten minutes into his watch. When my head hit the pillow in my hammock this time, I fell immediately to sleep.

It was already daylight, and only 6 a.m. on a bright sunny morning when I awoke to find myself being covered with large flakes of black soot floating down from the funnel. The 2nd Engineer had decided to 'blow tubes' and my bed was in a mess. I hastily rose, untied the hammock and took it indoors before crawling into my bunk and having about an hour's sleep before breakfast. Consequently the forenoon was spent scrubbing the hammock before returning it to the gunner. The escapade was not a total loss, however, as it gave everybody a laugh and, having seen what happened to me, Eric and the 5th handed their hammocks back unused.

But heat was not the only thing which kept me awake. The cabin which I shared with Caro was separated from the wireless room by only the Captain's shower room. The door of the wireless room was never shut and, during Caro's evening watch, Parkin and he listened to the Overseas Service of the BBC on the broadcast receiver. Night after night, I had to get out of bed between 8 and 9 p.m., and sometimes later, to ask them to keep the noise down. They were a pain in the neck and it was more the sound of their laughing at such programmes as *Mediterranean Merry-Go-Round* that kept me from getting to sleep. And, when I complained, the noise would be reduced for only a short period before it started up again.

Then there was the aforementioned problem of getting Parkin out of his bunk to take over his watch at 4 a.m. As he invariably ignored the one-bell call of the quartermaster, i.e. the call 15 minutes before a watch begins, I took to nipping along to his cabin before 4 a.m. to try to rouse him. Usually, this had no effect. He would mumble, but, when he still did not appear, I would have to go again and he would, regularly, not take over from me until 4.15. I suppose this would have been rectified had I complained to Gepp, but, as I have said, Parkin was not unpleasant and, at sea, you have to live with your colleagues.

I wrote an Air Letter home during the passage from Port Tewfik to Bombay. I began it at 5 a.m. on Saturday 7 April when I was on watch in the Red Sea and broke a sentence to say 'Gee, is this Saturday?' Weekends and public holidays have no meaning for seafarers. I completed the letter in the Arabian Sea and posted it in Bombay where all references to Bombay were obliterated by the purple ink of the censor. My parents, however, had no difficulty in deducing my whereabouts as, in the Red Sea, I wrote: 'How would you like to be aboard here Dad? Just think – in another fortnight or so I'll be having tiffin and reading the *Times of India*.' And this got through.

As we crossed the Arabian Sea, some of the fellows took pot shots, with rifles, at sharks although I never saw one of the creatures. We docked in Bombay to discharge the remainder of our cargo on 20 April.

CHAPTER 34

BOMBAY

India had been the greatest experience of my father's life. He talked about it throughout his life and, appropriately, it was a Sikh doctor who attended him during his terminal illness. In 1915, when he was seventeen, he joined the City of Dundee 2/1 Fortress Company of the Royal Engineers (Territorials). On the last Saturday evening of November 1916, they set off for France, but while at Overton in Hampshire he was transferred into the 9th Battalion of the Worcestershire Regiment who went to India. His love of India stemmed principally from his five months at Wellington Barracks in Ootacumund convalescing from a serious bout of malaria, and where he was free to tramp the Nilgiri Hills with his camera. He still used the same Kodak folding camera, but as the 130-type films were now hard to find, I tried throughout the voyage to get them without success. I was glad to see Bombay because I had been hearing about India all my life and both my father and I spent our twentieth birthdays in India.

We were disappointed to find that no mail awaited our arrival, but it did arrive on 24 April and I received eight letters. The oldest, with photographs from Inez in Saint John, was dated 19 February while the most recent was from my parents and dated 10 April. Because she was engaged, I was surprised to hear that Inez wanted to correspond (In 1947, Inez came to London to meet her fiancé and his family and the engagement was broken off).

At last, Captain Gepp received a reply to his second letter to Holts regarding my salary. The letter, dated 11 April 1945, read:

Wireless. With reference to your letter of the 14th March, 1945, we do not appear to have received your letter regarding the pay of Mr. I. Malcolm your 3rd Radio Officer. The position is that on and after 1st April 1943 all applicants holding PMG Special Certificates first entering

the Marine Wireless Service shall be known as Assistant Radio Officers
and shall be paid at the following rates:–

With less than 12 months' experience as an
Assistant Radio Officer at sea   £8. 0. 0. per month
With 12 months' and less than 24 months'
experience as an Assistant Radio Officer
at sea   £10. 0. 0
With 24 months' experience and over as an
Assistant Radio Officer at sea   £12. 0. 0

If an Assistant Radio Officer obtains a 1st or 2nd Class P.M.G.Certificate,
he will, from the date he obtains such a Certificate be paid at the
appropriate rate for Radio Officers shown in Clause IV (a) of the
Agreement and he will be credited with his accrued sea service.

   Mr. Malcolm unfortunately [the word 'unfortunately' was crossed
out] signed on Articles in July 1943 before we were in possession of the
above information. His seniority dates from 6th July 1943 and the rate
as shown on your Articles (£10. per month) is therefore correct. He is of
course entitled to War Risk Bonus.

Gepp was sympathetic and, of course, I had been fortunate in being
'overpaid' on the *Samite* and Holts made no attempt to recover the
overpayment. But it seemed that the ship owners had got together to
reduce our rates of pay as soon as the war was going our way and the
supply of radio officers was no longer critical. It would have been common
courtesy for Calverley to have informed me of my reduction in pay. I may
say that the contents of the letter did not come as a complete surprise. I
had seen a copy of the Agreement during the voyage, but thought that
Holts were paying rates above those laid down by the National Maritime
Board, which they most certainly did after the war. But, although Holts
was among the elite of shipping companies and I was proud to sail on
their fine ships, they were in no way philanthropic and we worked hard
for the extra remuneration when peacetime working was resumed and the
Ministry of War Transport was no longer footing the bill.

   It was some distance from the ship to the dock gate and the Army
captain whom we had carried from Port Tewfik put a jeep at our disposal
to convey us to the gate. I learned this when an enthusiastic young seaman,
at the wheel of the jeep, told a couple of us to jump in as we descended
from the gangway. As soon as we were in the jeep, we became aware of
the driver's inadequacy when he had trouble with the gears and banged
into some cases on the quay. When I enquired if he had ever driven one of

these things before he cheerfully answered in the negative, but managed nevertheless, to get us to the dock gate without further mishap.

Bombay takes its name from the Portuguese word *bombaim*, which means 'good harbour'. In Hindi it is called Bambai, but in Gujarati and Marathi it has always been known as Mumbai and this is now the official name of the City. The change was made on 1 May 1995 by a newly-elected state government, and without the required permission of the Indian Government which had, twice before, refused it. The same state government also changed the names of other cities, including that of Poona, which is now Pune. The reason for this is to get rid of the colonial legacy and Ootacamund, nicknamed 'Snooty Ooty', now suffers the significant handicap of being called Uthagamandalam! Although Hindi has replaced English as the principal language of India, a significant amount of the buisness in the India parliament, modelled on the British parliament, is still conducted in English. Situated on a peninsula known as Bombay Island, Bombay had a population of under two million. Today, with a population of over eight million, it has spilled onto the mainland and overtaken Calcutta in being the most overcrowded city in India.

I found central Bombay attractive with wide thoroughfares and beautiful buildings. Like my father before me, I roamed with my camera and soaked in the busy yet pleasant atmosphere. Ayahs tended white children on the lawn beside the University, men walked in sandals with their shirt tails hanging out (a fashion now adopted in Britain), and the traffic, impeded at times by unattended sacred cows, consisted of push carts, bullock carts, cyclists, horse-drawn gharries, single-deck trams and double-deck buses. Once outside the dock gate, we could take a tram or a gharri into town. I went by tram, but, on the odd occasion, returned by gharri when the driver always tried to overcharge.

Indian currency is now metric and there are 100 paisas to the rupee. Prior to metrication, there were 16 annas and 64 pice to the rupee. In 1945, the rupee was worth about 1/6d (7½p) and shop prices never included the humble pice. In the better shops you paid the price asked for, but in the lesser ones and in the bazaar, you always bargained. I bought two souvenirs for my parents. One was an engraved and painted brass powder bowl, which I got for 8 Rs after managing to knock the price down from 12. The other was a beautifully-carved ivory figurine of a man in a cloak playing a pipe. I got the latter from a salesman who was delivering figurines to the shop in the entrance of a Service club and he did not want to sell it to me. I saw it in his open suitcase when he was at the counter of the shop, but, when I asked how much he wanted for it, he explained that he sold only to shops and it took some persuasion to get him to part with it. He eventually let me have it for 15 Rs which, he said, was a little more

Young salesman, Bombay.

than the wholesale price and I later had it valued at between 25 and 30 Rs.

In retirement, my father did the dusting in the house and, to him, it was never a chore to dust the many ornaments from abroad, which he valued only for their association with the places from which they came. He broke the feather off the turban of the ivory figure and glued it back on. My mother's reaction was, 'He breaks everything' and, indeed, in his eighties, he did break a few things which he bitterly regretted. I now have the ivory figure, but, to me, the glued-on feather serves as a reminder of the pleasure he got from this souvenir of India. I also have the two soapstone figurines of Hindu gods which he was given in payment for photographic work done for a fellow soldier.

When Huw and I were in town one afternoon, we came across a shop where the proprietor claimed that all his stock had to be cleared by the 5 May although we rather suspected that the date was likely to be advanced! I bought a white tropical shirt for 3 Rs (knocked down from 4Rs 8As), but Huw was interested in a small attaché case, priced at 14 Rs 8 As. He got it, I thought too easily, for 12 Rs, so I hauled down a bigger one and offered the same price for it. The proprietor feigned incredulity. He explained that the case was larger so that it was impossible to let it go at the price of the smaller one. But, after leaving and returning to the shop two or three times, I got it for 12 Rs and all Huw could say was, 'Gee Whiz!' On the funny side, the shirt I bought did not fit me so that I went back to the shop a day or so later, ransacked it for one that did, and eventually got a replacement after finding flaws in the first half dozen examined. I also had to return to another shop with a high-necked, short sleeved cotton singlet (today it would be called a T-shirt) which I had bought the same day. I had been assured that it would fit perfectly, but it turned out to be size 32 instead of the 36 which I required. The proprietor of this shop tried to claim that I had bought the singlet somewhere else, but in the end I again left with a replacement. On the same day I made these purchases, I bought a pair of leather sandals for 7 Rs 10 As.

At last I managed to replace the record of the first part of Tchaikovsky's No. 1 Piano Concerto which had been broken during the rail journey to Avonmouth. I bought it in H.M.V. & Columbia Salon in Sir Phirozshah Mehta Road, Fort for 5 Rs 8 As, which was less than half the price it sold for in the UK. As in Larg's music shop in Dundee, the salon had sound-proof booths where you could listen to records, but in Bombay it was a stately, turbaned Sikh who held the door open for me to enter the booth. In Dundee, the girl sales-assistant had sat with me listening to records and was interested in the transaction. But the Sikh was not a salesman and his job was only to escort customers to the booths so that, in spite of the man's demeanour, there was a touch of servility which I found embarrassing.

Huw Davies (left) and self, Bombay.

The other record I bought that day was one of Victor Silvester and His Orchestra. On one side it had 'The Homecoming Waltz' and on the other, 'If I Had My Way'. Victor Silvester was always a favourite of mine and after seeing him interviewed on BBC Television in January 1978, I wrote telling him of how I had learned to dance to his music at Robertson's Palais de Danse in Dundee. I received a nice reply and am glad that I wrote as he collapsed and died only six months later on a beach near Nice. The records sold in Bombay were made at Dum-Dum, near Calcutta, better known for the production of its dreadful bullets.

I said earlier that Michael seemed to want to travel the world in order to learn the different dances, but the same accusation might be levelled at me as I went dancing at every opportunity. In Bombay, there were dances at some Service club or other every night of the week. I went by myself to dances at the YMCA and the Town Hall. All were from 7 to 9 p.m., and women were always in such short supply that the men rushed for partners. On the evening of Tuesday 1 May, I attended the dance at the Town Hall and had been up at a number of dances when Parkin and Caro appeared in white uniform, but were politely asked to leave as the dance was not for officers. I was also in uniform, but because I was in khaki, I was not noticed until near the end of the evening when I happened to land beside the elderly army captain, with a slight limp, who was in charge. He smiled and asked, 'How did you get in here?' and I cleverly replied, 'Through that door over there.' Although the pleasant captain ignored my cheek and told me that there was a dance for officers at the Taj Mahal Hotel, I immediately regretted my *clever* reply.

At the YM, I danced with white girls in European dress, ATS girls, Indian girls in saris and an Indian lieutenant in the Indian equivalent of the ATS. I particularly remember an afternoon dance when I asked an Anglo-Indian up to dance. When she rose from her seat, I found that she was only about half my size so that the dance was an embarrassment. Anglo-Indian women are among the most beautiful in the world, but Anglo-Indians, who were disparagingly referred to as chichis (chee-chees), suffered from being neither European nor Indian and, when independence came to India in 1947, they were treated very badly.

We went, by magnificent Marine Drive, to swim at Breach Candy which was exclusive to Forces personnel and where there were two pools: one indoor and one outdoor. To get to the outdoor pool, separated from the Indian Ocean by only the beach and a strip of concrete, you had to walk past the indoor pool and I wondered why people were swimming there in preference to swimming in the open air. I soon found out. The south-west monsoon had not yet broken. The air temperature was 86°F and that of the outdoor pool about 90°F. On the ship, awnings had been stretched across the central accommodation to shield us from the heat which, however, was not nearly so oppressive as the heat we had experienced in the Arabian Sea.

After swimming at Breach Candy on Saturday 28 April, a group of us had tea at the Excelsior Restaurant in Hornby Road before going on to the Eros Cinema to see *The Thief of Bagdad*. My meal cost me 2 Rs 6 As and the cinema seat 1 Rs 2 As, which included a 2 As tax. The latter was the reduced price for 'Defence Forces in Uniform' and, as seats were bookable, the ticket specified a particular seat. Although dances ended at 9 p.m., the last cinema performance began at 9.30 p.m.

The journey into town from the dock gate by tramcar cost only 1 anna. The tram company was the Bombay E. S. & Tramways Co. Ltd. and although the fare and 'Subject to the Company's bye laws' were printed in English, Gujarati and Marathi on their tickets, the stop names were only in English. The top part listed numbers while the bottom half named the stops to which the numbers referred. When I went from stop No. 4 at the dock gate, which was Ballard Pier, to stop 24, which was BYC Bridge, the conductor punched a hole in number 24 on my ticket.

Returning to the docks one dark evening with Arthur Hardaker, before boarding a tram on the dock road, we crossed a square where we had to run the gauntlet of a number of young Indians shouting abuse at us. I was carrying the large teddy bear which Arthur had bought for one of his children when the Indians were shouting 'Dirty British, go home'. While the incident was unpleasant, I sympathised with their wish for independence, but did not realise at the time so many of them would want to go 'home' with me! When we negotiated that Bombay square in the late evenings, we had to step over people sleeping on the pavement. But, when I mentioned this to an Indian student at Edinburgh University some fifteen years later, he insisted that these people were not homeless and preferred to sleep on pavements because of the heat indoors!

On Sunday 29 April, Bill Dawson and I failed in our attempt to hire bikes so that we settled for seeing the City from the open top deck of buses. We saw quite a bit of the poor districts and stopped off at various points in order to see the arch of the Gateway of India and the Prince of Wales Museum, where many locals were taking an interest in the exhibits. I formed the opinion that it was safer to walk through a native quarter in Bombay than down Sista Street in Alexandria.

The war in Europe was nearing its end. It was announced on 3 May that the Italian Campaign was over and rumoured that Hitler was dead. I wrote that day that I had spoken to a soldier who had been fighting in Burma and was waiting to go home on leave. He had told me that 80 per cent of the casualties were due to illnesses such as malaria and dysentery

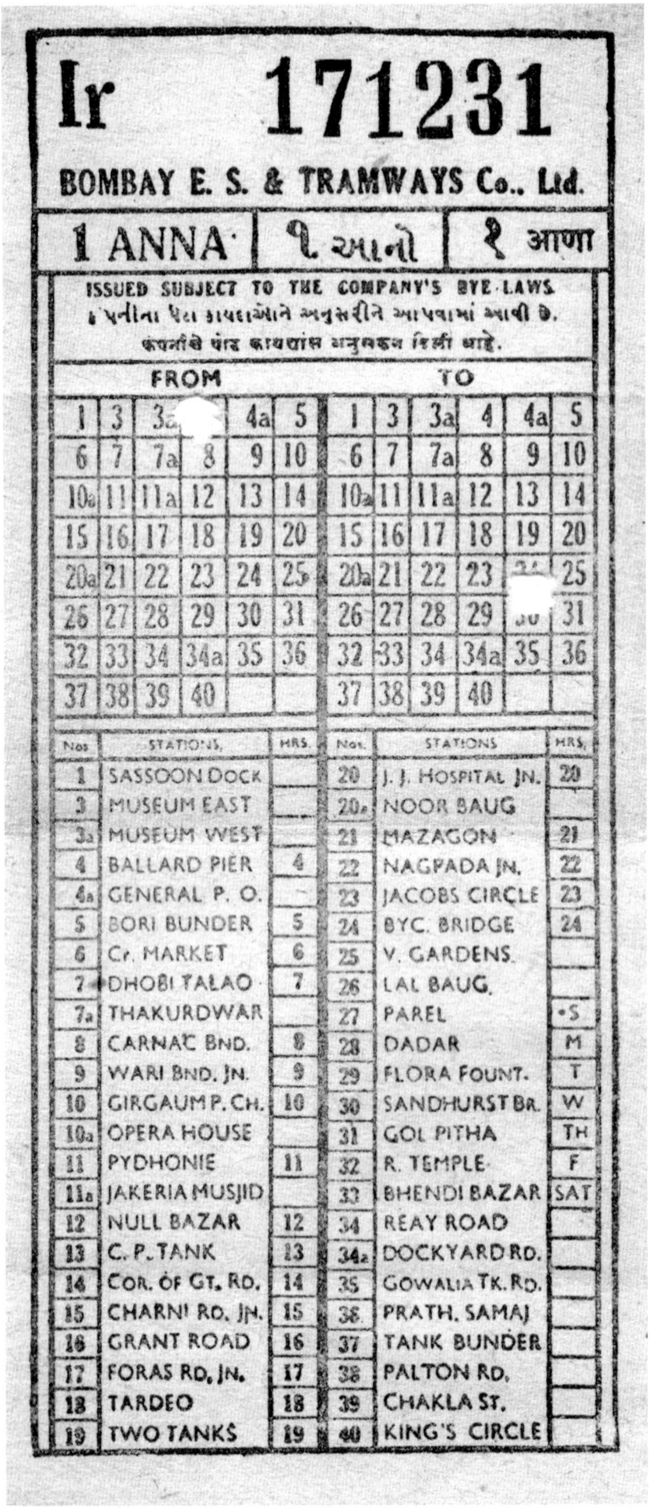

Ir 171231

BOMBAY E. S. & TRAMWAYS Co., Ltd.

1 ANNA	૧ આનો	१ आणा

ISSUED SUBJECT TO THE COMPANY'S BYE-LAWS.
કંપનીના પેટા કાયદાઓને અનુસરીને આપવામાં આવી છે.
कंपनीचे पोट कायदांस अनुसरून दिली आहे.

FROM						TO					
1	3	3a	[illegible]	4a	5	1	3	3a	4	4a	5
6	7	7a	8	9	10	6	7	7a	8	9	10
10a	11	11a	12	13	14	10a	11	11a	12	13	14
15	16	17	18	19	20	15	16	17	18	19	20
20a	21	22	23	24	25	20a	21	22	23	[illegible]	25
26	27	28	29	30	31	26	27	28	29	[illegible]	31
32	33	34	34a	35	36	32	33	34	34a	35	36
37	38	39	40			37	38	39	40		

Nos	STATIONS	HRS.	Nos.	STATIONS	HRS.
1	SASSOON DOCK		20	J. J. HOSPITAL JN.	20
3	MUSEUM EAST		20a	NOOR BAUG	
3a	MUSEUM WEST		21	MAZAGON	21
4	BALLARD PIER	4	22	NAGPADA JN.	22
4a	GENERAL P. O.		23	JACOBS CIRCLE	23
5	BORI BUNDER	5	24	BYC. BRIDGE	24
6	Cr. MARKET	6	25	V. GARDENS	
7	DHOBI TALAO	7	26	LAL BAUG	
7a	THAKURDWAR		27	PAREL	S
8	CARNAC BND.	8	28	DADAR	M
9	WARI BND. JN.	9	29	FLORA FOUNT.	T
10	GIRGAUM P. CH.	10	30	SANDHURST BR.	W
10a	OPERA HOUSE		31	GOL PITHA	TH
11	PYDHONIE	11	32	R. TEMPLE	F
11a	JAKERIA MUSJID		33	BHENDI BAZAR	SAT
12	NULL BAZAR	12	34	REAY ROAD	
13	C. P. TANK	13	34a	DOCKYARD RD.	
14	COR. OF GT. RD.	14	35	GOWALIA TK. RD.	
15	CHARNI RD. JN.	15	36	PRATH. SAMAJ	
16	GRANT ROAD	16	37	TANK BUNDER	
17	FORAS RD. JN.	17	38	PALTON RD.	
18	TARDEO	18	39	CHAKLA ST.	
19	TWO TANKS	19	40	KING'S CIRCLE	

Tram ticket,
Bombay.

Bill Dawson, Syd Thompson, self and W. Willsteed.

and I said in my letter that I had 'a bobby's job compared to these fellows' and that 'when the war in Europe does end, I hope the folk at home don't forget the boys of the 14th Army on the Burma Front'. They were largely 'forgotten' even then and history has not done them justice. In the evening of that day, Eric and I went ashore to have a haircut before going to the New Empire Cinema to see Boris Karloff in *Arsenic and Old Lace*. I did not really need a haircut, but had my hair cut very short because we were about to sail and it would be some time before we reached another port. The following day, I cancelled the allotment deducted from my pay on the grounds that I had some idea of where we were heading and needed the money to buy things to take home.

I told Captain Gepp about travelling to Liverpool with Mr Mitchell and how he had said to look him up if I were ever in Bombay. It turned out that Gepp had a friend employed by Shell and through him I learned that Mr Mitchell had been transferred to Rawalpindi in the Punjab. When Gepp informed me of this, he smiled and said it was a pity as 'It would always have been a free lunch'. But it would have been nice to have seen Mr Mitchell again and he might have shown me a bit more of Bombay. I was now sending home snaps which I had developed and printed myself and had purchased a book called *Photography in India* which provided some useful tips.

The rigid censorship to which my first letter home had been subjected was not applied to all subsequent letters. The word 'India' was left in

N° 11871

THE NEW EMPIRE
Direction : Western India Theatres Ltd.

Saturday.........9-30 p. m.

Defence Forces in Uniform

STALLS | Adm. Rs. 1-0-0
Tax , 0-2-0
Rs. 1-2-0

Row............ Seat.........

Cinema ticket, Bombay.

Showing
unlowered
torpedo net and
life raft, Indian
Ocean.

my second letter, but 'Bombay' and place names in the city were deleted
from my third letter. My final letter, however, written over 3 to 6 May,
went unmolested although I mentioned Bombay, the Taj Mahal Hotel, the
Gateway of India and the Prince of Wales Museum. My experience was
that censorship was seldom consistent and different censors had different
ideas as to what should be eliminated. On RN vessels, an officer was given
the job of censoring all letters from the ship, but, as it was only rarely that
an officer was entrusted with this job on merchant ships, I presume that
Armed Forces personnel censored our mail. But I was always responsible
and restricted myself in the use of information and of place names when I
considered it wise to do so. The day before we left Bombay, Michael and
I had tea at a Service club then came across a park where hundreds of

Indians were spending the evening playing hockey, football in their bare feet, and cricket. We enjoyed ourselves by joining in a game of cricket.

We sailed on the afternoon of Sunday 6 May and our departure from the quay is unlikely ever to have been forgotten by Michael Shaw. We had a number of cats on board and, when the ropes were cast off and we were moving slowly from the quay, our big tomcat, walking along the gunwale, missed its footing and fell into the dock. Michael, unfortunately, was doing something on the side of the ship directly below so that the cat fell onto his head, which it badly clawed in an attempt to save itself, before landing in the water. We were only a few yards from the quay and the cat had no difficulty in swimming to it and mounting the stone steps. Gepp put the ship back, had the gangway lowered and our pet climbed back on board. Now devoid of Sammy 1 and Sammy 2, we sailed independently and light ship. There was no secrecy about our destination, Lourenço Marques in Portuguese East Africa, and I never saw India again.

CHAPTER 35

THE WAR IN EUROPE ENDS AND LOURENÇO MARQUES

We were two days out from Bombay when, on 8 May 1945, Victory in Europe (VE) Day was proclaimed. There was no great rejoicing on the ship and I believe that everyone, like myself, was just relieved that that conflict was at an end. During my night watch, I listened to the Overseas Service of the BBC which gave commentaries on the celebrations in various cities throughout the world. The commentator located in London's Trafalgar Square described the wild scene there, where the crowd was so dense that individuals were carried along with it. But I felt no jubilation, and only a great sadness for those who had lost loved ones or whose lives had been destroyed in the protracted and senseless conflict. Most certainly Nazi Germany had to be defeated, but had Britain and France stopped Hitler from rearming Germany, in contravention of the Treaty of Versailles, when he came to power in 1933, there would have been no Second World War. A blight on the victory celebrations occurred in Halifax, Nova Scotia where about 1,000 navy men, assisted by some merchant seamen and dregs, including women, of the local population, rioted. It started by a streetcar being set alight, then liquor stores were broken into, shops looted and the centre of the town badly damaged. It was a shameful episode in the history of the town which had shown such hospitality to sailors and contributed so much to the winning of the Battle of the Atlantic.

As the *Samforth* was in the Japanese Theatre of War, we still sailed 'blacked-out'. The weather was good and it became pleasantly cooler as we proceeded south. During the passage, I made my first crossing of the Line/Equator, but nothing was made of the event other than that I bought soft drinks for a few shipmates who were not on watch in the early evening. We dropped anchor off Lourenço Marques on Sunday 20 May, berthed on Tuesday morning, but were sent out to anchor again the following day. And we remained at anchor in the bay until taken alongside again on Monday 28 May, to load coal.

The day after our arrival, I received nine letters, including one from A. & S. Henry & Co., Limited in Dundee. Dated 5 May 1945, it was a blurred carbon copy with my name inserted and read:

Dear Ian,

In view of present developments in Europe and elsewhere which hold out the prospect of the war with Germany ending shortly – perhaps even before this letter reaches you – we are preparing our plans for the resumption of peace-time trading.

We have no doubt that you have given this matter some thought and we should be glad to know by return airmail/mail whether you intend to apply for reinstatement in our employment.

While we cannot at this stage give you any indication of the nature of the employment that may be available, you will realise that in an organisation such as ours there are excellent opportunities for active young men.

If possible, please let us know your Group Number under the Age and Length of Service Scheme for demobilisation.

Yours faithfully,
A. & S. Henry & Co., Limited
(signed) G. Archbold

As I fully expected to return to the firm, I was surprised to learn that I had to 'apply for reinstatement'. But as the letter referred to 'excellent opportunities for active young men', it appeared that they wanted me back and I answered in the affirmative. I wrote home saying that I didn't intend 'pushing a pen around for a couple of pound a week' when I left the MN and that I intended making something of myself by learning a foreign language such as Spanish. My Group Number, commonly referred to as your Demob. (Demobilisation) Number, may have been 54.

Portugal had remained neutral throughout the war, and it was a unique experience to be in a neutral port. There was reputed to be a German merchant ship in port, but no reports reached us of any trouble between crews. The neutrality, however, had a direct bearing on my work and, instead of having all night in my bunk as I usually did when in port, I had to listen for instructions from RugbyRadio (GBR) at 2 a.m. every morning. Had we gone into Durban, an Allied port, these instructions would have been brought on board to Gepp, but, as it was, they were transmitted as BAMS Messages, in a 5-figure code. The first of these transmissions lasted the best part of an hour, so I copied an extremely long message which was decoded by Parkin and Caro after breakfast. Decoding was done by using our secret book and was quite simple. The key, which was varied, was contained in the first group of figures and the message notified all Allied ships on procedure now that the war was over in Europe. At the time, I just accepted that the broadcasts were made during my midnight to 4 a.m. watch, but in retrospect, and had I been No. 1, I would not have devolved responsibility to a junior while I lay comfortably in my bunk. When Gepp received the long decoded message, he made a point of congratulating me on my work.

The crew had been given a football by the Missions to Seamen in Bombay and, during our first day alongside, we had an enjoyable game on the quay. When we were taken out to anchor again, and as we had no cargo, we had a game at the bottom of No. 2 hold. But although this was great fun, we abandoned the practice when it was found that the ball was being destroyed by being kicked against the steel hull of the ship.

Lourenço Marques, on Delagoa Bay, was named after a sixteenth-century Portuguese trader. It had a population of about 100,000, including some 28,000 Europeans, and I considered it the best laid-out city I had visited. The cathedral, with its long, tapering tower surmounted by a cross, was the most outstanding building and the railway station, built in the same white stone, was aesthetically superior to New York's Grand Central. In front of the station was a garden with palm trees and trees, and the roots of the trees played havoc with the decorated mosaic pavements of the town's streets. I enjoyed the solitude of the Vasco da Gama Gardens and the whole place was beautifully clean. The Portuguese lived in lovely houses with Negro servants attending to their needs. All the menial work was done by the blacks and, as in Bombay, I saw native girls looking after white children. What I did not see was where the blacks lived, which was on the outskirts of the city and which I heard disparagingly referred to as 'Jungle Town'. The shops were well stocked and it appeared that the Portuguese had never wanted for anything throughout the war. But, for us, everything was expensive. I took pictures as usual, but when I ran out of film, decided to wait until another port before replenishing my stock. One dark evening, I steadied my camera on a telephone junction box and took a time exposure of the railway station. A bus, with headlights on, passed as I did this, but I let the camera run on and much to my amazement, there was no sign of the bus on the picture. The city was well lit by round white globes displaying 'white' electric light. This gave the place a cheerful appearance and, in my opinion, is vastly superior to the dismal orange lighting which 'experts' have inflicted on us in Britain, and which serves to increase the driechness of our towns in winter.

There were no dancehalls that I knew of in Lourenço Marques, but there were three cinemas. One of these, owned by African Consolidated Theatres, Ltd., was the Scala and the name of the owners suggests that they were not Portuguese. I visited the Scala on two occasions. Seats in the 'galeria' cost 7 escudos 50 centavos (1/6d or 7½p) and all seats were bookable. During our stay, two of the cinemas showed American films, with Portuguese subtitles, while the other showed a Portuguese film.

As our departure drew near, our thoughts turned again to haircuts and, two days before we left, Huw and I had a wander round town before having our hair cut and returning to the ship for dinner. In the evening, I sat late yarning with Eric, and the next day accompanied him on the same mission ashore. There was always a great camaraderie on the ship. We wandered into each other's cabins and, while I wrote a letter home, Huw played Hungarian Rhapsody, his favourite, on my gramophone. He also helped me consume the 2 kilos of peanuts which I had bought for 5 escudos (1s or 5p) and we amused ourselves by throwing them in the air and catching them in our mouths. The day before we sailed, I spent 44 escudos (roughly 9s or 45p) on mint Mozambique postage stamps for my father.

Loading coal is never a pleasant experience and, as all portholes have to be closed and ventilators blocked to keep out the dust, it is particularly unpleasant in hot weather. Fortunately, it was autumn in the Southern Hemisphere and only pleasantly warm. And Lourenço Marques, with its modern facilities, was one of the fastest coaling ports in the world. To load

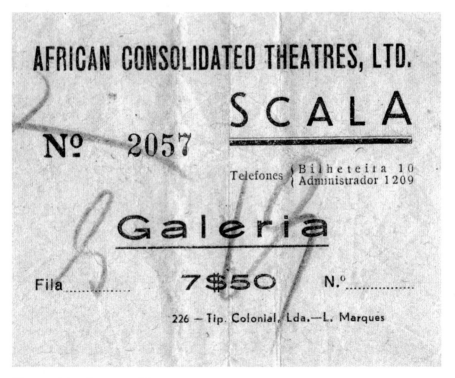

Cinema ticket, Lourenço Marques.

a 7,000 ton ship in 4/5 days was fast, but the loading went on day and night and was not only dirty, but noisy. The coal, brought by rail from mines in the Transvaal, was first loaded into large circular containers/buckets on the quay before cranes swung them over the holds. The explosions caused by the dropping of the coal from the buckets into our five holds were considerable. There was coal dust everywhere. Closed portholes and stopped-up ventilators could not prevent it from coming into our living quarters. There was a film of coal dust over everything in our cabins, and it even entered our hair and clothes. The evening before we sailed, half the crew went ashore to escape from it. Eric was one of them and he went to see the film *Above Suspicion* which he had already seen. 'Anything,' he said, 'is better than remaining on board here.' I, nevertheless, remained on board to write home. After all, I, too, had already seen the film!

It was therefore with considerable relief that we sailed from Lourenço Marques. The decks were hosed down to rid the ship of the coal dust and we showered and changed into clean clothes. But I was to undergo the same coaling experience in the port on two other occasions the following year and subjected to a great deal more discomfort in far hotter places.

Bill Dawson had purchased two chameleons in the port and it now amused us to watch the movements and colour changes of these interesting creatures who were generally on the white-painted large diameter pipes which ran through his cabin, just below the deck-head.

We sailed on Saturday 2 June and I looked forward eagerly to our next port-of-call – Montevideo, Uruguay! Blue Funnel was not a tramp company, but all ships were tramps during, and for sometime after, the war and I never liked the sea better than when tramping, as you never knew where you were heading next. It was an adventure and when I eventually sailed, voyage after voyage, on the same route to the Far East, I became bored. I enjoyed being on much finer vessels than SAM BOATS, but a regular route destroyed the adventure and I came to equate it with a bus run. Lourenço Marques was renamed Maputo after Mozambique gained independence from Portugal in 1975 and, no doubt, the imposing tall statue of 'Mother Portugal' suffered the same fate as that of de Lesseps at Port Said.

I neglected to mention that, during the passage to Lourenço Marques, a rash appeared in my crotch which became so bad and uncomfortable that I eventually consulted the Chief Steward – our medical officer in the absence of a doctor. Recognising it to be 'dhobi itch', he painted the affected area, on this and subsequent occasions, with a bright red substance. This did the trick, but the cure was worse than the complaint as it virtually burned the rash away. My discomfort didn't escape my shipmates. When, after a session with the Steward, they saw me standing with legs apart and in agony, their remarks were far from sympathetic!

CHAPTER 36

LIGHTS ON TO MONTEVIDEO

The instructions contained in the long coded message I had taken down in Lourenço Marques informed Captain Gepp of the line of longitude chosen to delineate the Japanese Theatre of War from the now peaceful ocean to the west. It is likely to have been 20° East, directly south of Cape Agulhas, and the evening of the day we crossed that line would never be forgotten by any of us on the *Samforth*. Everyone came on deck to see the deck lights switched on, and we stood like small children at a fairground to marvel at the fully illuminated ship. No longer would we have to close every porthole or use porthole ventilator covers, see that outside doors were closed and curtains drawn over them or be fearful of lighting even a cigarette which could disclose our presence to an unseen enemy. For us, it was the end of the war. But we were lucky. To the east of 20° East, in Burma and the Far East, the war continued. And the war against Japan seemed set to continue for a long time. In the distance, as we rounded South Africa, we had the added comfort of seeing lights twinkling from a friendly shore.

The passage across the South Atlantic seemed a long one, as the sea was against us all the way so that the ship pitched and rolled. It was nothing like the fearful weather experienced in the North Atlantic, but the continual motion of the ship tired us. The fiddles round the meal tables were up and tablecloths were dampened to prevent dishes sliding off. Walking on sloping decks required effort, and even sitting was tiring as we had to brace our feet against the roll of the ship. But there were days when the sun shone and we had the company of albatross and many small birds. I had never before seen albatross and it was a delight to watch these birds, with their large wingspan, gliding along beside us. They were there to collect food scraps thrown overboard and, at night, they rested on the ship.

As always, we listened to the Overseas Service of the BBC and, on 23 June, exactly three weeks after leaving Lourenço Marques, I was annoyed because, having already had a news bulletin at midday, the one o'clock news was extended into half the time allocated to the Merchant Navy Programme. During the passage I listened to election addresses by representatives of Britain's political parties and was impressed by the one made by Stafford Cripps, but the general feeling was that the Conservative Party would win because of the esteem in which Churchill was held as war leader. As we neared South America, I copied a weather report in Spanish and, with the aid of the Spanish/English dictionary I had bought in Saint John, translated it before sending it to the bridge.

Our ETA (Estimated Time of Arrival) in Montevideo was Saturday 23 June but, due to the adverse weather, it was Monday 25 June before we sailed past the exposed stern of the sunken German pocket-battleship *Graf Spee* in the estuary of the Plate and dropped anchor in the harbour. I stood on deck as we entered and saw the albatross and their cohorts leave us to hover together in the distance. They would latch onto a ship leaving the port and might well fly back across the same miles of ocean they had already crossed.

While at anchor, I took a picture of the city with the *Ocean Liberty*, alongside a quay, in the foreground. The *Ocean Liberty* was one of the first of the Ocean ships built in the US to the design of J. L. Thompson & Sons of Sunderland. The Canadian-built Fort 'boats' also stemmed from the Thompson design, as did the Liberties. The Liberties, however, differed markedly in appearance from the Oceans and Forts in that they had a single accommodation-block amidships. Another main difference was that they were oil and not coal burners.

After only a short time at anchor, we moved alongside and, within an hour of docking, eagerly awaited mail arrived. I received eleven letters and a postcard, and the best news I received that day was that John Noble's father had arrived home safely after six years as a prisoner of war. John had been my pal throughout those years and, of course, I knew his mother well. It was almost unbelievable their ordeal was over. When I met Mr Noble at the end of the voyage, I found him to be a most gentle and unassuming man and I had difficulty in extracting his experiences from him. He had spent most of the war working on farms in Poland where getting enough to eat was always a problem, and where he had swopped bars of chocolate, received in Red Cross parcels, for bread from the locals. According to him, the worst time was when the Germans surrendered and the prisoners were left to walk all the way west to the British/American lines. His home was in a now demolished tenement at the top of Dundee's Hawkhill, and his homecoming must have been overwhelming as the neighbours slung a large sign across the building which read 'Welcome Home John Noble'. He was a motor mechanic by trade, but, due to the Depression of the thirties, had become a bus driver and he resumed that occupation. When in his late fifties, he and Mrs Noble went on holiday to London to visit John who had gone to work there. But they had no sooner arrived than he had a heart attack and died. No doubt it was because their son had married a daughter of the sports reporter on the Dundee Courier that an obituary appeared in the paper. The obituary was brief and recorded the fact that Mr Noble had been given an extra day's leave of absence by the bus company. No mention was made of his war service.

Because Ian Smart was wearing the ribbon of the 1939-1943 Star, I had written to the ROU (Radio Officers' Union) from Canada about applying for the medal. They had sent me an application form to be completed and returned to the General Register and Record Office of Shipping and Seamen, Llantrisant Road, Cardiff. I had done this and now received the following standard (C. R. S.102) reply, dated 22nd May, 1945.

Dear Sir,
1939-43 STAR.

With reference to your recent application, I enclose herewith a supply of the ribbon of the 1939-43 Star for which you appear to be eligible.

If you hold a British Seaman's Identity Card you should take it with this form and your Discharge Book to any Superintendent of a Mercantile Marine Office, who will make the appropriate endorsement thereon. A change in your permanent address should be notified to this Office.

Yours faithfully,
W. J. KILLINGBACK,
Registrar General.

I. M. Malcolm Esq.

By the time I received my reply from the Registrar General, the name of the medal had been changed to the 1939-45 Star and the medal which I was subsequently given bore that name. The 1939-43 Medal was never struck, but I have the C. R. S. 102 which shows that I was awarded that medal for which I barely qualified and it is interesting to note that it was still being called the 1939-43 Star a fortnight after VE-day. Perhaps, by 1943, the British Government thought that it was about time that our Forces were given a campaign ribbon to wear as US servicemen were not short of them. Incidentally, the following notice appeared in the July 1995 issue of *Sea Breezes* Magazine: 'Merchant Seamen who didn't bother to collect the medals they earned during the war can still get them from the Registry of Shipping and Seamen!'

Montevideo, the capital of Uruguay, is situated on the northern shore of the Rio de la Plata which is not really a river in its own right, but the expansive estuary into which the Rivers Paraná and Uruguay and their tributaries flow. The name Montevideo means 'I see a mountain' and the city is reputed to take its name from a remark made by a Portuguese lookout on Ferdinand Magellan's ship as it approached the area in 1520. No doubt impressed by the flatness of the terrain, the seaman is said to have called out 'Monte vide eu' and the 'mountain', the only pimple on the landscape and no more than 500 feet high, was the Cerro hill which is now within the city limits.

The city, founded by the Spaniards in 1726, was cleverly planned with its wide central avenues running in the same direction as the prevailing south-east trade winds so as to take full advantage of their cooling influence. There are fine public parks and several plazas or squares. Plaza de la Independencia is the main square and the heart of the city. It is a large square with palm trees, grassy areas and several bench seats to allow people to rest awhile and, in the centre, high on a base, is an equestrian statue of José Gervasio Artigas, who fought to gain Uruguay's independence from Spain and is regarded as the Father of Uruguay.

The Hotel Palacio Salvo overlooked the Plaza and was a magnificent building with many of its rooms contained in a majestic tower. Leading off the Plaza is Calle Sarandi, the principal shopping street, and Avenida 18 de Julio (July), considered to be one of the finest boulevards in South America. Montevideo is reputed to be one of the cleanest cities in the world and, for the first time, I saw the walls of a building being cleaned by a steam process. I made full use of the eleven days we stayed in the port, walking the streets with my camera and enjoying using my limited Spanish.

On arrival in port, several of us gave our laundry to a lady who came on board looking for business. We did not ask the price and, when our clothes were returned, we found it so exorbitant that I discussed it with Huw and we decided to stand together and refuse to pay it. But, when the lady came to me for payment, I discovered that, without telling me, Huw had paid the price asked for so that I was left to do likewise.

The highlight of our visit was a concert and dance organised by the Uruguayan Red Cross, but run mostly by the about 1,000-strong British community, on Saturday 30 June. My evening, however, began on a rather sour note owing to the behaviour of some of our crew. I had gone with Eric and the 2nd Engineer and we were sitting at the table reserved for officers, to the right of the door on the ground floor, when Ian Smart arrived to sit at the same table with an AB. As the AB was a decent bloke, we had no objection to this, but shortly afterwards along came Chippy (carpenter) who planked himself beside us and not only had he too much to drink, but he was scruffily dressed. Although I was the most junior officer present, it was left to me to point out to him that the table was for officers, but it was only when the AB coaxed him that he departed with the AB and Ian. They had not long gone, however, when Parkin, Willsteed and Huw arrived with others and proposed to sit twelve at the table meant for about half that number. As Parkin and Willsteed were exuberantly vocal and Huw also was in his cups, I decided it was time to leave and look for another seat. I found one at a table on the balcony where I had a good view of the concert which proved most enjoyable. Apparently the pianist who was to accompany the singers had been unable to attend, and I agonised with the stand-in as he struggled with the music and had someone turning the pages for him. When the concert ended at midnight, dancing began and went on until 4 a.m. Eric left at the finish of the concert, but I stayed till the end and recollect only of dancing with a British teenage girl who was with her family. The ship had discharged her coal and was now lying at anchor well out in the harbour and, as it was barely daylight when I arrived at the quay, I had to wait for some time before I was able to get a launch to carry me across to her.

Trips to and from the shore were costly and late one afternoon I was returning to the ship as the sole passenger on a tender. We were half way to the ship when I learned the fare and, as I considered it excessive, refused to pay it. There was no argument. The boatman made no attempt to negotiate a price, but turned the boat round and took me back to the quay!

On Tuesday 3 July, I was ashore from 2 p.m. till midnight and wandered about taking photographs before meeting Eric in town. We dropped in first at the St Helen's Club, where Eric played the piano for the entertainment of all. We then went on to a dance in Lafone Hall, where dances were held one or twice a week for ships' crews, and enjoyed the pleasant atmosphere together with the tea and cakes served during the interval. It was in Lafone Hall that I met a 1st R/O from Dundee whom I had already met with his 2nd in a Bombay club. Many ships were on the same route and the *Samforth* had made the run from Bombay to Montevideo during her previous voyage. A year or two later, I met this fellow again on the top deck of Dundee tram. He had just graduated BSc, prior to entering teaching, and was temporarily employed parcelling up Beano Comics for D. C. Thomson.

Bill Dawson had found his way to the zoo, and this resulted in Ian Smart and I spending an afternoon there. It was a novel experience for us, although in my opinion the zoo was not as good as that of Edinburgh.

As most films were made in the United States or Britain, we could usually take it for granted that the dialogue was in English, but there was one occasion when I entered a cinema to find it in Spanish and without English subtitles. Most of the films, however, were in English, but I had to leave before performances ended in order to catch the last 'liberty' boat back to the ship.

Because I had cancelled my allotment home, my ship's account was much healthier than it otherwise would have been and I could take advantage of the well-stocked shops. I bought the watch requested by my brother, stamps for my father and a length of cloth which my mother had asked for in order to have it made into a bolero suit. The cloth was beautiful English worsted, unattainable at home where clothes were rationed anyway, and when my mother saw the material, she considered it too good to be made into a bolero suit and requested the tailoress to make a costume for her. As, however, the jacket of an ordinary suit requires more material, the result turned out to be rather too well fitting and allowed no room for expansion! The citizens of Montevideo, incidentally, were noticeably well dressed.

With the pampas on the doorstep, there was no shortage of food and Eric and I had an excellent meal in a very nice restaurant where the tables were covered with white linen tablecloths. The waiter who served us was a stocky man with close-cropped hair which made me think he was German. He had very little English and, trying to be helpful, suggested that I should have 'fiss'. I took his advice and was given a whole 'fiss' which was so big that its head and tail hung over the sides of the plate. It proved to be very good although I had no idea of its breed. Many of the public places displayed a poster of Churchill captioned 'El Hombre del Momento'.

Our last opportunity to go ashore was on Thursday 5 July and the ship was almost deserted that evening when there was a dance on at Lafone Hall. I should liked to have gone, but felt that I had a touch of flu and deemed it prudent to remain on board all day in order to be fit to stand my watch at sea. The US Navy Sailing Card shows the *Samforth* as being in Buenos Aires on 9 July, but this is incorrect as we did not call there. I regretted not seeing BA, on the opposite side of the wide estuary of the Plate and only 130 miles from Montevideo.

On the afternoon of Friday, 6 July, we sailed for Bahia Blanca in the Argentine to load a cargo of wheat for Norway. The port of discharge was unknown, but we knew that we were going via Kirkwall in Orkney.

CHAPTER 37

BAHIA BLANCA

The passage to Bahia Blanca was a short one and we dropped anchor in the bay on Monday 9 July. As we lay at anchor, the Swedish ship *Tonghai* sailed past us outward bound. During the war, ships of neutral countries clearly displayed their identity and TONGHAI – SVERIGE was painted in large letters on her hull. Shortly afterwards, a pilot boarded the *Samforth* and assisted by the tug *Navegador*, we were taken alongside.

It is likely to have been on the morning of the same day that my parents received the following communication from Holts:

DATE AS PER POSTMARK.

Ref. ss/AJD/54

We are glad to be able to advise you that according to telegraphic information just received from abroad your son, I.M.Malcolm is well and his ship has arrived safely in port. We hope to be able to advise you regularly as to his welfare but you must appreciate that it may not be possible for us to maintain complete regularity, and if there is any delay in advising you, you should not assume that anything untoward has happened either to ship or crew.

These advices are the result of a new arrangement for information to be sent regarding the welfare of crews.

ALFRED HOLT & CO.

54, Ullet Road,
Liverpool, 17.

The word 'son' and my name were inserted in what was a standard circular, folded and sent without being put into an envelope. The date of the postmark was 7 VII 45 and, strangely enough, the notice was addressed to me so that it is a wonder that my parents, who very much appreciated the thoughtfulness of the Company, opened it. The collapse of Germany was obviously the major factor in allowing Holts to instigate such a service and that communication is evidence of the fact that the war against Japan was expected to continue for some time.

On arriving in port, we had to fill in a Customs manifest declaring all dutiable goods in our possession. As we were taking the articles home and no-one had any intention of taking them ashore, many paid scant attention to the accuracy of their declarations. This, however, was a mistake. Customs officers boarded another ship and charged duty on everything which they found had not been declared, and we were spared their attention only by Captain Gepp plying the customs officers with cigarettes and whisky.

Bahia Blanca (White Bay), a principal port of the Argentine, was much smaller than Montevideo. It proved to be a pleasant town, but we considered it something of a let-down after Montevideo, where there had been so much to see and do. During most of our time in the latter, we had had the inconvenience and expense of being stuck out in the harbour, but now we could again walk ashore. This advantage was, however, tempered by the fact that we docked at Ingeniero White, four miles from the town, so that it was an hour's round trip to town and back by bus, over a bumpy road made only of stone. But there was a Mission to Seamen at Ingenerio White and the good people of the mission did a great deal to make our stay enjoyable.

Many sailors never went near a mission until they had spent all their money so that those who went to missions were often, usually jocularly, referred to as 'Mission Bums' because facilities were free. We were all Mission Bums in Ingenerio White and I certainly enjoyed several evenings at the mission, which was run by a rather prim and portly English gentleman who did his best to please us. The mission had snooker, billiards, table tennis, draughts and darts and was usually a very quiet place where the majority sat round a stove reading magazines in preference to remaining on board ship. There were, however, special evenings when there were whist drives, singsongs and dances. At an all-male whist drive, I had an average score while Huw collected the booby prize of a little cloth doll. After the game, we were given tea, sandwiches and cakes and, because all the food had not been eaten, one of our sailors was given a load to take back to the ship.

Eric was the pianist at a singsong on the evening of the day we arrived and we had great fun yelling our heads off. My buddies wanted me to take

Fotografía

Capitán
CAPTAIN

Firma del tripulante
SIGNATURE OF MEMBER OF CREW

Puesto que ocupa 3rd Radio Officer
RATING

Lugar y fecha Bahia Blanca
PLACE AND DATE

Shore Pass, Bahia Blanca.

my mouth organ, but I declined as I did not like the Swiss-made Thorens Chromatic Harmonica I had bought in the States the previous year. There was one evening which I remember particularly well. The crew of the *Samforth* were in command and there were no inhibitions. Eric was again at the piano while, in addition to being on the drums, Willsteed gave a rendering of Widecombe Fair when we all joined in the chorus, 'old Uncle Tom Cobbleigh and all'. It was a great evening and when my wife and I visited the village of Widecombe in the Moor in Devon ten years later, I had that evening in mind.

I went into Bahia Blanca the next afternoon to change Uruguayan pesos into those of Argentina for myself and three of my shipmates. Having no success in the first bank, I was talking to a teller in the second when I had the bright idea of asking the address of the British Consulate. Overhearing my request, the man standing beside me said that the Consulate was above El Banco de Londres and, as he worked there, he would show me the way.

I went along with him and he left me to go upstairs to tell the Vice-Consul (only Buenos Aires had a full Consul) that I would like to see him.

The Vice-Consul, a tall white haired gentleman, appeared within minutes and, on hearing that I had the equivalent of £24 to change, instructed a porter to take me to a place where I handed over the money and received a cheque which I had to take to El Banco del Rio de la Plata to be cashed. It was no doubt a cheek involving the Vice Consul in the transaction, but it paid off as I got a very good rate of exchange. Although the Vice-Consul made no objection to having been called upon to resolve such a trivial matter, his attitude was decidedly formal and he made no conversation whatever.

Thursday night's dance at the mission was considered to be hopeless, as it was to gramophone records and the Englishman in charge had no idea of what was suitable for dancing. In his attempt to get us all to mix, he favoured the Paul Jones and played his favourite record, 'Look For The Silver Lining' so often that we joked about it. Composed by Jerome Kern, it is a lovely tune, but there is a limit to hearing anything again and again. When I told the same gentleman that I was interested in obtaining stamps, he gave me a pile of used Argentinian and Chilean stamps and this delighted me until I discovered that they were nearly all the same!

The dance held on Saturday evening was, however, a different kettle of fish and we enjoyed it very much. The music was provided by a pianist and a drummer and I 'brought the honours back to the ship' by winning the elimination dance with a local señorita. My prize was a tie, and my father used to tell people that I won it by dancing the tango in Argentina! A day or two afterwards , I was accosted in the street in Bahia Blanca by a lady whom I had not noticed at the dance. She was from Glasgow, had previously lived in South Africa, and introduced herself by saying, 'You were dancing with my friend.' While we were talking, an acquaintance of hers passed by and I was amused to hear her pronounce 'buenos tardes' in her Glasgow accent. The girls at the mission dances had little or no English and, as it was the same in the shops, my limited Spanish proved useful.

Although the fascist Juan Perón was already Vice-President and Minister of War, there was considerable sympathy for the Allied cause and the people were just as friendly towards us as they had been in Montevideo. The sailor guard I encountered on my first re-entrance at the dock gate was an exception and refused to let me pass with two tins of pineapples because I did not have a receipt for them. His manner was objectionable and could have led me to believe that all the military were antagonistic, which they were not as the majority were conscripts merely working out their period of compulsory service. I subsequently learned, however, that the objectionable guard was right. He eventually allowed me to proceed, but the regulations demanded that we had to have three receipts for everything brought into the docks: one for the guard at the gate, one for the Customs who examined the articles in a hut and one for the guard on our gangway. But although I always obtained receipts after that incident, they were unnecessary if we gave cigarettes to the guards.

As in Montevideo, the people were dressed like ourselves, but occasionally I came across men in narrow hats, long jackets and long, baggy trousers tucked into boots, who, I surmised, were farmers or gauchos from the pampas. The shops were well stocked and things were cheaper than in Montevideo. But I saw evidence of poverty on the outskirts of the town and the people were not as well dressed as in Montevideo, as the good English cloth which I bought there was unattainable. There was, however, no shortage of inferior material made in the Argentine, which was trying to be as self-sufficient as possible. Because I had bought so much to take home, I invested in a suitcase which cost about 24s (£1.20p).

Bill and I spent most of Sunday afternoon in the lovely Parque de Mayo[9], where many people were out for a walk or in rowing boats on the small lake. It had been a surprise to me to see a street in the town called Calle O'Higgins, but in the park was an equestrian statue of General San Martín who had fought for freedom from Spain and had led the Army of the Andes across the Andes, together with Bernardo O'Higgins, to free Chile. O'Higgins was the illegitimate son of a Spanish Governor of Chile, of Irish extraction, and, born in Chile, he became the supreme director of that country when San Martín refused the office in his favour. Another surprising fact is that General José de San Martín was a freeman of Banff in Scotland.

Some of our evenings were dull, and one evening some of us told Bill that there was a dance at the Mission when there wasn't. We took delight in seeing him spruce up for the 'dance' and went along with him to see his reaction at finding that there was no dance and only sailors sitting in the quiet Mission reading magazines. It was childish behaviour, but without malice, and Bill took it in good part.

I had bought six films in Montevideo, at twice the price they were in Saint John, but was getting through them at such a rate that I tried to obtain some more. This turned out to be impossible, but, as I could get movie film, I hit upon the idea of buying a strip which I cut into lengths and fixed to the paper backing of used 828 films.

We were berthed beside grain elevators at Ingeniero White and going ashore one afternoon, I suddenly became vaguely aware of a movement on the ground when walking along a narrow path through an area of grass. The movement was so imperceptible that it did not immediately register

Ian Smart, Bill
Dawson and me,
Bahia Blanca.

and, when I went back to investigate, I found an army of ants crossing the path. Rows of ants were carrying grains of wheat in one direction while other rows were proceeding, unladen, in the other. I followed each of the rows and discovered that a quantity of grain had been spilt on the grass and the disciplined insects were engaged in conveying it over a distance of perhaps twenty yards to their anthill.

Although, due to pressure from the United States, Argentina had previously severed diplomatic relations with Germany, she had only recently become an ally when 'the writing was on the wall' for the Axis powers and she wanted to have a seat in the UN Assembly. I formed the opinion that everything 'official' was rotten and that the people were not behind their Government which, I was told, was taking advantage of the situation in war-torn Europe by charging an exorbitantly high price for the wheat we were loading. We sailed on the evening of Thursday 19 July and, in the radio department, only Caro left without winning a mission tie. Parkin had been given one when he had come 3rd in a whist drive at which the Chief Steward had won 1st prize. We were bound for Pernambuco, in Brazil, to bunker.

CHAPTER 38

PERNAMBUCO, BRAZIL

I began a letter home at 1.30 a.m., when on watch eleven days out from Bahia Blanca and nearing Pernambuco. The weather was warming up again. We had changed into tropical uniform four days previously and I had had difficulty in sleeping as our cabin was on the port side and the cooling breeze blew from the east. We had learned the election results. Churchill's name had not been sufficient to bring the Conservatives into power and out of the 640 parliamentary seats, the Conservatives won only 189 and Labour 393, and there were even 2 Communist MPs. It was a landslide for Labour: Clement Atlee, whose son later did one voyage as a midshipman with Blue Funnel, was Prime Minister with Ernest Bevin as his Foreign Secretary. With the exception of two senior officers, all on board were pleased with the result and, as Labour stood for nationalisation, perhaps even merchant shipping would be nationalised. As I wrote, I could hear Willsteed stirring his tea in the chart room which was on the starboard side, directly opposite the wireless room. We expected to be in port for only a matter of hours before continuing on our way to Kirkwall. My khaki shorts had just about reached the end of their tether, and during the passage I had darned holes in my stockings.

By 9 a.m. the same day (Monday 30 July), we were in Pernambuco and looking for the agent to come on board with mail. He arrived within half an hour when we were at anchor in the harbour, but there was no mail for us. It had been a month since I had received any and my most recent letter was two months old. At 10 a.m., a tug arrived to take us alongside and it was a short walk into town from our berth.

Pernambuco is near the most eastern point of the South American mainland and, now known as Recifé, it is made up of three districts connected by bridges. The district on the mainland is Boâ Vista, the one on the peninsula is Recifé (the Reef) and on an island between the two is São

Antonio. Only 8° south of the Equator, it is very hot in summer and even though it was winter, it was still hot.

Because it was expected that we would be in port for twenty-four hours at the most, there was no draw (i.e. we were not given the opportunity to draw cash from our accounts). This would have entirely restricted our activities if we had not resorted to using the international currency of cigarettes. And, as we had almost two full days in port and did not sail until Wednesday 1 August, this proved a godsend. My khaki uniform being now barely fit for wearing on board, I dressed in the immaculate new whites that I had bought when on leave in Dundee and had been saving.

Having been a colony of the Portuguese, Brazil is the only country in South America where the Portuguese language is spoken. I thought that there was such a similarity between Portuguese and Spanish that I could get along by using Spanish but, when, looking for a bank, my question "Donde esta un banco?" did not appear to be understood by either the person I asked or by other passers-by enlisted to help. Not knowing the town, I strayed into the 'red light' district where prostitutes called to me from balconies and where one had the swollen legs indicative of elephantiasis. I have a vague memory of being at an open-air function where an English lady, dressed in white, was serving tea and cakes.

Pernambuco, Brazil.

A thing which struck me about Pernambuco was that the colour of the people ranged through all shades from white to jet black. And, as far as I am aware, there was no colour problem in Brazil. Public transport was provided by dilapidated single-deck electric trams and it was a common sight to see passengers clinging to the outsides and no doubt travelling free.

As the port was full to capacity and there were no spaces at the quays, an American Liberty Ship tied up against us so that we were between this ship and the quay. Most of us were on deck to witness the manoeuvre, during which the US ship slammed into us and damaged one of our lifeboats. Someone immediately called out, but the Chief Engineer of the US ship, who, one would think, should have been in the engine room, calmly told him to 'keep his hair on' and that we would be compensated for the damage.

On the evening prior to departure, I bought two birds in a wooden cage. They were believed to be canaries and, as the weather was fine at sea the next day, I hung the cage in the open air on the small deck aft of our cabin. During the evening, however, Caro came into the cabin to tell me that both birds had gone. I was naturally angry, as the birds could not have escaped without someone opening the door of the cage. The following morning, Arthur said to me, 'I see one of your birds has escaped.' 'What do you mean one?' I asked, 'They've both gone.' 'Well,' said Arthur, 'there's one there now', and when I went out to look, there was a bird in the cage. I could not believe it, but the mystery was solved when the DEMS sergeant explained that he had caught it sitting on the stern rail and returned it.

I was cleaning out the cage the next day when the bird escaped again, and this time I caught it taking a stroll on the bridge. And, although I christened it Joe, its name was promptly changed to Houdini. During the next fortnight, when the bird uttered only a couple feeble chirps, I gave it to Arthur. Arthur was always cheerful and, when he reported to me about the bird's welfare, he stressed that, under his care, Houdini was singing beautifully! We again had the company of albatross and small birds all the way north through the South Atlantic and it was only when in the region of the Equator that they disappeared.

Brazil, incidentally, had been an ally since August 1942 and in July 1944 a Brazilian force landed in Italy to take part in the campaign.

CHAPTER 39

THE LONG HAUL TO KIRKWALL VIA VJ-DAY

The distance between Pernambuco and Kirkwall is over 4,000 miles and, when you are steaming at approximately nine nautical miles (just over ten land miles) an hour, that is a long way. The weather was generally fine and we arrived in the early morning of Sunday 19 August. Strangely enough, in a letter home which I began when off the west coast of Scotland on Friday 18 August, I did not even refer to the dropping of the atom bombs and the end of the war with Japan. It was already history.

We were somewhere off the coast of West Africa on 6 August when we learned from the Overseas Service of the BBC that an atomic bomb had been dropped on Hiroshima. We were stunned at the news and, like the rest of the world, had never heard of such a weapon which could destroy an entire city. All of us had seen, and most had experienced, the effects of the German bombing of British cities and because of this had no sympathy for the Japanese, whom we knew to be ruthless aggressors. And, when the second bomb was dropped three days later on Nagasaki, and the Japanese finally surrendered, we were just thankful it was all over and that we, personally, had survived.

What we did not know was that the atomic bomb was not just the equivalent of so many tons of what became known as conventional bombs. We did not know about radiation and its effect on future generations. I wish now that the bomb had never been invented, but why was it not dropped on the Imperial Palace in Tokyo and why was Emperor Hirohito not tried as a war criminal? When I visited Japan after the war, I liked the people who were polite and gentle and in no way antagonistic towards us. My travels led me to believe that people are basically the same the world over and that it is the politicians who create wars.

The radio silence which had prevailed throughout the war, when only the neutral coast stations could be heard working on the calling and distress frequency of 500 kcs, had already been relegated to the past, and peacetime working was in operation as we neared the UK. I was on afternoon watch when Landsendradio (GLD) called the *Samforth* (MYQN), and I took a telegram from the Office telling us that the charts to show us the way through the minefield across the North Sea to Norway would be awaiting our arrival at Kirkwall. And it was with some trepidation that, for the first time and after being at sea for over two years, I started up the transmitter and communicated with Landsend.

The weather had been fine the whole way from Pernambuco, but we were in thick fog when I went on watch at midnight on Thursday 17 August so that we proceeded cautiously with the ship's whistle sounding every few minutes. The fog, however, lasted only about an hour and when I came off watch at 4 a.m., I got my first sight of 'God's Country', as it was already daylight and St Kilda was visible to starboard. By the afternoon we were somewhere between the Butt of Lewis and Sule Skerry and the following morning reduced speed in order to arrive at our anchorage in daylight. As usual, our main interest was not so much in arriving at our destination, but in receiving mail and my most recent letter was dated 1 June.

I had a letter ready for posting and, as all our letters had to be stamped, was fortunate in having a stamped-addressed envelope which I had carried with me since crossing to Halifax, Nova Scotia, on the *Queen Elizabeth* in July 1943. I had retained it when I learned that all letters from the *Queen Elizabeth* went free and, bearing an embossed 2½d stamp with the figure of King George VI in its centre, it now came in useful.

The clocks on the ship had not been advanced sufficiently during our progress east so that the time on board was two hours behind that in the UK. The discrepancy was rectified by the clocks being advanced one hour on the Saturday night and another hour on Sunday morning and this state of affairs naturally gave rise to considerable criticism and discussion. Serving in the saloon, in his capacity of assistant steward, Arthur enquired what time it was in Japan. When someone asked why he wanted to know this, he said, 'If I know what time it is in Japan, I'll know what time it is in Burma and from that I can work out what time it is aboard here.'

Having negotiated a calm Pentland Firth, we dropped anchor in Shapinsay Sound early in the morning of Sunday 19 August and I wrote another letter home when Richard Tauber was singing 'You Are My Heart's Delight' on the radio. I said that I now knew that we were going to Moss on the Oslo Fiord and then to Oslo, and that I had received twenty-five letters and five postcards. Only the deck boy had beaten me as he had apparently received thirty-seven letters!

CHAPTER 40

AT ANCHOR NEAR KIRKWALL

The charts which we had been told would be waiting for us in Kirkwall were not there so that we swung at anchor awaiting their arrival until Saturday 25 August, when they arrived from Aberdeen. Although the US Navy sailing card states that we were in Kirkwall, we never saw the place as it was 'round a corner' and out of sight. The length of stay did not bother us, but we thought it a bit much that during that whole week and having been away so long, we were not given the opportunity to go ashore. Our spirits were nevertheless high. We had received such a tremendous batch of mail, brought out by a Wren 3rd Officer on an old tender, and it was good to be in sight of green fields again. We looked forward to Norway and knew that it would not be long before we were home.

On the night of our arrival, Huw came down from the bridge to tell me that there was a seagull sitting on a lamp and that he thought that it would be fun to try to catch it. I returned with him to the bridge when he quietly sneaked up on the bird, caught it and brought it down to the chart room. It was not an easy thing to do. The bird was a big strong herring gull and could have injured him. Having succeeded, he took the bird outside and released it.

A welcome diversion occurred when it was decided to calibrate our DF (direction finder) and I was sent off in our motorised lifeboat with our lifeboat transmitter and receiver. Huw was in charge of the boat, Bill operated the motor, Ian was on the tiller and Michael and three young sailors, D. Burton, G. Brown and E. Bailey, were with us. The calibration was done by me transmitting continuous signals while those on board took bearings on the boat by both ship's compass and DF as it proceeded slowly round the ship. Differences between the accurate compass bearings and those of the DF were noted and would in future be taken into account when the DF was used. Bill and I took our cameras and pictures were

D. Burton, G. Brown, Ian Smart (behind me), Huw and E. Bailey. Calibrating the D/F.

At anchor, near Kirkwall, Orkney.

taken of me 'at work' and of the rather dirty-looking *Samforth* in her grey wartime livery with the flags of her callsign flying. I have pictures of every ship on which I sailed deep-sea except the *Samite* as it was forbidden to take such pictures during the war.

Gepp and Guppy had had a sailing dinghy built during the passage from Pernambuco and we all watched as it was launched and they sailed it in the bay for the first time. It sailed beautifully and they often enjoyed themselves in it.

Our days at anchor were pleasant and I spent a great deal of time on photography, developing and printing photographs taken in South America and cutting off lengths of the movie film I had bought in Bahia Blanca to fix onto old 828 backing paper.

When making my bed one morning, Arthur asked if I had been ashore and I couldn't think what gave him that idea until he pointed to the thistle at the head of my bunk. But, although the thistle looked real, it was a crocheted one given to me by a friend when on leave and had been there throughout the voyage.

Among the letters I had received was one from David Cathro, who was now stationed forty miles from Cairo and had spent a fortnight's leave in Alexandria at the end of June. He had been as far west as Rabat in Morocco and to Cyprus and Palestine. In his letter, David said that I should let him know immediately if I were ever in the area as he would try to come to see me. Although our paths had crossed on several occasions, it seemed we were destined not to meet, but a reunion in Greece lay ahead. David had also received the circular from the Henry's asking if he wished to return and he too had answered in the affirmative. Unlike me, however, he did return to the Company and became Managing Director, two years prior to its closing in 1972.

A letter from Robert South contained the news that he was now with the US military police in France and awaiting transportation back to the United States. But as the US Government was offering jobs in either France or Britain, plus a free passage home when the work terminated, this option was open to him. Other news I received was that my brother, Eric, had passed the National Certificate exams in bookkeeping and another subject at night school.

Shortly after receiving the charts showing the minefields of the North Sea, we weighed anchor on the afternoon of Saturday 25 August and headed for Norway. During the passage, a floating mine was seen and our gunners fired at it with rifles in an effort to explode it. As mines could be exploded only by hitting one of their horns, this was not an easy thing to do. But, although we knew this, it did not prevent the crew shouting derisive remarks as the gunners failed to hit the target. We then sent out a mine warning to all ships and also reported the position of the mine to the GPO coastal radio station at Wick (GKR) so that the Royal Navy would be alerted and dispose of the mine. Floating mines continued to be a danger to shipping long after the war and mine warnings were commonplace. Preceded by the XXX (Urgency) Signal, they were repeated by coast stations until the mine was destroyed.

CHAPTER 41

NORWAY

We anchored off Moss, on the east side of the Oslo Fiord, at 3 a.m. on Tuesday 28 August when I was on watch. It was dark and I could see only the shore lights, but when I rose later in the morning, I was struck by the beauty of our surroundings. It was like being in a Scottish loch. There were hills all around us and Jel Island obscured the passage through which we had entered. The setting was absolutely idyllic and we were taken alongside later in the day.

Moss was a lovely little town. Its main industries were fishing, timber and papermaking and there was a granary into which we had come to discharge part of our cargo of wheat. As I believed we were only the second merchant ship to arrive since the end of the war, I thought that, because we had brought much-needed food, we would receive a great welcome. But we received no such welcome and, although the people were reasonably friendly, they seemed somewhat shy of us and I was disappointed by our reception. There may, however, have been a reason for this as we were led to believe that a Scottish regiment had occupied the town and had taken too many liberties. In spite of the privations they had suffered, the predominantly blond people looked healthy. Rationing was more severe than that in Britain, but there had been plenty of fish to eat. Some of the people had been shot during the German occupation and they absolutely hated the Germans.

As it was the school holidays, many of the children were out in cobles and, before we went alongside, some rowed to the gangway and came on board. We had no difficulty in hiring boats and when I spent a couple of hours enjoying myself rowing about the fiord, the ship's motorised lifeboat, with Gepp at the tiller, came deliberately close to rock me. Everybody was laughing and the lifeboat towed a plank of wood in an attempt to provide water-skiing. In the evening, Eric and I went for a walk in the country and as the scenery was similar to that around Pitlochry, we felt very much at home.

The following morning, I went for a haircut, bought a small Norwegian–English dictionary and tried to buy a fishing line. Fishing lines, however, were unattainable although it was possible to get hooks and flies. In the afternoon I walked for about five miles in the country and climbed through heather and blaeberries to the top of a hill to get a magnificent view of Vann Lake, into which the River Moss flows before it passes through the town into the fiord. After being so long on board ship, I revelled in the surroundings and gathered a bunch of heather, half of which I gave to Eric.

Although cigarettes could bring a high price, I was not prepared to sell them to the Norwegians who had suffered so much and when I gave I packet of twenty to an elderly man who leant on his bike as we chatted one evening, he called me a 'hero'. Later, however, when I was charged an astronomical price for photographic printing paper, I came to the conclusion that I was a 'mug'. But, although my salary could not cope with the prices in Norway, I still did not sell cigarettes.

Before we left Moss, we knew that, after Oslo, we were going to load in a Baltic port in either Finland or Sweden. Oslo was barely forty miles away. We sailed from Moss at 4 a.m. on Saturday, 1 September and three hours later arrived in Oslo.

Oslo, known as Christiania until its name was changed in 1925, stands at the head of the sixty-mile long Oslo Fiord and I found it a fine city. Parkin knew his way around and advised me where to go to obtain a good view of the city so that on Tuesday 4 September and after consulting a plan which I bought, I set out for Holmenkollen, which hosts the annual ski-jump competitions. To get there, I took what was called the subway although only five minutes of the half-hour journey was underground. The train was short and wide and would have been comfortable if it had not been so crowded that I had to stand all the way. On the train, I met a young chap in the Royal Army Service Corps who was also sightseeing and who had only recently arrived in Oslo after home leave. We teamed up for the afternoon and I learned that he had been in North Africa with the 8th Army, and then in France and the Netherlands. At the summit, from which we indeed had fine views, I met the Skipper and the Chief Engineer so that we all returned to town together. On another occasion, I visited Frogner Park, unique because of many sculptures by Gustav Vigeland which it contains.

Our stay coincided with the reopening of the University which, I was told, had been closed for some time during the Nazi occupation. Every student wore a black cap with a cord suspended from it and at the end of which was a large tassel worn on the right shoulder. All spoke English and I had a conversation with one of the girls. The Royal Palace was close by, but, although there was no admittance, I walked through the grounds without hindrance.

We had received no mail in Moss, but when mail arrived in Oslo, I received two letters, one from Barbara and one, dated 24 August, from my father. My father's letter carried the information that Dundee was getting a zoo and I replied that Dundee could be doing with a lot of other things before it started collecting wild animals! On a visit to a cinema I saw the film *Road to Singapore*, which I had seen years previously.

Having discharged the remainder of our wheat, we left Oslo on Friday 7 September bound for Kotka in Finland, via Copenhagen. As we sailed out of Oslo harbour, the house which had been the home of Vidkun Quisling, whose name has become synonymous with the word 'collaborator', was pointed out to me. Some ten miles south of Oslo, we bunkered at a small fuelling station before proceeding out the Fiord and through the Kattegat to Copenhagen.

Three sailors had missed the ship in Oslo and, while we lay at anchor in Copenhagen harbour, they were brought out in a launch. Their folly cost them dear as not only was the price of the airfare docked from their wages, but they were fined for their misdemeanour.

Oslo University.

CHAPTER 42

KOTKA

After spending about four hours at anchor in Copenhagen, we began coast crawling all the way to Kotka and I never again made a passage which required the services of so many pilots, as they numbered about twenty. The majority were Swedish, but first there was a Dane and the Finns took over from the Swedes when we arrived in their territorial waters off the southwest coast of Finland. Each pilot was on board for an average of six hours, and the launch which took him ashore brought out his replacement who knew the next stretch of water. A night was spent at anchor in the harbour of Malmö in Sweden, and the night of Monday 10 September at anchor off the Finnish town of Hanko (Hangö). We anchored again at about 10 a.m. the following morning, when in the midst of islands somewhere between Hanko and Helsinki, the delay this time was to obtain clearance from the Soviet authorities who controlled the waters east of our position. The lights of Helsinki were seen as we passed during the evening and the following morning, Wednesday 12 September, we arrived in Kotka. The final part of our journey was quite hazardous as we had to pass between islands which were little more than a stone's throw away and much more numerous than those shown on any ordinary map. This caused Captain Gepp to make out a report to the Office, which I typed, saying that it was unwise to send such a large ship (laughable by today's standards) this way again.

Regarding the typing, I objected to Parkin making use of my typing skill when he was the Purser and I the junior 3rd Sparks. He must have reported this to Gepp as, months later, Calverley made a brief reference to it.

With peace restored, it was again necessary that the Silence Periods, already described in Chapter 7, be observed. But all too many continental coast stations were continuing to work through them and this so incensed me that, on two occasions, I sent QRT SP (stop sending, silence period) to Finnish stations. Although infringing maritime law, they completely ignored my protests.

Kotka, on Kotkansaari (Kotka Island) at the mouth of the Kymijoki (Kymi River), is only about twenty-five miles from the Russian border. We were taken alongside almost immediately on arrival and Michael and I had a walk through the town in the afternoon. In a letter home, I said that my first impressions were that it was a poor place with bad and often cobbled roads and that what there was in the poorly-stocked shops was of poor quality. I also said that the people weren't very well dressed and did not appear to be particularly friendly although, in mitigation, I must say that I added the rider, 'However, we don't know them yet.' I say 'in mitigation' because that first impression of the people could not have been more wrong, as nowhere did I meet more friendly folk than the Finns and our reception turned out to be in marked contrast to that which we had received in Norway. During the evening, I listened to a boxing match on the BBC between Jim Brady and Jackie Paterson. Paterson won, but it was my considered opinion that this was because of his hard punching as Brady seemed to be the more scientific boxer!

We had come to load cut timber, and Caro and I were given the job of counting the lengths on the quay before they were loaded. We counted every piece of timber which went into the ship and which was stowed by women dockers. And when we left Kotka, not only were our holds full, but we had such a mass of deck cargo that you could hardly see the ship for wood. To begin with, I found the counting quite difficult, as when I started at the top of a row in the pile, I soon found that the planks did not continue in a straight line to the ground, but wandered into next row. The foreman, however, showed me how to go about it. A man in his fifties and of Slav appearance, he had fought in the Russo-Finnish War of 1939-40 and we became friends. The hours of work were from 7 a.m. to 4 p.m., and there was no work on Saturdays and Sundays.

Finland was a poor country with very little other than timber – the major resource and exploited to the full. An office chap, who came on board regularly and with whom I also became friendly, told me to feel his shirt. It felt like cloth, but was made of paper and was apparently washable. When the foreman arranged for me to go round a paper mill, I visited its chemical laboratory and learned that even soap was made from oil extracted from timber. There was no petrol or coal so that the buses and trains were fueled by it. Perhaps I was the only merchant seaman ever to take wallpaper home! I also took home a sheath-knife for my brother, a bone paper knife and a record of the slow foxtrot, 'It can't be wrong', from the film *Now Voyager*, which I had seen in Port Tewfik. The record was made in Finland by the Rytmi Company, and Raija Valtonen sang,

Women stowing our cargo, Kotka.

in English, to the music of the Rytmi Orchestra conducted by Erkki Aho. 'You'll Never Know' was on the other side.

Clothes were rationed, but although the people had clothing coupons, there was very little to buy in the shops. Food was also rationed and coupons were necessary even to eat in restaurants. My friend from the office gave me coupons and Eric and I went for a meal in a restaurant in the main square. The waitresses knew no English so that we took what came and helped ourselves from a large platter containing a variety of fish dishes. We thought this was the meal then regretted eating so much when we found that it was only the hors d'oeuvre and was followed by soup and a meat dish.

There were two Soviet ships and another British vessel in port, but we were the largest ship and most of the town came to have a look at us. A party of students from the Technical College came on board to see round and the College reciprocated by inviting us to a dance. Language was no barrier at the dance. Although we did not understand the words, we understood the speech of welcome and had a good time. It was probably there that I learned a few words of Finnish. I remember 'kiitos' (thank you) and 'Minä olen surullinen' which I thought meant 'I am sorry', but which, I believe, means 'I am sorrowful' and was definitely not the case! A plumpish girl took a fancy to me. She was a telephone operator who was on duty all night after the dance and asked me to accompany her to the exchange. I did this, but, when I learned that she expected me to stay the night, I ran like billyo to catch up with Bill and another shipmate who were making their way back to the ship! 'Didn't expect to see you again tonight,' said Bill. My admirer, however, was not put off by my behaviour. I had to resist her advances at another dance and somehow or other Bill learned that she lived in a large, palatial-looking house. Many of the girls were keen to get hold of a British sailor and one of our officers, standing beside a pleasant-looking blond woman, smirked as he said to me that he'd have to come back to Kotka to see his son. I cannot recall if he were married, but rather think that he was and, as he remained with Blue Funnel, it is extremely unlikely that he ever returned, or wanted to return, to Kotka again.

CHAPTER 43

HELSINKI

As Helsinki was only about 100 miles away, I made enquiries and found that it was possible to make the journey if I could stay overnight. Gepp gave his permission and a pal of Parkin's got a bus ticket for me. Seats had to be booked two days in advance and the bus left at 7 a.m.

It was cutting it fine when I rose at 6 a.m. on the morning of Friday 21 September as we were now out in the harbour, loading from lighters because the water at the quay was too shallow to accommodate the ship as she sank deeper in the water under the weight of the cargo. The foreman had arranged for a boat to collect me and, after a hurried breakfast of two eggs, a piece of poor bacon and bread and tea, which I was lucky to get at that time in the morning and which Arthur may have provided, I was taken ashore. I had no idea where to meet the bus, but when I asked at the Custom's hut, someone took me in a lorry and I boarded the bus five minutes before departure. It was an old bus, with a 'clapped-out' engine and a charcoal burner on the back, and the journey, which took 5½ hours, was an experience in itself.

My seat was at the front, on the right-hand side of the door, and as there was a considerable amount of luggage lying in the area, I had to lift my legs whenever anyone got off or on. To begin with, people seemed to be leaving or boarding every five minutes. When one lady boarded with a large, loose basket of small fish, a handle broke and there were fish everywhere. The bus broke down on two occasions and the driver poked at the works with a spanner. When we stopped in a village for about half an hour, the engine was given a rough overhaul. We arrived in Helsinki at 12.30 p.m. I had no idea where to go, but had been told by the chap who procured the bus ticket for me that the first thing to do was to book a seat back to Kotka. But, when I enquired at the ticket office, where I made myself understood with the aid of diagrams, I was told that the Saturday bus was already fully booked and that I would have to join a queue at 5 a.m. to obtain a seat on the Sunday one.

My adviser had told me that there was an English Club diagonally across from the bus station, but I couldn't find it and this was not surprising as I learned later that the Club had moved to other premises. I realised that I had to get hold of someone who spoke English and, when I saw a travel bureau, went in to try my luck. Fortunately the girl in her twenties who attended to me spoke English and gave me the address of the Finnish–British Society, with instructions of how to get there. I went by a single decker tramcar where fares were collected by the conductress at a desk at the entrance. When I held out money, she seemed embarrassed and I made the journey without paying. Had I been in uniform, I might have thought this was the reason, but I was not. I showed her the diagram supplied by the girl in the travel office and she saw that I got off at the correct stop.

The Finnish-British Society was quite luxurious and the gold-braided commissionaire took my coat and showed me up a marble staircase to the office of Mr Von Hartman, who was in charge. Mr Von Hartman was most courteous and greeted me by saying, 'It is not often that one finds a British subject in Helsinki these days.' He then said that there was no hope of finding a hotel room and that he was unable to put me up as all spare rooms had been commandeered by the government. Helsinki was overcrowded due to so many people flooding into the city from former Finnish territory in Karelia, now occupied by the Russians. However, after one or two phone calls, Mr Von Hartman contacted Mr Roper, the British Press Attaché, who said to send me to his office at the British Mission. I went there, climbed a stair and knocked at a door. A girl in her twenties answered it and, when I asked the perfectly reasonable question, 'Do you speak English?' she replied in a snooty and abrasive manner, 'Of course I do, I *am* English.' Mr Roper said he would put me up for the night and gave me coupons so that I could obtain a meal in a restaurant, as he said that he and his wife had plenty as they were given treble the Finnish ration. He told me to meet him and his wife outside the railway station at 9 p.m. And having secured a bed for the night and learned that I could return to Kotka by train, I went off to see the city.

Mr Von Hartman had told me that I could eat at the Club, and after spending hours walking about taking photographs, I returned there for evening dinner. No coupons were asked for, but the service was so slow that I wrote postcards between the courses. I had intended spending the evening at a cinema, but finished dinner so late that this was impossible as performances, as in so many other places in the world, were not continuous and began at 7 p.m. I spent the time in the Club conversing with a porter who spoke reasonable English. He told me that he had fought against the Russians, but that he had had no choice in this and said that he, like most Finns, liked them. I took this information with a pinch of salt as I suspected that this was what he thought I wanted to hear as the USSR was Britain's ally.

I was at the railway station at the appointed time, but the Ropers, who had been to a symphony concert, did not appear in their petrol-driven car until about a quarter to ten to drive me to their villa which lay fifteen to twenty miles from the City centre. Their house was beautiful. None of its eight rooms, containing mostly solid oak furniture, had been commandeered by the Government and they were living in luxury. I estimated the Ropers to be about forty and, although they were hospitable to me, we did not really hit it off. Mrs Roper was a dreamy sort of person, the daughter of a pukka-sahib who had spent the first nine years of her life in India. Mr Roper enquired if my ship could take passengers, as he had a friend who had been given a job as announcer, script writer and programme arranger in the Finnish section of the BBC and was looking for a passage to England for himself and his family. The BBC was prepared to pay his airfare, but not those of his wife and children. I said that I thought the *Samforth* could accommodate them and to give me a letter to take to Captain Gepp. After a light supper, we went to bed and, for the one and only time in my life, I slept between paper sheets. Mrs Roper explained that she had only two pairs of linen/cotton sheets and that 'the other pair' were 'in the wash'. Before falling asleep, I heard the Ropers laughing and giggling in bed.

The maid wakened me in the morning with, 'It's 8.15, sir.' I had slept well and found the paper sheets very warm, but was embarrassed to find a big piece torn out of the top sheet, although I don't suppose it mattered as the sheets would be thrown away. I was reading a Penguin paperback in the lounge when Mr Roper came in and we had breakfast together. It was served by the maid and when I had finished the unsalted porridge, I pushed my plate aside, waiting for the bacon and eggs. Sensing my anticipation, Mr Roper then said, 'You know, I don't think we're going to get anything else' and, when I looked crestfallen, added, 'Would you like some more porridge?' I declined the offer and satisfied my appetite with bread and marmalade. Mrs Roper was having a lie-in and did not even appear to bid me goodbye.

Mr Roper had phoned his BBC friend, a bald-headed man of about forty who arrived shortly after breakfast to consult me. The three of us then drove into town together and I asked to be dropped off at the Stadium which Mr Roper had said was worth seeing. The other two continued to the Press Office to compose a letter to Captain Gepp which I was to collect later in the day.

It cost only 10 marks to enter the tower which over looked the Stadium and two Finnish policemen and I were the first at the top that morning. The climb was worth the effort as we obtained fine views although it was a dull and rainy morning and the rain continued throughout the day. I took some photographs and several more when I walked about the City. I expected to see evidence of the bombing which Helsinki had experienced during the Russo-Finnish war, but saw very little of this as, of course, several years had gone by, allowing repairs to be made. There were no Soviet troops in Kotka, but I saw a group of Soviet officers in Helsinki.

I went to the railway station to buy a ticket to travel on the 3 p.m. train to Kotka before calling at the Press Office at 11.30 a.m. I expected to see Mr Roper, whom I wished to thank and offer payment for my overnight stay, but the letter was handed to me by a secretary and, similar to his wife, he did not appear to say goodbye. On return to Kotka, I sent a letter of thanks to the Ropers and enclosed a pair of stockings. No acknowledgment was received and I cynically wondered if they saw me only as someone who could be of use to them. And I was. The letter, signed by a Finnish Government Minister, which I conveyed to Captain Gepp, resulted in the Finnish broadcaster and his family travelling to England as passengers on the *Samforth*. But, throughout the passage, the broadcaster barely acknowledged me.

After lunch at the Finnish–British Society and a bit more sightseeing, I went to the station in good time for the train and was surprised to see British magazines on the bookstall. I bought copies of the *Picture Post* and *Illustrated* magazines, both dated 15 September, before boarding the train. I had opted to travel 2nd Class rather than 3rd and there didn't appear to be a 1st Class. I was pleased with my choice as 2nd Class was comfortable while the seats in the 3rd Class were merely bare boards. And as the journey lasted 7½ hours, two hours longer than the journey by bus, to travel 3rd must have been very uncomfortable. The reason for the length of the rail journey was partly due to the fact that there is no direct link between Kotka and Helsinki and the line lies well inland by way of Lahti and Kouvola. Another factor was that I had to change trains at Kouvola.

Although divided into compartments, the carriage was open-plan and I sat beside a Finnish Army captain of about twenty-five who spoke reasonably good English. He and I got on fine together and, until he left the train two or three hours after its departure, we entertained each other by talking about our various experiences. Opposite us was a lady with two children and she also was friendly and spoke English. About half an hour after these companions left the train, I was sitting on my own reading my magazines when a gentleman, sitting diagonally across the passage from me with a lady, came over and offered me two copies of the *Daily Mail*!

This man spoke very good English and told me that he had bought British papers throughout the war and that he had been a fireman on both Finnish and British ships before the war. We talked of places we had both visited and, although the lady, whom I took to be his wife, knew no English, she communicated through him. When a conductor entered the carriage, I knew before the translation that she was telling him to look after me; he was to show me to the dining car and to see that I was put off at Kouvola. They left the train at Lahti at about 7.30 p.m. and I went to the dining car. I remember the meal, for which I gave coupons, because I could not make the waiter understand that I wanted water and eventually settled for a beer! When the train reached Kouvola, the Kotka train was waiting in the station. It pulled into Kotka at 10 p.m. and, somewhat tired, I was back on board by 11 p.m.

The man with the lady had asked me to correspond with him and I did. He was Paul Palkonen, who worked for the Ministry of Agriculture in Helsinki, and in a letter to me dated 7 January 1946, he said that the lady had been his fiancée, but had broken their engagement two weeks before Christmas due to pressure from her parents who did not approve of him. According to Paul, this was because he had been married before and had a different background from that of their daughter. He said he was very unhappy and had spent Christmas alone, then added, 'And now, if you know some good girls, who will begin a correspond with me, so please, give my address to her, you know me.' But, as I had formed a good opinion of his intended bride and didn't know him, I did not reply.

Over 23 and 24 September I wrote a long letter home telling of my trip to Helsinki and ended it, as usual, with 'My love to Granma and Grandad'. Always when I received mail, I put the letters in date order before reading them and I did this when I subsequently received letters in Kotka. The first letter I read, from my parents, said that my grandmother was ill and in Dundee Royal Infirmary. The second letter said she had died. And as I loved my grandparents dearly, I went out into the darkness of the deck that night and shed tears.

CHAPTER 44

THE LAST LEG

The small tugs of Kotka were not sufficiently powered to handle the heavily laden *Samforth* and this resulted in the death of an engineer on one of the tugs assisting us out of the harbour on Friday 28 September. The tug was pulled under water and the engineer drowned. It was a sad end to our stay in a port where we had been made so welcome.

A flurry of snow blew over the harbour as we slowly made our exit, looking like a timber yard as only the central accommodation was clear of cargo. The flurry heralded the approach of the long winter, when the nights would be long in the Land of the Midnight Sun and the Baltic would freeze over, due to the many rivers which discharge fresh water into it and its exclusion from the warming effect of the North Atlantic Drift. We were homeward bound now and our destination was Immingham in Lincolnshire.

We anchored all night in Helsinki harbour before continuing on to the Kiel Canal. The eastern entrance of the Canal, sixty-one miles long and connecting the Baltic with the North Sea, is a mile and a half north of Kiel and we anchored in Kiel harbour for the night. And when we began the voyage at Avonmouth, we little thought that, ten months later, we would be in a German naval base.

Although Kiel had been largely destroyed by the RAF, we were too far from the shore to see evidence of the bombing in the daylight of the following morning. But when we continued into the Canal, we saw the U-boat pens which had housed the sinister monsters which we had feared and which had sent so many seamen to their deaths during their 'Happy Time'. We exited the Canal at Brunsbüttel, at the estuary of the River Elbe, and saw Cuxhaven on the distant southern shore as we proceeded into the North Sea.

We docked in Immingham, on the west shore of the Humber, in the early morning of Saturday 6 October. Customs officers came on board and my pink custom's slip, which gives the ship's name as *Samworth*, reads: One watch v (value) £1 - - 6s 8d (duty), Six pairs art. (artificial) silk hose v 15/- - 6s 6d (duty), One powder compact v 5/- - 1s 3d (duty), The same allowances applied irrespective of the length of time you had been out of the country and I paid a total of 14s 5d.

Having been given a rail voucher to travel 3rd Class to Dundee, I was free to travel home overnight and went by taxi to the railway station in Grimsby, from where the train left in the evening. I deposited my cabin trunk, the case I had bought in Bahia Blanca, my portable gramophone and grip at the left-luggage office before having a wander round the town and then tea in a restaurant. The restaurant was busy and there was a happy atmosphere, due mainly to a number of girls in the WAAF (Women's Auxiliary Air Force) who had pushed several tables together to make one long table and were having a great time laughing at the prognostications of the girl at the head of the table reading their tea cups. The scene seemed to epitomise the mood the country after six long years of war.

As I had learned from experience that wartime trains on the main routes were always overcrowded, I decided to pay the extra to travel 1st Class from York, where I had to change and board the train from London at 2 a.m. The train to York was half empty and a young nurse and I had a compartment to ourselves. But even at 2 o'clock in the morning, York station was a hive of activity and there was a great crowd of mainly service men and women awaiting the arrival of the London train. When it pulled into the station, it was already so full that there were no seats in even the 1st class carriage and I had to stand almost all the way to Edinburgh.

Even the corridor was crowded and I stood, first of all, with an opulent-looking gentleman who offered me a drink from his flask of whisky, and then with an RNR lieutenant travelling to somewhere in Tyneside. At that time, railway compartments had three seats on each side with arms dividing the seats, but, when trains were crowded, it was the rule that the arms should be put back to allow four people to sit on each side. When I saw that the compartment outside which the lieutenant and I stood had only three on each side, I went in and asked the occupants to lift the arms and give us a seat. But everyone in the dark compartment feigned sleep so that we returned to our position in the corridor. It was daylight and the lieutenant had already left the train when someone left the compartment; I went in and sat down. It was occupied by RAF officers, some of whom were wearing the DFC, and shortly after my entrance, one loudly and brazenly said to a companion, and obviously for my benefit, 'What gets me is someone coming into the compartment in the middle of the night, looking for a seat and waking everybody up.' I did not hesitate. 'I suppose you're referring to me,' I said, 'but if I had been sitting in a compartment with only three aside, nobody would have needed to ask me to put up the arm.' The man made no reply.

My continuous Certificate of Discharge shows that I was discharged from the *Samforth* at Immingham on 6 October 1945, but that I signed off, by form C. R. S.3, at the Mercantile Marine Office in Dundee on 8 October. The end of the voyage signified a watershed for me as I knew that a continuous, twenty-four hour radio watch would no longer be kept on ships. This meant that thousands of radio officers were redundant and the wartime Special Radio Certificate would no longer be accepted as a qualification to serve on ships other than trawlers. The Radio Officers' Union (ROU) tried long and hard for the continuance of a twenty-four hour watch and even in 1948, the following notice was appearing in their monthly official organ, *The Signal*: 'SEAFARERS!! A Twenty-Four Hour Human Radio Watch is essential to Safety of Life at Sea. Insist upon a Twenty-Four Hour Human[10] Radio Watch being kept on your Ship.'

I don't know if the notice appeared anywhere other than *The Signal*, read only by radio officers, but, anyway, nobody was in a position to 'insist' and I knew that I had to obtain a 2nd Class PMG (Postmaster General) Certificate if I were to remain in the MN. And because my demob number was above that of 45, I was not yet 24 and had not completed four years at sea, I was still liable for call-up into one of the Armed Forces of the Crown.

CHAPTER 45

UNCERTAINTY

I wasted no time in going to Dundee Wireless College to study for my 2nd Class PMG. The College had now transferred from Windsor Street to a much smaller building in Airlie Place, but Drew Mackenzie was still the instructor and there were at least a couple of students who had been in my class in 1943. Holders of the Special Certificate had to sit only the written part of the exam and because I knew that I had about four weeks leave, I went through to Leith to attempt it after three weeks' study. I failed and later, when I had a bit more knowledge, cringed at some of the answers I gave. It was now only a question of waiting until a letter arrived from Holts telling me I was axed.

I could not believe my luck when the following telegram arrived on the evening of 16 November: 'REPORT OFFICE NINE AM TUESDAY READY DUTY ACKNOWLEDGE = ODYSSEY.' I was to get one more voyage and it was with considerable elation that I set off for Liverpool with all my sea-going gear. I travelled overnight and, as always, had to change trains at Perth and Preston. There was time to spare in Perth so that I gave my heavy luggage into the care of a lady porter, who said she would put it on the train, before setting off to look up Sandy McPherson who had been a friend at Wireless College. But as he wasn't at home, I had a wander through the fairground on the South Inch before boarding the train.

The train arrived in Preston at about 2 a.m. and I ran along the platform to the luggage van to find that my luggage wasn't there. There was nothing for it but to continue to Liverpool without it and, obviously worried, I immediately reported my loss at the left luggage office upon arrival in Lime Street Station. And, having given the attendant a description of my luggage plus a half-crown to keep a lookout for it, I went off to report at India Buildings.

Calverley usually dealt with us at the office counter, but on this occasion he said that Mr Gleave wanted to see me and I was ushered into the latter's office behind a glass door in the main office. Gleave and I stood facing each other as he told me that I was redundant and, when I protested about the contents of the telegram and how I had lost my luggage, he told me to take my hands out of my pockets when I was speaking to him. He knew I was vulnerable. I took my hands out of my pockets and left the office with a feeling of despair.

When I returned to the left-luggage office, the attendant said that there was no sign of my luggage, but, looking behind him, I spotted the cheap suitcase I had bought in Bahia Blanca and which had been found on a train from the north. I never saw the rest of my luggage again, but that suitcase proved the most valuable to me as it contained all my irreplaceable photographic negatives which were, of course, of no interest to thieves. But, apart from my grip and portable gramophone which I carried, all my clothes, including brand new whites and everything of material value, had gone, including my Kodak Bantam camera.

After booking in at the Officers' Club in Lime Street station, I went to a news cinema where there was a brief rumpus when a woman interrupted the performance claiming that a man had tried to interfere with her. But as I was dog-tired and found myself falling asleep, I returned early to the Club and went to bed in the large empty dormitory full of camp beds. On rising early the next morning, the room was full of sleeping men and I had heard nothing.

When I got back to Dundee, my father had me write a letter of complaint to Lawrence Holt to which I received the following reply, dated 28 November 1945:

Dear Sir,

Mr. Lawrence Holt has handed your letter of 26th inst. to us.

We are rather surprised to learn that you feel agrieved* at the termination of your temporary employment with us. The Admiralty War-time regulation compelling all shipowners to maintain a continuous human watch, thus necessitating the employment of three operators on each ship, has now been withdrawn and we are therefore dispensing with the services of junior operators as their ships come in. We are, however, sorry for sending a misleading telegram to you which caused you to bring your gear to Liverpool.

We understand you propose sitting for your 2nd Class certificate and as indicated to you when you were last in this office if you are successful there is no reason why you should not make application to us for a position, although we cannot, of course, guarantee, that we shall have a vacancy at the time.

Yours truly,

Alfred Holt & Co

*Spelling as in letter and they also got my name wrong.
As the reference on the letter was SS/EG, it was dictated by Gleave.

My war, therefore, ended on an unnecessarily sour note. As we all knew the position, Holts could have dismissed me by letter, but, even if they wanted to do this in a more personal manner, their incorrectly worded telegram cost me my belongings. While Gleave apologised for the misleading telegram, he made no enquiry as to whether or not my luggage had turned up and also no mention of compensation so that I was left to battle this out with the London, Midland and Scottish Railway Company. But by the time his letter was received, I was already back at the Wireless College.

EPILOGUE

Although the civilian Merchant Navy suffered a higher percentage loss than any of the Armed Services in the Second World War, there is no memorial to it within the Scottish War Memorial in Edinburgh Castle as that which is deemed to represent it bears the incorrect title 'The Mercantile Marine'.

Due to the good service given by the Mercantile Marine in the First World War, George V conferred the title Master of the Merchant Navy and Fishing Fleet on the Prince of Wales in 1928. From that date, therefore, the correct title has been HM Merchant Navy and the silver lapel badge given to all of us, and which we proudly wore, bore the letters MN.

In case this should be regarded as pedantry, I would point out that the name change of our military air service was recognised as there is a memorial to 'The Royal Air Force' under that of 'The Royal Flying Corps'.

When, in 2000, I requested the Trustees of the Memorial to rectify the omission, they declined to do so on the grounds that their predecessors of 1945 had taken the decision not to make any changes. They did, however, agree to add a Red Ensign to the colours, but while I am pleased about this, it does not make up for the lack of a memorial to the Merchant Navy.

ENDNOTES

1. In his report, Captain Woodruff said: 'Eliminate entry of New York section into Hampton Roads. After decision as to sailing date fly commodore from Hampton Roads to New York for sailing conference and issue orders to masters. Fly him back to Hampton Roads for sailing conference of Hampton Roads section. Have sections rendezvous outside the Chesapeake Bay approaches. There is nothing which cannot be given all hands by this procedure. There would thus be eliminated: (a) Work of piloting New York ships into Hampton Roads. (b) Work of boarding these ships to secure information. (c) Work of boarding these ships to bring masters ashore to conference. (d) Work of returning masters to ships. (e) Work of piloting these ships from Hampton Roads to sea. All orders for passage can be taken to New York by the Commodore and he can secure all available information for inclusion in folder for Commodore and Vice-Commodore. New York ships could sail two days later, eliminating the day it takes to get the section into Hampton Roads and anchored and the day of the conference at Little Creek.'

2. Postscript: In his letter to me dated 7 May 1992, Mr R. M. Coppock of the Directorate of Naval Staff Duties (Foreign Documents Section, Ministry of Defence) wrote:

   I can find no instance of an attack on a convoy with glider bombs before that on UGS 18.
   Admiralty records do not reveal whether the HIRAM S. MAXIM and the SELVIK were hit by glider bomb or torpedo. Unfortunately, Admiralty Trade Division tended to interview the survivors from

British vessels only, and none of the reports of the various escorts of UGS 18 indicates which ships were bombed and which torpedoed. There can, however, be no doubt that the SAMITE was the first <u>British merchantman</u> to be hit by a glider bomb since the FORT FITZGERALD was damaged by an aerial torpedo.

The first British ship to be sunk by a glider bomb was the sloop EGRET, on 27 August 1943 off the west coast of Spain. The Canadian destroyer ATABASKAN was hit by a glider bomb in the same attack. Two days earlier the sloop BIDEFORD had been damaged by a near miss with a glider bomb off Cape Ortegal, on what is believed to have been the first occasion when the weapon was used operationally.'

Glider bombs, manufactured by Henschel, were known as Hs.293 bombs. They had a wingspan of eleven feet and one could be carried under each wing of a heavy bomber such as the Focke Wulf 200, Do.217 or He.177. Their small jet engines started after release, the parent aircraft guided them by radio control then cut off the engine and it coasted to the target. Their range was eleven miles, speed about 370 mph and the explosive head weighed 1,100 lbs. The notice beside the one in the RAF Museum at Cosford in Shropshire states 'The HS 293 was the first ASM (Air to Surface Missile) in the world to sink a ship.

3.   Postscript to explain the chapter heading.

Ministry of War Transport Notice No. M. 279 headed 'Notice to Masters, Officers and Seamen of Merchant Ships' and dated June 1945 lays down the conditions necessary to qualify for the various campaign medals. In the Merchant Navy the qualifications for the Italy Star are:

20(a) The 1939-45 Star must have been earned by six months' service at sea and be followed by service in a vessel landing troops, stores, etc., at ports in, or on the shores of the Mediterranean, excluding those in Spain, the Balearic Islands, North Africa, Palestine, Syria, Turkey (East of 30°E) and in Cyprus. Service in vessels passing through the Mediterranean will not be a qualification.

According to these regulations, therefore, being torpedoed on the way to and within two days of Italy is not a qualification so that you could have been blown to bits on the way, yet denied the medal awarded to those fortunate enough to reach their destinations.

But there is a corollary to this.

In October, 1997, Douglas Cameron sent me a copy of the regulations pointing out that paragraph 19 seemed to cover those on ships which failed to arrive in Italy due to enemy action as it reads: 'The Italy Star will be awarded for service at sea in the Mediterranean during the campaign ... irrespective of the length of that service, provided the service was directly connected with active operations in the Mediterranean theatre'.

I took this up with the Maritime and Coastguard Agency in Llanishen, Cardiff, but when, during protracted correspondence, they continued to deny me the medal and kept ignoring my reference to paragraph 19, I asked for the name of a higher authority to which I could refer. I then received the following letter dated 28 April 1998.

Dear Mr Malcolm

THE ITALY STAR

I write further to my letter of 26 March, 1998. I now have the findings of our legal advisor and I am pleased to tell you that he has found in your favour.

Our advisor noted that you appear to qualify under paragraph 19 of M279 and to this extent paragraph 20 (a) does not fully reflect paragraph 19. This is something of which we were both aware but he does go on to say that 'It seems to be that 20 (a) should be construed as if "landing" included "or sent to land stores etc. but unable to do so because of enemy action"'.

Although this is only one opinion we have taken the view that in your peculiar* circumstances, and the legal view enables us to do so, the Italy Star should be issued to you ... and it is with pleasure that I inform you that the Italy Star is enclosed herewith.

So I got the Italy Star almost exactly fifty-four years after the event. I have Douglas to thank for it and, when acknowledging its receipt and, referring only to the correspondence, I said I had fought hard for it! Douglas, a Blue Funnel midshipman on the *Samharle* at the time, collapsed and died of a heart attack in April, 1999 shortly before he, his wife and I were going on holiday to Liverpool, principally to visit the Maritime Museum.

*Not a word I would use to describe them!

4. British ships generally carried alcoholic drinks, but US ships were 'dry' and we had been fitted out as one of the latter.

5. The Algerians called upon the Turks to free them from the Spaniards, but the Turks merely replaced the Spaniards as conquerors until they, themselves, were ousted by the French in 1830. It was not until 1962 that Algeria gained its independence, after a bloody war against France. And a right mess they have made of governing themselves as its citizens live in fear due to an oppressive government and the ruthless Islamic fundamentalists who oppose it.

6. I subsequently heard that the *Samite* was damaged by a V-bomb in London and that, at a later date, she suffered an explosion in her engine room when off the coast of Italy. I cannot, however, substantiate these reports. When the war was over, many British ship owners bought the Liberty Ships they had managed for the Ministry of War Transport, but, although Holts bought a number of these vessels, the *Samite* was not one of them. She was returned to the US Maritime Commission in 1947 and I was told by her 1st R/O that their representative said to the Master, "I'm surprised you're returning this one, Captain. She looks in very good condition." "Wait till you see her bottom," was the reply! But it was not until March, 1963 that the *Samite* was reduced to scrap metal in Panama City, Florida. Hundreds of Liberties were then surplus to requirements and neglectedly swung at anchor in bays around the United States until eventually scrapped.

   The frostbite which had caused Mr Thomas to wear heavy boots eventually resulted in him having to drag himself along on sticks. And, unfit for further service at sea, he was given an office job. Mr Ball's leg injury left him somewhat lame, but able to walk reasonably well.

7. Spelling as on slip.

8. The day in 1830 when the constitution of the new nation was approved.

9. It is common in South America to name places, and particularly streets, after significant dates a country's history. 25 May is Independence Day in the Argentine as it was on 25 May 1810 that the *criollos* rose against their Spanish masters and took over the country.

10.   This word was inserted because, when the radio officer went off watch after the war, he switched on an auto-alarm device which responded to four-second-long dashes preceding a distress call and set off a bell in the wheelhouse and another at the head of his bunk. He would then race to the radio room, switch on the receiver and listen for the distress message which was sent two minutes after the auto-alarm signal in order to give him time to get to his post.

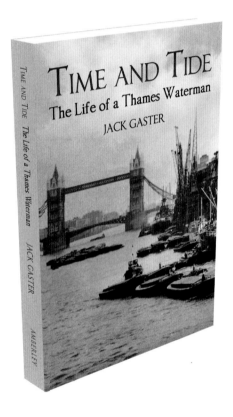

ALSO AVAILABLE FROM
AMBERLEY PUBLISHING

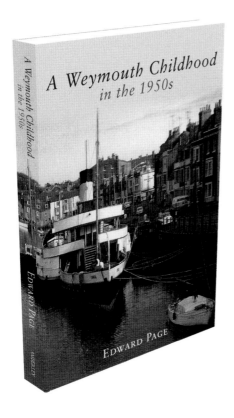

A WEYMOUTH CHILDHOOD IN THE 1950s

Edward Page

Price: £14.99
ISBN: 978-1-84868-878-0
Binding: PB
Extent: 224 pages

Available from all good bookshops or order direct
from our website www.amberleybooks.com